Literature Circles

Voice and Choice in Book Clubs and Reading Groups

SECOND EDITION

Harvey Daniels

Stenhouse Publishers
Portland, Maine

Pembroke Publishers Limited
Markham, Ontario

Stenhouse Publishers
www.stenhouse.com

Library of Congress Cataloging-in-Publication Data
Daniels, Harvey, 1947–
Literature circles : voice and choice in book clubs and reading groups / Harvey Daniels.—2d ed.
      p. cm.
Includes bibliographical references and index.
ISBN 1-57110-333-3 (alk. paper)
1. Group reading—United States. 2. Literature—Study and teaching—United States. 3. Children—Books and reading—United States. 4. Group work in education—United States. I. Title.
LC6631 .D36 2002
371.39'5—dc21   2001049385

Published simultaneously in Canada by
Pembroke Publishers
538 Hood Road
Markham, Ontario L3R 3K9
ISBN 1-55138-139-7

Cover photographs by Bob Tanner
(Elementary students [left to right]: Meiko Zhang, Eva Coleman, Keegan Dufty, Anna Takada, Rachel Esrig. High school students [left to right]: Maria Gama, Darris Bailey, Oscar Gonzalez, Roza Gama)

Manufactured in the United States of America on acid-free paper
08 07 06   10 9

Contents

▼ ▼ ▼ ▼ ▼ ▼ ▼ ▼ ▼ ▼ ▼ ▼

Acknowledgments

Some things just don't change. As with the first edition, this book owes its biggest debt to all the teachers I'm privileged to call colleagues and friends. In my roles as teacher educator, author, writing project codirector, and researcher I spend a lot of time in other people's classrooms, borrowing ideas. Sometimes they make me work for the privilege, by reading the kids a story, talking about the process of writing books, or joining in a book club. Other times, I just pass through and collect ideas.

From Chicago's inner city to its cosmopolitan suburbs to the rural schools downstate to a host of other schools across the country, scores of generous teachers have lent me their students, their time, and their space to try out and observe ideas about literature and learning. They've also inundated me from every corner of the country and many places around the world with e-mails and letters detailing their personal adaptations of literature circles. Some of these professionals' best ideas appear in their own words in Chapters 6, 7, and 8, and their many other insights strand through every page of this volume. To all of these treasured colleagues, my deepest thanks.

Since this book was first published, in 1994, I have spent most of my time working in Chicago public school classrooms, a location toward which very few compliments have been launched in recent years. Well, let me tell you something. Among the 27,000 educators who work in the CPS are some of the bravest, smartest, most dedicated teachers in the world. To a great extent, the idea of literature circles has been gestating in Chicago public schools for the past decade, and it has proven to be a most fertile environment for innovation and growth.

Among dozens of inspiring schools and faculties, the family of Washington Irving School stands out. Every day of every school year, Irving contradicts the negative myths propounded about inner-city schools, minority students, and urban teachers. Highlights of our collaboration have included countless after-school workshops, "family album night," a PBS documentary, and the many summers when we went on retreat together to the woods of northern Michigan. It was principal Madeleine Maraldi who first encouraged my colleagues and me to start a new high school, so that the kids graduating from Irving would have a progressive alternative for their teenage years.

Tomas Revollo and the teachers at Waters School have also shown what true believers can achieve. Over eight years of steady and steadfast commitment, they have turned a drab and ordinary school into an extraordinary environment for children, filled with art and books and nature and ideas. They have energized the parent community, enlisted local artists, planted a beautiful community garden, tended the nearby river—and raised their test scores. Their school slogan really fits: "Waters School, where fresh ideas flow."

In 1995, after fifteen years of working mainly in elementary education, I returned to my old secondary haunts to help plan and eventually open Chicago's first new high school in thirty years, which we most unwisely dubbed Best Practice High School. Among their many other commitments, the faculty at BPHS have been dedicated to experimenting with literature circles, and many of their voices appear in this book.

My professional family for the past decade has been the Center for City Schools at National-Louis University, in Chicago. We began with three of us, Steve Zemelman, Marilyn Bizar, and me, who devised and shaped the center. Since the beginning, we have worked so closely that we often joke about being "three bodies with one brain." Some days, when grant reports are due and eighteen principals are calling, we can't even seem to muster one brain between us. Steve, with whom I've written four books, has undoubtedly enjoyed this respite from collaboration with me, but he nevertheless chipped in his usual assortment of valuable ideas and constructive challenges. I've also written a couple of books with Marilyn, who has ideas for ten more and the energy to make them happen. The rest of our CCS family includes teachers we have temporarily stolen from the CPS and an incredible staff of university people: Barbara Morris, Yolanda Simmons, Toni Murff, Marianne Flanagan, Pete Leki, Jessica Swanson, Linda Bailey, Lynnette Emmons, Mark Rodriguez, Natasha Schaefer, Chris Sorenson, Brenda Bell, Lilia Moreno, Mirlene Cadichon.

At the Center for City Schools, a central part of our work is helping teachers implement literature circles in several overlapping networks of Chicago schools. Recently, we started our own in-house book club, which we schedule for our first staff meeting of each month. Since we were going around encouraging everyone else to start literature circles in their classrooms, it seemed sort of hypocritical not to practice what we preached.

An unexpected benefit of our doing a book club together is that we have demonstrated some of the most dysfunctional group behavior ever seen in the annals of literature circles. Ours is a very unruly group. The first time we met, on *The Color of Water,* no one could get a word in edgewise—literally, because there was an absolute, deafening wall of sound, thirteen people talking at once and not one single person listening. We had to institute a "talking stick" rule right away, passing around a little teachers' apple that someone found. You weren't allowed to speak until the apple was in your grasp. This tool slightly moderated the interruptions and talk-overs. But when Lynnette offered the scandalous and totally unfounded opinion that the mother in the book was "just a mess," look out! The crowd hooted down her incorrect interpretation unmercifully, and there were barely veiled threats of bodily harm.

Well, you could be charitable and say that our group is just "too eager" and that we are "passionate readers." But the fact is, we had a lot to work out. Maybe we were chronologically adults, maybe we'd read a lot of books, maybe we knew a thing or two about group dynamics theory, and maybe we were out there every day telling other people how to behave in book clubs. So what? We still needed training. We needed to go through a developmental process of problem solving, adjusting, and fine-tuning, just like kids do when they begin literature circles. Our problems might have been a little different (too much talking instead of not enough), but the structural process was remarkably parallel. For each dysfunction, we had to find, test out, refine, and adopt a strategy to address it. And yes, we have gotten better over time. There's hardly any hitting any more.

So who would encourage this feisty group of people to work together? Over the past few years, our projects have been supported by the Joyce Foundation, the DeWitt Wallace Readers-Digest Fund, the Annenberg Challenge, the Prince Charitable Trusts, the Chicago Community Trust, the Fry Foundation, the Polk Bros. Foundation, the MacDougal Family Foundation, and others. We thank them for their funding—and their sense of humor.

No college faculty members can enjoy this kind of deep involvement in public school reform without the support and encouragement of their administration. At National-Louis University, the backing has been strong and consistent. Our provost, Linda Tafel, is one of those rare teachers who has risen to a top administrative post without forgetting her roots in the classroom; she always puts kids first and the bottom line second. We have also been joined by our president, Curt McCray, and board chair, Jeff Louis, who not only approve of what we are doing, but roll up their sleeves and work with the kids, right beside us in the schools.

Back in 1994, when I heard that Philippa Stratton and Tom Seavey were starting Stenhouse Publishers, I immediately knew that I wanted this book to be on their first list. It has been a treat to see Stenhouse grow from a tiny start-up to a major force in the educational world, now home to some of the most influential and popular professional books in the nation. With a little "Martha magic" the books always look good, and Brenda the book doctor makes sure they make sense.

My personal literature circle contains three dedicated and insightful members. Nick's extensive reading in the genres of crime, psychology, forensic science, and criminal detection (along with the requisite college degree) has led him to an important job with the medical examiner of St. Paul, Minnesota. His proud parents hope that he will someday write about the bizarre and horrific crimes that he is helping to solve every day. Marny, the child raised on literature circles, may be the only sixteen-year-old in America to have experienced book clubs for the first nine years of school and to have taught teachers in summer institutes just how to run them. As she says, "Literature circles provide an arena for the venting, development, and analysis of a novel that is as integral a part of the digestion of a book as the reading itself." Marny's own reading taste now knows no bounds; she's read most of the adult books on our favorites list (p. 248), and there are few greater experts on the works of Pat Conroy.

Elaine, the mother of all readers, is the other teacher educator in our house. She's solved the puzzle that so many educators fret over: how to be a connected and caring teacher while still maintaining a rich reading life of your own. Every spring, Elaine triages the year in contemporary literature for me, boiling it down to eight or ten summer must-reads, thus helping extend the public impression that her husband is a well-read person. She also comments very favorably on almost everything I write, which makes her my first, best, and most trustworthy audience.

The first edition of this book was dedicated to my father, who died in 1994. Dad was a dedicated but unusual reader. He had a cheap hardback set of Zane Grey westerns in his library, about fifty volumes in all, which he read over and over again. Aside from the occasional Louis Lamour paperback that he might pick up on a trip, this was all the fiction my father read throughout my entire life, as far as I know. Each time he finished one of those Zane Greys, he would put the date of completion in a crisp pencil notation on the inside cover of the volume. Over the years, each of the titles accumulated a series of notations: "May 1978, August 1981, December 1984, April 1986." Many were read eight and ten times, usually at two-year intervals. Why my father confined himself to this narrow universe of literature, I have no idea. Perhaps for him, as Don Graves puts it, repetition was the spice of life. But Dad was a steadfast reader of Zane Gray novels all of my life, and that rugged landscape of brave cowboys formed a big part of his interior world. He found a way that books worked for him and he stuck to it—and, along the way, he passed along his love of reading to his children.

I hope this book helps launch many other idiosyncratic reading careers. I hope that as teachers invite kids to pick their own books and talk freely in book clubs, children will feel welcome to make personal and even peculiar choices, to find the way that books work for them, to make reading a special part of their interior and exterior lives, forever.

Contributing Teachers

Primary, K–2

Angie Bynum
Jenner School, Chicago, IL

Lynn Cherkasky
Foundations School, Chicago, IL

Debbie Gurvitz
Lyon School, Glenview, IL

Mary Ann Pegura
Deer Path School, Cary, IL

Norma Rocha-Cardenas
Seward School, Chicago, IL

Intermediate

Judith Alford
Maplewood School, Cary, IL

Barbara Dress
Illinois Writing Project, Arlington Heights, IL

Marianne Flanagan
Metcalfe Magnet School, Chicago, IL

Teresa Bond Fluth
Round Rock Independent Schools, Cedar Park, TX

Sandy King
Marion Jordan School, Palatine, IL

Theresa Kubasak
Baker Demonstration School, Evanston, IL

Sara Nordlund
Hart Upper Elementary School, Hart, MI

Melissa Woodbury
Hart Upper Elementary School, Hart, MI

7–12

Margaret Forst
Lake Forest High School, Lake Forest, IL

Kathy LaLuz
Washington Irving School, Chicago, IL

Marline Pearson
Madison Area Technical College, Madison, WI

Becky Abraham Searle
Whiteley School, Hoffman Estates, IL

Nancy Steineke
Victor J. Andrew High School, Tinley Park, IL

Sharon Weiner
Baker Demonstration School, Evanston, IL

▼ ▼ ▼ ▼ ▼ ▼ ▼ ▼ ▼ ▼ ▼ ▼

1

Welcome to Literature Circles

BACK IN 1993, when I joined with twenty great teachers to write a book about literature circles, we didn't quite know what we were getting into. We were a loose confederation of colleagues working from kindergarten through college, in city and suburban schools around Chicago. What brought us together was our excitement about the student book clubs meeting in our classrooms, which we called "literature circles."

Using a variety of different structures and procedures that matched our grade levels, we'd been dazzled by what the kids could do when given choices, time, responsibility, a little guidance, and a workable structure. Our students were reading lots of good books, thinking deeply about them, writing notes and journal entries, and joining in lively, informed literature discussions. They shared responses with peers, listened respectfully to one another, sometimes disagreed vehemently, but dug back into the text to settle arguments or validate different interpretations. In short, our kids were acting like real readers, lifelong readers. Oh, sure, there were problems, too: kids who didn't do the reading, off-task discussions, and really noisy rooms. But mostly, it was working. And our group of colleagues was really excited. Literature circles were a pretty nifty little invention that we had created all by ourselves, right here in the rarefied climate of Chicago. Of course, we soon found out that we were not alone at all. All across the country, we had plenty of unmet company, teachers and kids who were inventing and reinventing literature circles of their own.

Today, things have really changed. The world has changed, schools have changed, and literature circles have changed. What used to be a quiet, home-grown activity in a few scattered classrooms has become a trend, a boom, almost a fad. Now tens of thousands of teachers are doing something they call "literature circles." And many other teachers are using classroom activities that look very much the same, which they call "book clubs" or "reading groups." This means that now literally *millions* of students are involved in some kind of small, peer-led reading discussion group.

Over this period of phenomenal growth, the basic definition of LCs has stayed the same, at least for us. Literature circles are small, peer-led discussion groups whose members have chosen to read the same story, poem, article, or book. While reading each group-assigned portion of the text (either in or outside of class), members make notes to help them contribute to the upcoming discussion, and everyone comes to the group with ideas to share. Each group follows a reading and meeting schedule, holding periodic discussions on the way through the book. When they finish a book, the circle members may share highlights of their reading with the wider community; then they trade members with other finishing groups, select more reading, and move into a new cycle.

Members of our teacher team have been able to visit, work in, and steal ideas from hundreds of classrooms around the country where creative teachers are pioneering personalized versions of book clubs. Over the web, we hear from teachers in Australia, Asia, and all corners of Europe who are developing and enjoying some form of literature circles in their classrooms. We were amazed and warmed when we recently received this e-mail from a Chinese educator:

> I'm sure it will be hard to open students' mouths back in China because it has been five thousand years that we have been taught to respect experts' opinions and accept them with no doubt. But I'm confident that literature circles will finally make a difference in teaching reading because it represents the nature of literary works, which is life itself. . . . I wish my brave idea will someday come true in China.
> —*Bingbing Fan*

Along with all this fast-spreading popularity have come some wonderful new resources, many improved insights, countless inspiring stories—and some worrisome problems, too.

So that's what this revised edition is for: to share what we have learned from ten years of doing literature circles. Among the questions I want to address are, What do we know about literature circles that we didn't understand eight or ten years ago? What new resources and procedures can help teachers organize their classroom book clubs better? What are the most common pitfalls, potholes, and stumbling blocks to successful kid-led discussion groups? Beyond the basics, what do mature or "advanced" literature circles look like? And what just plain errors did I make in the first edition of the book? There's plenty to say in each of these categories.

The core of the book is still a comprehensive and practical description of literature circles: what they are, where they came from, how they operate, what they mean for young readers, and how teachers can integrate them into the broader literacy program, K–12. All these topics have been revised and updated to reflect a decade of practice, problem solving, and refinement.

But there is also lots of new material here, which explains why the book is a bit thicker than the previous incarnation. Among the added ingredients:

New, more effective activities for preparing students.

A major reconsideration of role sheets with new guidelines for their use.

Descriptions of "second-generation" literature circles in various grade levels.

Dozens of variations on the basic version of student-led book clubs.

More models and procedures for primary grades.

A visit to a whole-school literature circle program.

Key strategies for ensuring deep and sustained discussion.

An inventory of common management problems and solutions.

New scheduling patterns for group meetings and reading time.

Sample mini-lessons for literature circle sessions.

New materials for assessing and grading literature circles.

Ideas for using literature circles with nonfiction across the curriculum.

Plans for starting and sustaining a teachers-as-readers group.

Notes on the role of parents as at-home reading models and literature circle helpers.

A review of recent professional materials and research on literature circles.

An explanation of how literature circles match the national standards for literacy education.

The Literature Circles Boom

This has been a great decade for literature circles. Over the past ten years, a host of positive conditions, both in schools and in the wider culture, have coalesced to support the rapid growth of book clubs for students. Out in the general culture, some of these supportive trends include the following:

Adult Book Clubs Are Burgeoning

Over the past decade, reading groups have become a renewed American pastime. In 1990, there were about 50,000 book clubs in the United States; by the turn of the millennium that number had just about doubled. For many of us teachers trying to bring literature circles into our schools, these adult book clubs have been our implicit model—our prototype. And what a powerful template they are. Our adult book clubs are voluntary groups of friends who meet monthly in one another's living rooms, in church basements, or in the back rooms of bookstores. We select and read great books, books that move us, that change us as people, that create a powerful and caring community among us.

Then when we go back to our jobs as schoolteachers, we are trying to transfer the energy, the depth of thought and emotion, the lifelong commitment to books and ideas we have experienced ourselves. Whenever we run into problems translating book clubs to the school world, our own grown-up book club experience serves as our management touchstone. We can always ask ourselves first, Well, how do we deal with this problem in our own reading groups? In short, many of us who have been experimenting with literature circles are simply trying to import a powerful, beautiful, naturally occurring literacy structure called "book clubs" into the public schools—without messing them up.

Publishers' Support

Trade book publishers have recognized and fed the book club boom, and now offer free reading group discussion guides for their major "quality" titles. Scan the cover of almost any contemporary novel and somewhere you'll see a headline announcing "reading group guide included." Some guides are conveniently printed right in the back of the book, while an even larger inventory is available on publishers' websites. The Random House website, for example, lists more than 100 book club study guides, all immediately downloadable. All these discussion guides, of course, are not just a selfless service to book clubs, but a very low-cost way to promote multiple-copy sales.

The Internet Grows

The Internet has supported the book club trend in a number of ways. Most obviously, there are now countless websites where any reader from around the country can jump into a virtual book discussion at will. There are other sites that tell you step-by-step how to set up and run a book club. Even many traditional face-to-face book clubs have developed websites as a means of communicating with their members, keeping a record of their group's work, and sharing the group's ideas about books and about club procedures with a wider audience. The simple miracle of e-mail has unleashed a torrent of pent-up letter-writing activity throughout the country, and is a wonderful tool for talking about books. Meanwhile, websites like amazon.com and bn.com offer readers not just speedy shipping of books but information about authors, reviews by previous readers, sales information, and links to related sites. In the near future, e-books will become another part of our reading lives; we'll be able to load chosen texts directly into a light, legible, lap-friendly reader, either through our home computer or at a kiosk in the bookstore. Whatever delivery systems may emerge, it is comforting—and perhaps slightly ironic—to note that all this technology, all this marvelous silicon and plastic and bandwidth, are merely taking us back to the basics: to stories, to good old-fashioned flesh-and-blood books.

Oprah Takes the Lead

No single person gets more credit for the book club boom than talk-show host Oprah Winfrey, who founded an on-the-air book club in 1995, recommending one book a month for her viewers and holding periodic book discussion meetings on the show. Since that time, Oprah's Book Club has sparked the sale of tens of millions of books—and made a lasting contribution to our national literacy.

The broadcasting of book club meetings has opened a window into a world that Oprah's audience might never have seen. These on-air discussions usually feature a handful of lucky viewers who have written in about the book, nominating themselves for the taping, along with Oprah and the book's author (who typically keeps quiet during the first phase of the discussion). For people who have never attended a book discussion group, whose vision of book clubs harks back to reading groups in school, this could be a revelation. Instead of chalk and worksheets, there are snacks and candles and comfy chairs and— Toni Morrison! The meetings are held in Oprah's Chicago apartment, in restaurants, and other cozy locations, and they are casual, spontaneous, free-ranging. Far from being a dry, academic exercise with right answers and grades, these are informal, lively gatherings where everyone can speak their mind—but no one is forced to perform. It isn't unusual to see group members weep over a passage in a book, pass the tissues, hug one another, sit through a long silence, shout disagreements, or laugh uproariously. The sessions not only make you want to join a book club, but show you how to act when you get there: how to take turns, how to build on other people's ideas, how to use specific passages in the book to back up your interpretations, and scores of other discussion skills that are used by adults in effective book clubs.

It was back in the mid-1980s when our team in Chicago started experimenting with literature circles in our classrooms. That means a lot of years have intervened, and some significant developments in the school world have favored the spread of book clubs for kids.

Reading Instruction Has Improved

In spite of the notorious and energy-sapping "reading wars" that have pitted phonics fans against literature advocates for the past few decades, reading instruction has generally improved. Kids are reading much more good literature than they were a generation ago. Basal selections are of better quality, longer, and more authentic. In the classroom, having kids read aloud and answer factual recall questions no longer passes for good instruction. Teachers now ask kids to engage text at higher levels of thinking, drawing inferences, forming hypotheses, making judgments, and supporting conclusions about what they read. Independent reading time is sanctioned within virtually all school schedules, with activities like reading workshop, SSR (sustained silent reading) and DEAR (drop everything and read).

Indeed, this literature-centered reading-as-thinking mentality is even reflected in some state standards and assessments. Some progressive states like Michigan have mandated that children be able to "connect what they read to their own lives" and other goals harmonious not just with skill development but true lifelong reading. All these activities are a long way from the old-fashioned basal-driven, round-robin, drill-and-kill instruction of a generation ago. Even amid today's conservative educational climate, progressive practices with deep merit for children continue to spread into classrooms anyway. Indeed, though the whole-language movement seems to have lost many recent reading battles, it may have won the war; many of its key ingredients, like book clubs for kids, are becoming established in the majority of American schools.

Children's and Young Adult Literature Is Blooming

The past decade has been a terrifically fertile one for kids' books. For the youngest readers and prereaders, countless picture books of depth and beauty have been published in recent years, led by authors like Kevin Henkes, Eric Carle, and Anthony Browne. Many of the biggest hits—like the works of Lane Smith and Jon Scieszka—have tapped the age-old formula of appealing both to children and to the adults who read the books to their kids. For older youngsters, there has been plenty to pick from. The Harry Potter series, with its challenging, lengthy, and twisty plots, has millions of young devotees. Young adult books seem to get better and better—indeed, the artistry and quality of many is indistinguishable from that of "real" adult literature. Emblematic of this new wave of sophisticated YA literature was the 2000 Newbery Medal winner, *Bud, Not Buddy,* by Christopher Paul Curtis, a novel about a homeless boy's quest for a family during the Depression, set amid rich historical details of riding the rails, hobos, jazz, and the Negro baseball leagues.

Teachers Are Reading Themselves

Right along with the boom in children's literature circles, teacher reading groups are on the upswing, too. It has always been one of the great ironies of reading instruction in America that so few teachers actually read themselves. Indeed, very few of us habitually read books—novels, biographies, history, current events—as a steady and routine part of our lives. Of course, we have a thousand excuses why we don't: our teaching lives are so overstuffed with duties, including tons of take-home work that usurps all our potential reading time. And, hey: we are also trying to have our own families and children and lives outside of school—and maybe even plunk down in front of the tube once in a while. Reading just gets squeezed out.

But now, more and more teachers are coming back to books: they are joining with colleagues in their classrooms, in the faculty lounge, or in one another's homes to read and savor great books. Sometimes they choose current adult titles, maybe an "Oprah book" or a long-neglected classic; sometimes they read professional books that can inform their classroom practice; and sometimes they choose children's titles they may someday want to use with students. In many school districts, such teacher book clubs and study groups have become an official and encouraged form of staff development, offering a more personalized and peer-driven kind of growth experience—and a refreshing change from mass lectures or cattle-call workshops. In many of our Chicago network schools, we now work to develop simultaneous book clubs of teachers, parents, and kids—sometimes having all these groups read the same book and come together for a festival of sharing.

The National Literacy Standards Have Endorsed Lit Circles

In 1996, the National Council of Teachers of English and the International Reading Association issued the long-awaited national Standards for the English Language Arts. The standards strongly endorsed literature-based, collaborative classrooms where students take increasing responsibility for choosing, reading, and discussing books (and other texts). The document stressed the need for students to explore a wide range of books representing different cultures, periods, and regions—and to read for "personal fulfillment" as well as for information. Accompanying the NCTE/IRA standards were detailed scenarios of exemplary instruction provided by classroom teachers who were implementing the standards in their classrooms. Among these features was a detailed description of how Deb Foertsch of Champaign, Illinois, sets up and runs her fifth graders' literature circles (Sierra-Perry 1996). For literature circles to be explicitly sanctioned by the national literacy standards, identified as one of the "best classroom practices" in the teaching of reading and writing, was certainly another boost to its professional popularity.

Literature Circles Have Developed an Abundant Professional Literature and Research Base

Accompanying the boom in the practice of literature circles has been a boom in their documentation. We are growing a robust written record. Where ten years ago the research was sketchy, we now have qualitative and quantitative research studies, teacher accounts, journal articles, graduate dissertations, videotapes, and plenty of books. Now when we say that literature circles work, we can back it up with proof. We can offer teachers a dozen different models for getting started and moving forward. We have variations, adaptations, translations. We have collections of forms, tools, and assessment rubrics that teachers around the country have devised. We have conversations and resources on the web. We can show how book clubs fit into a complete and well-balanced reading program. And, sometimes most urgently of all, we can show how literature circles can improve students' scores on standardized tests.

The body of research on literature groups is growing quickly. Unfortunately, these studies appear under so many different names (literature studies, book clubs, literature discussion groups, literature circles, cooperative book discussion groups) and often combine so many divergent ingredients (teacher control versus student autonomy, assigned versus chosen books) that one has to read very carefully. But all sorts of evidence, support, and teacher testimonials are accumulating about literature circles.

Our own research in Chicago has linked literature circles to improving student achievement scores. Between 1995 and 1998, our Center for City Schools received a grant from the Chicago Annenberg Challenge to support the development of instruction in a group of struggling Chicago schools. Our intervention was very focused: we helped teachers implement literature circles, as part of a reading-writing workshop approach, in as many classrooms as we could. Our training involved summer institutes and school-year support, delivered by peer consultants, veteran Chicago teachers who had used these strategies in their own classrooms. Even though our consultants worked with only a fraction of each school's faculty, schoolwide results were encouraging. In reading, our schools outstripped citywide test score gains by 14 percent in third grade, 9 percent in sixth grade, and 10 percent in eighth grade. In writing, they topped citywide gains by 25 percent in third grade, 8 percent in sixth grade, and 27 percent in eighth grade. Now, there was a lot of good work going on in these schools, and it is never possible to tell exactly what treatments caused what gains. But the teachers were convinced: their literature circles were working, not just to help kids become readers but also to *prove* they are readers on the mandated measures of proficiency.

Other researchers have been finding similarly promising outcomes. A 1998 study of fourth graders by Klinger, Vaughn, and Schumm found that students in peer-led groups made greater gains than control groups in reading comprehension and equal gains in content knowledge after reading and discussing social studies material. This effect was confirmed through a standardized reading test, a social studies unit test, and audiotapes of group work. Interestingly, the researchers found that students' small-group talk was 65 percent academic and content-related, 25 percent procedural, and 8 percent feedback, with only 2 percent off-task.

Martinez-Roldan and López-Robertson looked at the effect of literature circles in a first-grade bilingual classroom. They found that "young bilingual children, no matter what their linguistic background, are able to have rich discussions if they have regular opportunities to engage with books." Interestingly, they found that many of the Spanish-dominant children were more eager and ready to make personal connections with stories than the English speakers, who tended to stick closer to the text on the page. The Hispanic children manifested their connections through the telling of extended stories, a style of response that the English-speaking kids rarely utilized.

Dana Grisham, of San Diego State University, has been an indefatigable recorder of emerging literature circle research. Her 1999 bibliography was a major contribution to the field, and can be found in its entirety on the literature circles website, at www.literaturecircles.com. She also organized the first panel at the American Educational Research Association to focus on literature circles. Grisham has catalogued literature circle research documenting benefits for inner-city students (Pardo 1992), incarcerated adolescents (Hill and Van Horn 1995), "resistant" learners (Hauschildt and McMahon 1996), homeless children and children living in poverty (Hanning 1998), second-language learners (MacGillivray 1995), and English-as-a-foreign-language (EFL) learners (Dupuy 1997). Various versions of book clubs and literature study circles have been found to increase student enjoyment of and engagement in reading (Fox and Wilkinson 1997), to expand children's discourse opportunities (Kaufmann et al. 1997), to increase multicultural awareness (Hansen-Krening 1997), to promote other perspectives on social issues (Noll 1994), to provide social outlets for students (Alvermann 1997), and to promote gender equity (Evans, Alvermann, and Anders 1998). Other than that we don't know much about lit circles!

Literature Circles Schoolwide: Washington Irving

Washington Irving used to be a typical Chicago school. Located in a tough neighborhood on the near west side of the city, with housing projects to the north and crumbling three-flats to the south, Irving had a long record of mediocre academic results. Although the succession of historic graduation photos hanging in the hallway showed that Irving had been a welcoming landing area for a succession of immigrant groups, only about 15 percent of its current students were achieving at national norms in reading and mathematics.

Then, in 1987, a couple of important things changed. The dilapidated three-story brick building dating from the 1890s was torn down and replaced with a bright and pleasing blond brick structure. Madeleine Maraldi, a veteran math teacher and Irving assistant principal, was named principal. And then Irving was selected as the site where Governor James Thompson would sign the state's ambitious school reform legislation. Amid great hoopla, balloons, and media lights, the governor gazed around Irving's spanking new multipurpose room and addressed the teachers. "We've built the outside," he said. "Now it's up to you to build the inside."

Madeleine and her teachers took this charge seriously. A few days later, the staff gathered in a big circle, and Madeleine challenged everyone to make a new commitment to teaching the children, to put aside the blaming of families from nonmainstream cultures. "Let's look at *us*," she declared. "The question is, How can we teach better? What do we need to focus on, to learn, get better at?" In the searching conversation that ensued, it became clear that language arts, writing, and reading needed to be at the center of Irving's rebirth.

Today, the number of Irving students reading at national norms has nearly tripled, and the state assessment of writing puts Irving among the top schools citywide. Now when Irving kids go on to high school (like the one where I work, a few blocks away), the teachers find them to be able readers, fluent writers, and skillful collaborators. As a result, educators come from all around the country to see how this faculty of smart and dedicated teachers has bucked the odds, growing class after class of lifelong readers and writers, in a half African American, half Hispanic school with an 85 percent poverty rate.

Obviously, any school improvement this dramatic must have many components and causes. But a central ingredient in Irving's formula for success has been literature circles. If you look at the weekly schedule posted outside every classroom, you'll see that third through eighth graders have literature circles every day of the school year, for forty minutes a day. Look in any classroom, and you'll see another indicator of the commitment to book clubs: half-size classes, with about fourteen or fifteen students each. Irving has not only scheduled its school day to include LCs, but has also honored their importance by giving teachers a more favorable situation in which to grow their book clubs. Where do the other kids go? Madeleine, a master of both budgets and scheduling, books students into a writing lab, science lab, and P.E. classes, where outstanding "special" teachers engage half-classes while the other halves meet in LCs back in their classrooms.

With five forty-minute sessions dedicated to literature circles each week, there's time for young readers to do everything. To browse, sample, and pick books; to read, alone or in groups, silently or aloud; to learn from teachers in mini-lessons before group meetings; to debrief processes and problems after book clubs; to bring in special people who can enrich their experiences with books; and to gather periodically to share and celebrate books. And the teachers have the latitude, indeed the encouragement, to invent their own variants of lit circles, for themselves and their students.

Sure, Irving is an ideal situation, with a near-perfect alignment of progressive leadership and dedicated teaching. We can grouse about how our school doesn't enjoy these advantages. But isn't it nice to see what an activity like literature circles can accomplish—indeed, what *kids* can accomplish—when it is steadily supported, fully funded, and consistently implemented, when it is continued, unswayed by fads or mandates, for ten solid years?

Problems with Literature Circles

Compared with the all these assets, strengths, and constructive trends, the problems with literature circles seem relatively minor and mostly solvable. Among the concerns I'll be addressing:

Assessment Mania

Probably the most malignant influence in education today is the testing frenzy that is misdirecting our school system from top to bottom. In the name of accountability and standards, people mostly from outside the educational system (read: politicians) are mandating that teachers and students spend more of their time on "standardized" tests that distort instruction, mismeasure kids, reward economic advantage, and punish cultural difference. When you are working in a city school system like Chicago, where many black and Hispanic kids, for several dozen perfectly understandable reasons, consistently score in the bottom half, bottom quartile, bottom decile of these discriminatory and meaningless tests, it can get pretty discouraging. When you see students in the lowest-scoring schools spending months, repeat months, studying test-coaching booklets and filling out sample tests instead of actually reading anything, you realize that the tests have *literally* become the curriculum. For the schools with the lowest test scores, the test results ensure that the kids will never get what they need, which is books, experiences, conversations, ideas, interaction, and learning.

So how does this testing mania affect literature circles and similar progressive, student-centered classroom practices? At the most superficial level it increases pressure to grade everything. Indeed, in workshops one of the most urgent and frequent questions teachers ask is, How can I get a grade out of this? The testing fad puts extra pressure on any innovation to "prove" its value, to justify any expenditure of time other than straight test coaching. As we noted earlier, there's good news on this front; research has been accumulating that literature circles do work, and that literature-based reading programs are best for kids.

On a wider scale, excessive testing threatens all our time allocations. It's hard to defend the big chunks of time that good activities like lit circles require when test coaching seems more relevant to test outcomes. While we may know that kids who join literature circles over extended periods of time will acquire vocabulary, build concepts, practice inferring, and develop a dozen other key reading skills, the effects are indirect. Book clubs look like the long way around to higher scores. They don't look quite as practical as opening a practice test and blackening some circles.

Terminology Drift

In education, we have a recurrent problem that might be called "terminology drift." Here's what happens. First, a new pedagogical practice—take "writing workshop," for example—is invented, described, and introduced to the profession. There are originators, there are definitions, there is literature specifically describing the practice. In "writing workshop" the innovation was outlined back in the 1980s by authors like Nancie Atwell, Don Graves, and Lucy Calkins. They identified the key, defining features of a workshop: student choice of topics, a big chunk of writing practice time, teacher as mentor and coach, a process approach featuring formative conferences, using peers as editors and collaborators, helping kids develop a portfolio of ongoing work, and so forth.

Then the idea of "writing workshop" starts to spread around the country. It gets popular. The term "writing workshop" just trips off the tongue. It sounds good, current, with-it. Suddenly, there are teachers who call it "writing workshop" when they assign kids to write a five-paragraph theme on the color symbolism in *The Scarlet Letter* or a story titled "How It Would Feel to Be a Butterfly." All the essential, defining ingredients of true writing workshop—student choice and responsibility, teacher mentoring—are absent; the only ingredient of writing workshop that's present is the name.

Now, I'm not saying that the above writing assignments are evil, wicked, sinful, or even wrong. But they are *not writing workshop*. And the same thing has happened to literature circles, big time. Today, it seems that any time you gather a group of students together for any activity involving reading, you can go right ahead and call it a literature circle. It doesn't matter if the teacher has picked the story, if the book is a basal (or a science textbook!), if the teacher is running the discussion, if the kids have no voice—it's just cool to call it a literature circle. There are even traditional round-robin reading groups being called literature circles, even though this activity is about as antithetical to the lit circle idea as you could imagine.

This is dangerous territory for me as a proponent of literature circles. I don't want to be a purist. I don't want to beat on anyone. I'm acutely aware that when you advocate a particular innovation, there's a dangerous tendency to get stuck on your own original model. I once saw a Very Famous Educational Author fall into this trap at a professional conference, and it was not a pretty sight. He looked out at a packed ballroom of adoring teacher-acolytes, with overflow participants sitting on the floor, standing against the walls, and clustered around the six propped-open doors. "As I have traveled around the country visiting so many of your classrooms," he intoned, "I have been saddened to see that so many of you are *doing it wrong*." There was a stunned silence and a bowing of heads. A pall settled over the room as teachers silently scourged themselves for squandering the gift. Observing from the very back of the room, I started to wonder whether these 1,500 shamed disciples were really the problem. Maybe if an impartial visitor (like me) visited some of their classrooms, he'd think that their adaptations of the Great Man's strategy were just terrific. Maybe the guru was having trouble letting go of his baby, of allowing the second wave of his idea to happen.

I have tried to keep this lesson with me as I become more and more identified as the lit circle guy. I try to remember to count to ten when I see the advertisement for another thirty-dollar compendium of handy-dandy role sheets. I bite my tongue during the workshop on "Infusing Punctuation Skills into Literature Circles." But while letting everyone have their own meritorious adaptations and second-generation versions, I'm also going to oppose severe terminology drift. If people don't know what the thing really is, they can never try the real thing. And if they think the things they have always done are really the same as the latest thing, what's the reason to experiment and change? In the following chapter I will again define, with even more care than the first time, exactly what a literature circle is and what it is not.

The Joy and Jeopardy of Role Sheets

Among the most popular features of the first edition were some little handouts called "role sheets" (see pages 107–132). These simple tools, adapted from standard collaborative-learning practice, gave book club members temporary jobs like "connector," "questioner," and "literary luminary." I know these role sheets have been popular because they have been revised and republished in countless professional journals, in school district curriculum guides across the country, and in every corner of the Internet.

Back in 1993, when the first edition of this book was in manuscript, one of the outside readers predicted that the role sheets were likely to be misused and might end up stifling interaction in student groups instead of nurturing it. Even though I doubted the wisdom of the reader's foresight, I added some extra warnings to the role sheet section and then launched the book into the school world. It turned out that the reader was right: in some classrooms, the role sheets did become a hindrance, an obstacle, a drain—sometimes a virtual albatross around the neck of book club meetings. What had been designed as a temporary support device to help peer-led discussion groups get started could actually undermine the activity it was meant to support.

The rationale for role sheets still makes sense. When students are first learning to operate in peer-led discussion groups, many teachers find it helpful to offer some intermediate support structures to ease the transition. That's how we started assigning a different, rotating task to each group member—setting a cognitive purpose for the reading and an interactive one for the group discussion. Each of the roles was designed to support collaborative learning by giving kids clearly defined, interlocking, and open-ended tasks. And the sheets also enact a key assumption about reading—that readers who approach a text with clear-cut, conscious purposes will comprehend more (Keene and Zimmerman 1997). So the role sheets had two purposes: to help kids read better and discuss better.

But, glorious rationale or not, "role sheet backfire syndrome" has turned out to be disturbingly widespread. Today, as I visit schools and talk with teachers about book clubs, one of the most frequent questions I hear is, Why are my kids' book clubs so mechanical? It seems like the kids just go around the circle, reading their role sheets one after the other, and never get into a real conversation. Sometimes, I ask how long the students have been using role sheets and the answer comes back denominated in months or years. Even though the book's first edition, from which these sheets are typically photocopied, clearly states, "The role sheets are supposed to be transitional, temporary devices" (p. 61), something tempts teachers to cling to them for way too long.

Kids are giving us the same warning about role sheets, if we will listen. Lesley Fowler's class of fifth graders in Waterville, Maine, tried meeting both ways, with and without role sheets. Lesley conducted a survey and found that 90 percent of the kids preferred discussions without the sheets:

> I think that we had better conversations without the sheets in our hands. We were able to say what we were thinking right then instead of what we wrote when we thought of it as an assignment.

> We had better conversations without the sheets because it makes it seem like a play and you can't say other things because you will get in trouble.

> When you have the papers, you are too lazy to think. But without the papers you are thinking hard to know what you wrote, and then suddenly something else pops up.

> I think we had better discussions without the role sheets. I think this is because it made for better conversations and it made it cooler for people to talk when we don't have papers to stick to.

> I think without, because it's more natural, and when you finish going around the circle you keep things going with things that aren't from the sheets.

> In my opinion when we had our sheets the discussion seemed a bit dull. Now, when we used only our books the discussion seemed to flow a lot better. I think this happened because it is just like a music concert. If you are reading a sheet it sounds groggy, but if you look up it will be clear and smooth.

> I think we had better conversations without our role sheets because we think of fresh ideas instead of trying to figure out what to say.

> I think we had better conversations without the sheets because we made up better things as we went along. We didn't have a script to stick to and be boring.

Interestingly, an equally large majority of kids felt it was valuable to prepare the sheets after the reading anyway—just not to use them during group meetings. As one kid put it, "I think it is good to prepare before you do the reading groups, because if you don't have anything, then what are you going to say? I think you need to prepare then leave your papers alone and go to the reading groups. If you don't, the discussion will go down instead of getting good." These kids are telling us that some kind of written preparation really *does* help them think, read, and discuss better. They are also warning us to be careful how such tools get used. In other words, the problem isn't the roles, it's the sheets.

For what it's worth, today in our own network of Chicago schools, we generally don't use the role sheets for very long, or at all. Often, we just start our literature circles using open-ended reading logs as the main tool for collecting reading responses. This switch hasn't been too hard, since these days most of our kids are already experienced lit loggers. They've used reading journals, dialogue journals, or written conversation in their reading workshop programs for years, and it's no big deal to transfer them to literature circles use. So instead of beginning with role sheets, we use a training process like the one outlined on pages 55–71, and save the roles to spice up ongoing groups later on.

Later in the book I'll try to sort all this out in detail, offering some alternatives, adjustments, and procedures. In the meantime, yes, the role sheets are still included in the book—in substantially improved form—because so many teachers find them to be constructive when used properly, either for brief initial training or as a later variation for experienced book clubs.

Learning by Doing

Oh, yes. One more thing that's happened since the first edition of this book. In 1996, four colleagues and I started a new school in Chicago. After many years of working with mostly elementary kids and teachers, I returned to my original (and uneasy) home in secondary education, to help design and open the Best Practice High School, on the city's west side. One of the key "best practices" we have been trying to explore at BPHS is—you guessed it—literature circles. Working with these very wonderful and very normal kids from all corners of Chicago has provided a great, ongoing lesson for me as the author of a teacher how-to book. In teaching BPHS kids about literature circles, I've had some transcendent classroom moments, and I've also had some days when I needed a really long nap after school. Working with our kids over weeks and months and years, I feel grounded in a new way. Now I will never underestimate what kids can do in peer-led groups, because I've seen what our students can accomplish. Neither will I underestimate the amount of effort it takes for teachers to get good literature circles up and running in classrooms. There's work involved here, for both teachers and kids. But it's good work, work worth doing, and work with very large rewards.

So where do you go from here? Depends on your past experience and your learning style, I guess. If you are already sold on literature circles, and you're ready to jump right in, you may want to skip right ahead to Chapter 5, where we "get practical" with four different training models, and carry on from there with basic strategies and advanced variations. If you need a little bit more background and explanation, continue straight ahead. In the next chapter, we will concisely define literature circles and explain how they fit into the broader language arts program, K–12. Then, in Chapter 3, we'll share the history and origins of LCs, a surprisingly exciting tale that begins on a ship bound for the American colonies. If, on the other hand, you are someone who needs to see and hear and smell how classroom activities really work, you may want to dive into Chapter 4, where we take a "field trip" to three very different state-of-the-art literature circle classrooms.

As you work your way through the book, you will encounter a variety of Variations, highlighted with a ▼. These are quick explanations of special lit circle adaptations or refinements developed by teachers around the country.

You may also want to view sections of the videotape *Looking into Literature Circles,* which was designed to accompany this book. Because genuine student-led book clubs have subtle sights, sounds, and dynamics that no book can quite communicate, we created this video to offer glimpses into three real literature circle settings, one elementary, one secondary, and one with parents. To show you where the video may be most helpful or relevant, we'll place a television icon like this one in the margin.

And you can find company and support at **www.literaturecircles.com**. This is an on-line resource where teachers can gather to exchange ideas about book clubs at all grade levels and across the curriculum. Please join us to share your questions, concerns, materials, samples of kids' work, and stories of classroom crashes or triumphs.

So welcome, readers, old and new. However you read it, I hope this book works for you all, grizzled literature circle veterans and eager newbies alike. Welcome—or welcome back.

▼ ▼ ▼ ▼ ▼ ▼ ▼ ▼ ▼ ▼ ▼ ▼

2

A Closer Look:
Literature Circles Defined

HERE IN THE Midwest, our loosely knit team of teachers has been developing one version of literature circles for almost fifteen years, combining our local inventions with national models appearing in the professional literature. We have been especially concerned with issues of management, the preparation of students, and enacting the principles of group dynamics. Perhaps our most unique and important contribution has been to infuse the key elements of effective collaborative learning into our reading models. Most of the rest of this book explains how and why we've evolved into setting up and running literature circles the way we do.

Do we think our model is better? Certainly not. We are genuinely impressed by the diverse ways that other teachers around the country have created and supported literature discussion groups. When this book was first published in 1994, just about the only company we had was *Grand Conversations,* a lovely report on book clubs and classroom community by Ralph Peterson and Maryann Eeds. Today, there are a dozen meritorious and helpful books about different aspects of literature circles, feeding good ideas to all of us.

My Seattle-based colleagues, Bonnie Campbell Hill, Nancy Johnson, and Katherine Schlick-Noe, in varying combinations, have issued several valuable books: *Literature Circles and Response* (1995), *Getting Started with Literature Circles* (1999), and *The Literature Circles Resource Guide* (2000), which includes a CD-ROM of forms, record-keeping tools, and an annotated book list. Susan McMahon and Taffy Raphael's *The Book Club Connection* (1997) has descriptions of many different classroom book clubs, with a strong focus on teachers doing their own research in them. Katharine Samway and Gail Whang's *Literature Study Circles in a Multicultural Classroom* (1995) offers a clear model of teacher-led book clubs. Kathy Short, Jerome Harste, and Carolyn Burke's chapter on lit circles in *Creating Classrooms for Authors and Inquirers* (1995) has been the starting point for many teachers around the country. And in *The Art of Teaching Reading* (2000), Lucy Calkins offers a new spin on literature circles, where groups stay together through many books and focus more on literary analysis than personal connections.

But even among these esteemed colleagues, we still believe we have some contributions to make. We think our approach makes it easy and safe for more kids (and more teachers) to try literature circles. We have developed four good ways of getting started, so that teachers can implement student-led discussion groups quickly and successfully, whatever kind of preparation their students may need. We have created a variety of structures and procedures for managing literature circles over the long run, strategies that solidify and deepen the role this special activity can play in a balanced curriculum across the grade levels. Our overarching goal is to "grow the club"—to enlarge the number of classrooms in which teachers can comfortably reallocate big chunks of class time to genuine student-led small-group book discussions. And if that's the result, we're happy.

Eleven Key Ingredients

So what is our distinctive version of literature circles? Here's our "official" eleven-point definition. While some of the defining ingredients of literature circles may be intentionally omitted when students are first learning the activity or when the group is applying lit circles to some mandated curriculum, authentic and mature literature circles will manifest most of these key features:

1. Students *choose* their own reading materials.
2. *Small temporary groups* are formed, based on book choice.
3. Different groups read *different books.*
4. Groups meet on a *regular, predictable schedule* to discuss their reading.
5. Kids use written or drawn *notes* to guide both their reading and discussion.
6. Discussion *topics come from the students.*
7. Group meetings aim to be *open, natural conversations about books,* so personal connections, digressions, and open-ended questions are welcome.
8. The teacher serves as a *facilitator,* not a group member or instructor.
9. Evaluation is by *teacher observation and student self-evaluation.*
10. A spirit of *playfulness and fun* pervades the room.
11. When books are finished, *readers share with their classmates,* and then *new groups form* around new reading choices.

1. Children Choose Their Own Reading Materials

Student choice tops the list, because the deepest spirit of literature circles comes from independent reading. One of the gravest shortcomings of school reading programs is that assignments, choices, texts to read, are usually all controlled by the teacher. This contrasts sharply with what we know of good home-based teaching, where parents intuitively provide kids with choices in their reading and discussion of books. Parents do not snuggle up to their offspring at story time and then announce, "It's October 19, so today the curriculum says we have to cover *Stellaluna.*" Caring parents simply say, "What do you want to read?" and even if the child selects the same book for the tenth night in a row or a book that's too hard or too easy for her to understand, the parents still let the kid lead. What parents know in their hearts, even if they cannot explain it, is that you can't fall in love with books that someone stuffs down your throat. For reading to become a lifelong habit and a deeply owned skill, it has to be voluntary, anchored in feelings of pleasure and power.

In the classroom, teachers who really want to meet this need for genuine choice and self-direction must provide two kinds of independent reading: time for *individuals,* through structures like sustained silent reading (SSR) and reading workshop; and time for independent reading in *groups,* when kids select, read, and discuss books together, as in literature circles.

2. Small Temporary Groups Are Formed, Based on Book Choice

Literature circle groups are formed around several people's desire to read the same book or article—not by reading level, ability grouping, teacher assignment, or curriculum mandate. These groups are temporary and task-oriented. They often mix children of different "abilities." Once they have finished their job—reading and discussing a book of common interest—the group disbands and individual members find their way into new, different groups by picking their next book. Group size can range from two to six, although the optimum seems to be four or five. This number guarantees a variety of perspectives on the text, a range of responses that enlivens discussion.

In real schools, our ideals of book choice and group formation are sometimes compromised. To begin with, kids will not be picking from all the books in the world but from those fairly handy in the classroom or the school or the local public library. The teacher may not be able to provide enough copies of a chosen book, and then kids will have to read their second or third choice instead. When teachers are just starting a class off with literature circles, they may decide to limit students' choices to a few books—or even assign a single title to all groups—in order to focus students on learning the structure. Sometimes, parents or teachers may limit the choices by refusing to let kids read books they consider inappropriate.

There may also be compromises or imperfections in the formation of groups. Of course, smart teachers know that many kids will pick books not out of genuine curiosity but to create a group of their friends. But these teachers also realize that as long as kids do the reading, invest in the conversation, get into the book, this needn't be a problem. Students tend to act exactly like adult reading groups—a group of people first decide that they want to be together, and then they pick some books as the centerpiece of their gathering. Other teachers have kids pick books through secret ballots that ensure a more authentic expression of interest in particular books. Sometimes teachers have to mediate, guide, and counsel in order to get groups formed and make things come out even. Groups may have to include some kids who are reading a first-choice title and others for whom it's a backup or secondary choice. Some teachers feel that in order to get a good, rich discussion going it is important to have three or four people in a group, so they try to talk kids out of pairs, even if that's the true first-choice grouping. While all these compromises may not be ideal, they are realistic. Even as teachers give classroom time to creating the groups and solving the difficulties democratically, they are explicitly demonstrating their commitment to honor student choice and make it work.

3. Different Groups Read Different Books

Obviously, when kids (or adults) are given a genuine choice of what to read, not everyone will pick the same book. More and more teachers realize that this variety is long overdue. In traditional American schools, virtually every single book, article, story, text, poem, chapter, novel, and play that students read throughout their first twelve or thirteen years is assigned by a teacher, dictated by the curriculum, and backed by the authority of grades. Now, this everybody-reads-the-same-thing approach isn't always bad. After all, it can be very helpful to be part of a wider community that has all read the same text, giving readers a wide range of different responses to hear and ponder.

However, our best research on the development of readers is very clear: assignments are not enough. Children need a mixture, a balance between teacher-chosen and self-selected materials (Zemelman, Daniels, and Hyde 1998). They need substantive opportunities to develop and pursue their own tastes, curiosities, and enthusiasms in the world of books. In fact, choice is actually a matter of educational standards and rigor. Students must learn to take full responsibility for locating, selecting, and pursuing books, rather than always expecting teachers or other adults to choose for them. Since choice is an integral component of literate behavior, if we don't require students to be constantly assigning reading to themselves, we have set our educational standards far too low and are nurturing dependency and helplessness. By providing structures and schedules to promote student-chosen reading experience at all levels, activities like literature circles, reading workshop, and sustained silent reading offer a way to redress our schools' dangerous imbalance between assigned and independent reading.

4. Groups Meet on a Regular, Predictable Schedule

In order to work most effectively, literature circles must be regularly scheduled—not as an occasional "treat," but continuously throughout the school year. If LCs are introduced as a one-time-only special event, teachers and kids will just have time to learn the procedures, go through one book (probably a bit mechanically, since the first time through is always a mixture of learning the process and discussing the book), and then quit just when the real payoff is in view. Lit circles hit their stride when everyone has internalized the norms and warmed up as readers. Teachers need to see this as a long-term classroom investment: literature circles require a modest "down payment" of time for training, but once they're installed in your portfolio of strategies, they pay big dividends in the reading program all year long.

The daily and weekly meeting schedules are important, too. Any lit circle session needs a good chunk of time—for meeting, reading, discussing, or a little of each. Even with the youngest or most distractible kids, anything less than twenty minutes doesn't allow the possibility for a natural conversation to open up. When sessions are too short, kids tend to rush mechanically through the meeting, and the session can become a kind of oral workbook with everyone hurrying to jump over each hurdle in the allotted time. For older kids and more focused groups, thirty minutes is a healthy chunk of time, while forty-five minutes will be welcomed and well used by lit circle veterans.

▼ V A R I A T I O N : **Try Book Clubs On-Line**
Sara Nordlund and Melissa Woodbury have been convening voluntary e-mail book discussions with some of their fourth graders. The interested kids agree on an extra book in addition to the one they are reading for their regular face-to-face book clubs during the school day. Then they set a time in the evening (7:30 P.M. on Wednesday, for example) when everyone gathers on-line to talk about the book for half an hour based on a list of prompts the teachers have created and e-mailed to everyone. Because everyone is on-line at the same time and gets everyone else's comments, the messages pile up pretty fast and there's plenty to read, think about, and answer.

Predictability is another factor. If kids are going to self-assign parts of a book, read with purpose, make notes in a reading log, and come to class ready to take an active part in the discussion, they need a sensible, predictable schedule. Circles can meet every day, with kids doing a chunk of reading each night as homework. Or groups can meet every second or third day, allowing time for kids to read bigger sections of text between meetings (and allowing the teacher to slide in some other curriculum in the intervening days). Some teachers have kids do their reading and prepare their notes on nonmeeting days during the same class time that the circles otherwise meet. This kind of schedule is especially helpful in the training stages or for kids who don't do well reading their books as homework. This pattern also allows the teacher to support students' reading, circulating to go over their written notes, model open-ended questions, reassure kids that their own real responses are truly invited.

5. Kids Use Written or Drawn Notes to Guide Both Their Reading and Discussion

Writing and drawing play a vital role in all stages of literature circles. While reading, students use response logs, Post-it notes, or role sheets to capture, record, crystalize, and play with their thinking and responses to the text. This kind of writing is open-ended and personal; it invites kids to generate extended, original language, not to jot "correct" phrases in response to workbook blanks or story-starter prompts. Later, when members come to the group, they use their own writings as a starting place for conversation and sharing. When the group gathers, these materials are a source ready to be drawn upon for discussion questions and ideas. Once a book is completed, groups or individuals often undertake a project as a way of synthesizing the reading for themselves and extending its reach to a wider audience. Sometimes such projects involve more formal, polished, audience-centered kinds of writing, such as a book review, a "missing chapter" of the book, a book poster, or a readers theater script. Across the whole cycle of a literature circle, then, writing and drawing are used to drive—and to record—the meaning constructed and the ideas shared.

6. Discussion Topics Come from the Students

One of the signal features of literature circles is that *kids develop their own discussion topics* and bring them to the group. The teacher does not provide the questions, whether verbally, on worksheets, or in study guides. Now, it may happen (and often does) that the topics kids come up with match the ones the teacher would have asked. But ownership makes a big difference: this way, students are in charge of their thinking and discussion.

Sometimes people mistake this element of literature circles as a kind of "permissiveness." But this is not a matter of "letting" kids choose their own discussion topics, or "allowing" or "permitting" them to do so. On the contrary, in literature circles, we *require* that students find and develop their own topics for discussion. In these challenging discussion groups, kids must perform all the acts that real, mature readers do—from picking their own books to making their own assignments to selecting issues for discussion, all the way through to sharing and expressing their views of the book to fellow readers. After all, if kids never practice digging the big ideas out of texts themselves and always have teachers doing it for them, how can they ever achieve literary and intellectual independence?

7. Group Meetings Aim to Be Open, Natural Conversations

Schools have traditionally favored convergent, objective questions—tasks in which the answers are fact-based and verifiably "correct." In literature circles, while we are always interested in the details of what we read and always take care to build our interpretations on a close reading of the text, we begin our conversations with personal response. We connect with one another around divergent, open-ended, interpretive questions—questions of value:

Does this book seem true to life?

How is this character like me?

Does this family remind me of my own?

If faced with this kind of choice, what would I do?

Could the people in this book have risen above their circumstances?

We take seriously the literary theory of reader response, which says that students cannot effectively move to the level of analysis until they have worked through, processed, savored, shared their personal response (Rosenblatt 1938).

But more than this—and here I part company with some other proponents of literature groups—much of the time, *sharing responses is enough.* Rather than forcing students onward to an explicit structural analysis of the literary components of the work, it's often fine to say, "That was great. Let's read another one." After all, if students have worked through a book together—sharing their views from a variety of angles, listening to selected passages read aloud, looking at one another's drawings, talking over particular vocabulary, connecting the work to their own lives, searching out questions of common interest among peers—is not the writer's craft being studied in a very deep, though implicit, way?

Though some teachers do seek ways to infuse literary terminology and analytical procedures into their literature circles, I do not see this as one of the structure's defining ingredients. Indeed, the distinctive value of literature circles is that it enacts another paradigm of learning. It is based on a faith in self-directed practice. Literature circles embody the idea that kids learn to read mainly by reading and to write mainly by writing and by doing so in a supportive, literate community. Of course we trust that kids' appreciation of the author's craft will grow as they read more, and that their own writing will, over time, reflect the deep, unconscious influences of all they have read. But the starting point, the way in, and the base for everything is "just reading" and "just responding" to lots and lots of books.

8. The Teacher Serves as a Facilitator

The teacher's main job in literature circles is to *not teach,* at least in the traditional sense of the term. For this special student-centered classroom activity, we bring back, with pride and respect, the abused term *facilitator,* taken from the work of Carl Rogers. As the many stories in Chapters 4, 8, 9, and 10 show, the teacher's work in literature circles is complex, artful, and absolutely essential. But it doesn't happen to include very much lecturing, telling, or advising.

Aside from initial mini-lessons and closing debriefing sessions (which are important but brief), the teacher isn't on stage. Instead, most of the teacher roles in literature circles are supportive, organizational, and managerial. We collect sets of good books, help groups to form, visit and observe meetings, confer with kids or groups who struggle, keep records, make assessment notes, and collect still more books.

In some literature circle classrooms, teachers also elect to play another key role: that of fellow reader. They join a group not as the teacher but as an equal, reading right along with kids a book they haven't previously read—and want to read. Obviously, teachers can make this choice only when the room's other lit circles are running smoothly enough that they can stay in one group over a couple of weeks' time. A teacher's becoming a fellow reader, honestly reading, responding, predicting, and sharing meaning-making processes right along with the students, offers a radically different and powerful demonstration of how grown-up readers really think.

Perhaps the one element most grievously lacking in the experience of most American schoolchildren is regularly seeing a mature adult reader connecting with a book for the first time, constructing meaning, talking about the thinking process, and sharing here-and-now responses. This mandate to model can be threatening to teachers, who assume they must be a paragon of cognition, of elevated literary taste, and authoritative interpretation. But this kind of modeling doesn't require perfection. On the contrary, we want kids to see how real readers really operate, which is far from neat and tidy. Effective adult reading is a complex constructive process, full of false starts, recursions, fix-ups, dead ends, blind alleys—not to mention personal quirks, tastes, strengths, and weaknesses. It's valuable for kids to see how all these attributes of real working readers go together day after day—not to be copied, but as one sample to build on, to vary from, to improvise off. If teachers are secure enough, they can "teach" their students a great deal simply by joining a group as an equal and reading a new book right along with the kids.

9. Evaluation Is by Teacher Observation and Student Self-Evaluation

Because literature circles do not aim to "cover material" or teach specific "subskills," the evaluation methods tied to those kinds of instruction are irrelevant. For literature circles, we need high-order assessment of kids working at the whole thing, the complete, put-together outcome—which, in this case, is joining in a thoughtful small-group conversation about literature. So how do we assess a student's achievement in such a complex event? Drawing on the burgeoning research and classroom lore of "authentic assessment," we use the tools of kidwatching, narrative observational logs, performance assessment, checklists, student conferences, group interviews, video/audiotaping, and the collection in portfolios of the artifacts created by lit circles. Because the structure of lit circles frees teachers from being the center of attention, they actually have time to conduct some of these more qualitative forms of evaluation while circulating through the classroom.

But evaluation in literature circles is not just the job of the teacher. Just as we require that kids take responsibility for their own book selections, topic choices, and reading assignments, we also want them involved in the record-keeping and evaluation activities of literature circles. Because self-monitoring is such a key ingredient in the reading process, it only makes sense that kids in literature circles are regularly asked to write and talk evaluatively about their own goals, roles, and performances in literature circles.

10. A Spirit of Playfulness and Fun Pervades the Room

It is a tenet of much modern learning theory—especially in the field of psycholinguistics—that young children learn most everything of importance to them by *playing at it* first. Indeed, *fun* is the factor that most effectively keeps learners engaged in complex learning tasks outside school, whether it is learning to speak one's native language or to water ski. Educators have recently come to recognize that the playful early childhood activities of "scribble writing" and "pretend reading" play a central role in the development of preschool children's literacy. Indeed, playing with books and playing with writing and drawing are not mere precursors to literacy but are real reading and writing. Similarly, the research on interaction in families, from the scaffolding work of Jerome Bruner (1961) to more recent family studies (Taylor 1998), shows that caring, playful adult-child relationships are crucial to nurturing learning. The "lap method," in which a parent gives a child full and loving attention and models the use of language for a real purpose, may be the most effective instructional strategy ever documented.

Teachers who implement literature circles in their classroom are recreating for their students the kind of close, playful interaction that scaffolds learning so productively elsewhere in life. They develop their classroom as a kind of analogous family, a substitute lap, another kind of dining-room table. It's no surprise, then, that teachers are energized by literature circles, that they so often comment on how much they and their students *enjoy* the time together. And when fun is unleashed in the classroom, can learning be far behind?

11. New Groups Form Around New Reading Choices

While we have recently been experimenting with lit circles that stay together for a while, especially during the second half of the year, we still believe in variety. Like many groups in the nonschool world, literature circles form when there is a job to do together, and when the job is done, the group disbands and its members move on to other projects. This allows for a constant mixing in the classroom, with different combinations of children being thrown together with each new book choice. From a literary point of view, this regular reshuffling of personalities and perspectives in discussion groups is enriching and challenging. With each new book comes a new set of coreaders, complete with their unique, sometimes unexpected views and interpretations.

The constant recombining of people into new groupings also enacts the principle of group dynamics whereby widespread, diffuse communication and friendship patterns in a classroom build cohesion and productivity. While it may seem more comfortable for kids to stay in the same literature circle and not switch, it is in the long-term best interest of the whole group (and the individuals it comprises) that everyone be brave and move on. Indeed, many teachers come to value this mixing phenomenon so highly that they work skillfully through book recommendations and personal persuasion to ensure that kids don't place themselves back into the same groups over and over.

▼ VARIATION: **Form Permanent, Not Temporary, Groups**
As valuable as it is to stir up book club membership, to make sure that kids work with lots of different classmates, there's a contradiction inherent in forming temporary groups. We keep saying that adult reading groups are the template that guides our translation of book clubs to school settings. But these "real" reading groups tend to keep the same members and stay together for a long time. People like Lucy Calkins argue that kids, too, need long-term, stable book clubs in which the same members work together over a long stretch of time and read several books together. Some of our Chicago schools have arrived at this compromise: they mix kids up first semester, then let them establish a "permanent" group for the next quarter or even for the rest of the year.

At a deeper level, this regular mixing of student groups is also important because literature circles offer a model of detracking, of how heterogeneous classes can work. Even if a classroom includes wildly diverse reading levels or "academic abilities," everyone can still pick books that group them at their own level. But this kind of leveling is self-chosen, temporary, and still within a mixed class—a huge difference from the permanent, official, and involuntary segregation of most school tracking systems. Further, in lit circle classrooms, kids can (and do) switch levels; they can pick harder or easier books, depending on their interest in certain authors, topics, or genres. Teachers encourage and support this kind of risk taking and stretching. The various comprehension tools we use can help different kinds of kids contribute successfully. For example, a student who isn't strong on verbal analysis may still offer her group an illustration that surprises and enriches the conversation. Or a special education student who needs to have the novel read aloud to him at home can still come to a discussion group and make arresting connections between the characters and his own life. In other words, literature circles, when done well, help make official ability grouping unnecessary. They show how heterogeneous, diverse student groups—including mainstreamed special education kids—can work together effectively.

How Literature Circles Fit in a Balanced Reading Program

When we discuss literature circles, we're talking about just a fraction of the school day, week, and year. So the question naturally arises, what *else* goes on during those days, weeks, and years? What other kinds of activities, structures, and strategies are going on that grow the whole range of literacy skills and habits?

Today, everybody talks about "balanced" reading instruction. The question is, a balance of *what*? One of the most popular models comes from Irene Fountas and Gay Su Pinnel as presented in a family of books about guided reading (1997, 1999, 2000). In Fountas and Pinnell's primary grades model, a balanced reading program includes eight elements (with my own terminology annotations):

1. Reading aloud.
2. Shared reading (visible text).
3. Guided reading (groups reading leveled texts).
4. Independent reading (kids on their own; reading workshop/literature circles).
5. Shared writing (teacher scribe).
6. Interactive writing (teacher/kids share pen).
7. Guided writing or writing workshop (teacher-guided, includes conferences and mini-lessons).
8. Independent writing (kids on their own).

In this version of balanced reading for young children, independent reading activities like literature circles have an important place, but they are only part of a larger puzzle.

In *The Art of Teaching Reading* (2000), Lucy Calkins offers a very different view of a balanced reading program. While she acknowledges the importance of the many teacher-directed elements in the Fountas and Pinnell model, she insists that independent reading, both individually and in book clubs, is a "central part of the reading curriculum," and not just one of many ingredients. "The independent reading workshop," she argues, "provides that opportunity for mentoring children in the project of composing a literate life, for teaching children to choose just-right books and to monitor for sense, to carry books between home and school, to not have a lonely reading life, to read a second book by an author in a different way because they've read the first, to have and develop ideas from books." For what it's worth, I lean toward Calkins's view that kid-driven independent reading, rather than teacher-driven leveled groups, is the most promising path toward passionate, lifelong reading.

My own model formula for balance in a reading and language arts program includes three other factors:

- Balance between teacher-guided and self-directed reading.
- Balance between wide and close (what Peterson and Eeds [1990] call "extensive" and "intensive") reading.
- Balance in the kind of social interaction students experience around books.

We can represent these kinds of balance on three parallel continuums:

Student-Directed		Teacher-Directed

Individual	Small Group	Whole Group

Extensive		Intensive
(fast, quick reading; focus on enjoyment and quantity)		(careful, deep reading; focus on author's craft and literary elements)

We can now use this device to illustrate the problem of balance by laying out some of the most widely used classroom structures for teaching reading. Obviously, the "accurate" location for any real classroom activity depends mightily on the teacher and kids who use it. Most of these structures can be shaded quite far in any direction—after all, some teachers give quizzes in SSR and others conduct genuinely nondirective whole-group discussions. But still, if we envision the usual manifestation of each model, we'll get a sense of how they sort out.

SSR RW LC	LSC	TDR GR RR
Student-Directed		Teacher-Directed

SSR RW	RR LSC LC GR	TDR
Individual	Small Group	Whole Group

SSR RW	LC	LSC GR TDR RR
Extensive		Intensive

RR = Traditional three-group round-robin reading

SSR = Sustained silent reading

GR = Guided reading; small groups in leveled books

RW = Reading workshop (Nancie Atwell model)

LC = Literature circles (this book's model)

LSC = Literature study circles (Katharine Samway and Gail Whang model)

TDR = Teacher-directed whole-class books (typical high school English class)

Perhaps this illustration helps point up the role that literature circles can play in a balanced reading program. It is the only structure that combines the elements of student direction, small groups, and moderately intensive reading.

There's not a "right side" to this chart. It's not meant to raise one structure above another, but to help us all build balance into the days, weeks, and years we design for kids. However, while there is no correct side, if you are running a classroom in which all the reading activities fall on the right-hand side (or the left-hand side) of this chart, then your program may be unbalanced. If you are doing nothing but reading workshop, SSR, and literature circles, you may want to rebalance by adding an element of intensive reading, making sure kids linger longer and more thoughtfully over some texts with some teacher input. If you are doing lots of guided reading lessons with leveled book groups, and also teacher-directed whole class books, then you might want to add an element of student direction to the mix, starting up some literature circles or initiating a reading workshop. If you believe, as we do, in balance, then the goal is not to be right but to offer our students a rich diversity of reading experiences.

▼ ▼ ▼ ▼ ▼ ▼ ▼ ▼ ▼ ▼ ▼ ▼

3

Ancient History and Current Research

ALTHOUGH MANY of us believe we "invented" literature circles with our students, peer-led discussion of written texts has been going on for many centuries. Though there is no official record, it wouldn't be surprising if book clubs were meeting in ancient Sumeria, where the world's first known writing system was created. I'd be willing to bet that some kind of proto–book club convened about five minutes after the first clay tablet was inscribed.

Closer to home, book clubs have had a surprisingly dramatic history in America, which has been aptly sketched by David Laskin and Holly Hughes in *The Reading Group Book* (1995). The first recorded "literature circle" in the New World convened in 1634, aboard a boat bound for the colonies. During her voyage to America, the noted Puritan figure Anne Hutchinson gathered a women's study group to discuss each Sunday's shipboard sermon. Once she was established in Boston, Hutchinson continued the practice, holding twice-weekly theological discussions in her parlor.

It didn't take long for the Puritan males to start worrying about what the Puritan females might be talking about in these study groups. An edict was promptly issued to the effect that Hutchinson was "maintaining a meeting and an assembly in your house that hath been condemned by the general assembly as a thing not tolerable or comely in the sight of God nor fitting for your sex." For running America's first literature circle, and thus "troubling the peace of the commonwealth," Hutchinson was banned.

In spite of this somewhat chilling start, book clubs became a vital element of the women's intellectual tradition in America. Early colonial women combined book discussions with their appointed chores, talking ideas over quilts or cooking. As the norms loosened in the early nineteenth century, book groups and book parties became popular women's events in New England. The first known bookstore-sponsored club began meeting in 1840, in Margaret Fuller's Boston shop. By the mid-1800s, book clubs were spreading to the Midwest, popping up in towns like Rochester, Michigan, and New Harmony, Indiana.

And though many of these early women's book clubs were the hobby of relatively well-off white women, there were also African American book clubs in some cities, which members used as one way to rise beyond slavery and educate themselves.

After the Civil War, these women's study groups enjoyed a major boom. What had been a scattered pastime now became a national movement. As Laskin and Hughes describe it:

> From El Paso, Texas, to Caribou, Maine, from Elmira, New York, to Madison, Indiana, women were gathering on weekday afternoons to discuss American and English literature (the Brownings, George Eliot, and John Stuart Mill were favorites), as well as the masterpieces of classical antiquity. They also debated the burning issues of the day, such as socialism, the Russian political system, and the tariff. Meetings generally lasted about two hours and usually took place during the day on weekdays—never on Sunday and rarely at night, since a woman was still not supposed to be seen outside her home after dark unless escorted by a man (and men were firmly barred from these gatherings). Roll call was taken as the meetings came to order; members were fined for absences.

Around the turn of the century, the focus of book clubs gradually shifted from cerebral pursuits to social service. Women started to take the social skills and worldly knowledge they had acquired in their book clubs and put them to use in the real world. They turned their attention from books to social reform, the suffrage movement, and prohibition. The foundation was laid for women's clubs as we know them today in many communities across the country, as agencies mostly dedicated to service projects rather than intellectual pursuits.

Of course, book clubs never completely died out during this century. They perked along at a lower level, with occasional spurts caused by the Great Books movement of the 1950s, and more recently by Oprah Winfrey's TV-driven book clubs. Thankfully, it has now become more common for book clubs to enroll members of both sexes. A recent study in Texas showed that about 30 to 35 percent of today's book clubs are mixed gender, while about 10 percent are men-only, with the rest clinging to the traditional women-only rule. A good account of contemporary American book clubs, including a variety of models, meeting procedures, and lists of favorite books, can be found in the aforementioned volume by Laskin and Hughes, as well as in *The Book Group Book,* by Ellen Slezak (2000).

Book Clubs Come to School

So now we know that book clubs weren't invented by American teachers in the 1980s. Instead, bringing literature circles to the classroom mainly involves importing book clubs from the wider adult culture into schools, translating them for young people without messing everything up. But that's a lot of translating. So maybe we should say that many teachers and students are *reinventing* literature circles together. But hey, if you believe in constructivist learning theory, you know that reinventing is pretty much as good as original inventing!

One original classroom reinventor was Karen Smith, now at the University of Arizona. It was the summer of 1982, and Karen was preparing for another year of teaching fifth grade at Lowell School, in Phoenix, Arizona. Claire Staab, a friend and teaching colleague who was moving to British Columbia, came by to offer Karen some classroom leftovers. Among the castoff items was a box of assorted paperback novels—three copies of this title, four or five of that, six of another. Because she could always use extra books for independent reading in her class, Karen cheerfully accepted her friend's donation. She stuck the box of books in the back of the room, and then, amid the turmoil of starting a new year, forgot about them.

A couple of months later, a group of students discovered the box. Sifting through the books, the kids got excited and approached Ms. Smith for permission to read them. Assuming the kids were simply prowling for more independent reading titles, Karen casually gave her approval. But within a few days, she noticed that the students had chosen books, established groups around their choices, assigned themselves pages to read, and were meeting regularly to talk about their books. She sat in on a couple of the groups and was dazzled by the quality, depth, range, and energy of the talk she heard. Karen's ten-year-old students had just invented their own literature circles.

In 1982, Karen was also a graduate student at Arizona State University, so she invited colleagues and professors into her classroom to observe the kids' groups at work and help her puzzle out the next steps. First among these was Ralph Peterson, who helped Karen figure out how to join the kids' book-talks without dominating the interaction. Soon, other leaders of the profession, including Dorothy Watson and Jerome Harste, came to visit, were impressed by the students, offered their insights on the process, and began to spread the word around the country of the wonderful structure invented by Karen Smith's fifth graders. A few years later, Karen herself told the story of these literature groups and the rest of her reading program in *Talking About Books* (Short and Pierce 1990).

Even though the classroom activity we now call literature circles is a new iteration of some ancient structures and ideas, the name is relatively new. Kathy Short and Gloria Kaufman get credit for assigning the name *literature circles* to the contemporary school-based book clubs, kid-led groups that show the genuine features of cooperative learning and student-centeredness. Short wrote about this innovation in her 1986 dissertation, titled "Literacy as a Collaborative Experience," which she prepared under the supervision of Jerome Harste and

Carolyn Burke, at Indiana University. A couple of years later, literature circles appeared as a featured activity in Short, Harste, and Burke's excellent book *Creating Classrooms for Authors and Inquirers* (1988; 2d edition 1995). All these progenitors seem to agree that the activity called literature circles draws on three main streams of thinking: independent reading, reader response theory, and collaborative learning.

Independent Reading

Today, most American elementary schools have made a daily commitment to independent reading, whether they call it reading workshop, SSR (sustained silent reading), or DEAR (drop everything and read). Whatever the name, this is a scheduled and sacred chunk of time, ten minutes to an hour, when everyone in the building—sometimes including cooks and janitors—"just reads" books of choice. There is no assigned reading, no quizzes, no strategy lessons, no grading, no book reports, and little or no record keeping. It is simply an official, scheduled acknowledgment of the research showing that reading achievement is more highly correlated with independent reading than with any other single factor.

The centrality of independent reading to students' lifelong literacy development has been underscored in every major report on reading issued over the past two decades. The landmark study *Becoming a Nation of Readers* (Anderson et al. 1985) stated: "Children should spend more time in independent reading. Independent reading, whether in school or out of school, is associated with gains in reading achievement. By the time they are in third or fourth grade, children should read independently a minimum of two hours per week. Children's reading should include classic and modern works of fiction and nonfiction that represent the core of our cultural heritage" (p. 119).

Of course, the value of independent reading wasn't exactly a hot news flash when the Commission on Reading endorsed it. Twenty years earlier, around the time I started teaching high school, "hooked on books" became an educational phenomenon. Daniel Fader, a former high school teacher and professor at the University of Michigan, came up with a simple idea for energizing secondary reading programs: jettison the thick anthologies and fill the classroom with lots of single copies of novels, especially current adolescent literature. Then, he said, use class time to let kids read and talk about books.

Though Fader's plan lacked the elaborated roles and structures of modern literature circles (or reading workshops), it worked. "Hooked on books" became a movement. All around the country, eager young teachers started scrounging school bookrooms, garage sales, and used-book shops, carrying armloads of books to school. We built our libraries and kids started reading more real books. While Fader's furor eventually faded, he legitimized classroom libraries and independent reading—lasting gifts to the profession. For many young teachers, Fader's book sparked our first classroom libraries and made independent reading a permanent part of our teaching repertoire.

More recently, the new *Standards for the English Language Arts,* issued by the International Reading Association and the National Council of Teachers of English (1996), place independent reading at the center of the curriculum, officially recommending both reading workshop and literature circles as structures for delivering this important experience. And even the 2000 National Reading Panel, whose controversial recommendations were considered highly conservative and whose main agenda was the promotion of phonics instruction, acknowledged that

> there has been widespread agreement in the literature that encouraging students to engage in wide, independent, silent reading increases reading achievement. Literally hundreds of correlational studies find that the best readers read the most and that poor readers read the least. These correlational studies suggest that the more that children read, the better their fluency, vocabulary, and comprehension.

Still, the panel called for more research to ensure that these strong correlations were actually causal.

The evidence for independent reading keeps accumulating. Richard Allington (2000), Patricia Cunningham and Richard Allington (1998), and Leslie Fielding and David Pearson (1994) have reported a number of studies linking independent reading to heightened comprehension and overall reading achievement. Kids need more time to actually read in school, to be able to choose their own materials and talk with fellow readers. This kind of time—time to "just read"—has been largely absent from most skill-and-worksheet-driven classrooms. These researchers also agree that independent reading time needs to be well structured, that teachers should help students pick books at their fluency level, and that when activities shift to teacher-guided instruction, the focus should be on demonstrations of comprehension strategies rather than so-called subskills. Literature circles are one orderly and manageable structure for ensuring that this kind of substantial independent reading—well beyond the levels customarily supported by SSR programs—happens in school.

Collaborative Learning

The collaborative/cooperative learning movement is so well established (or at least honored) in American schools that it requires no introduction here. There are ample and useful resources for teachers to read and learn about the underlying theory, the key classroom practices, and (for those who need "proof" in terms of the customary measures of educational success) the huge body of research documenting achievement gains across the curriculum (Johnson et al. 1994). Literature circles are a part—a quite sophisticated and highly evolved part—of the wider collaborative learning movement.

As most professionally active teachers are well aware, the epicenter of the collaborative movement is Minnesota, where brothers David and Roger Johnson, along with a host of colleagues, have developed a wide array of cooperative learning resources. While there are many other cooperative learning experts, authors, agencies, consultants, and workshops around, the Johnson group is always worth listening to because in their work they consistently adhere to the true, student-empowering potential of genuine collaborative structures. Unlike other popularizers who harness the energizing social processes of small groups to the memorization of the same old pointless trivia— constructs like Robert Slavin's (1985) "team games tournament"—the Johnsons generally apply cooperation to higher-order thinking about worthwhile topics.

As noted earlier, the widespread corruptions and misapplications of cooperative learning have given rise to a growing professional polarization. Today, the term *cooperative learning* is increasingly coming to denote skills-oriented, break-it-down, traditional school tasks assigned by teachers to student groups, while *collaborative learning* is the term preferred by teachers who are trying to sponsor true inquiry in small-group work by designing higher-order, student-centered, open-ended activities. Obviously, all the teachers who contributed to this book feel that our kid-run discussion groups represent authentic collaboration. Varied as they are, all of our literature circles display the characteristic features of true collaboration: student-initiated inquiry, choice, self-direction, mutual interdependence, face-to-face interaction, and self- and group assessment.

Collaborative learning draws heavily on a well-developed field of study called group dynamics, which remains largely unknown to schoolteachers. My work with several colleagues (Daniels and Zemelman 1985; Zemelman and Daniels 1988; Zemelman, Daniels, and Hyde 1998; and Daniels and Bizar 1998) tries to drag the insights of group dynamics into discussions of instruction and school reform. The overarching insight of group dynamics is that there are certain *predictable and controllable elements* in the development of highly productive groups. Since any school classroom—and any subgroup within it— is subject to these dynamics, it is very helpful for teachers to understand and "steer" these elements. For just one example, group dynamics research tells us that there are six ingredients in the development of a mature, interdependent, productive group (Schmuck and Schmuck 2000):

- Clear expectations.
- Mutually developed norms.
- Shared leadership and responsibility.
- Open channels of communication.

- Diverse friendship patterns.
- Conflict resolution mechanisms.

Therefore, if we want to have effective classroom literature circles, we would be well advised to ensure that each of these factors is explicitly provided for in the training, development, and maintenance of the discussion groups. Indeed, the very *essence* of literature circles involves predictable structures and events; clear, student-made procedures; kid leadership and responsibility; classwide friendships; constant public and private talk and writing among everyone in the room; and *inviting* disagreements and conflicting interpretations to emerge within a safe and comfortable structure. In other words, from a group dynamics point of view, literature circles are a very well-structured activity, one that we would expect not only to be successful in accomplishing its goal—which is the clear and deep understanding of a book—but also to contribute to the general cohesiveness and productivity of the wider classroom community.

One of the reasons literature circles have coalesced so strongly and generated so much excitement among teachers is that *they make heterogeneous classrooms work.* You can have a very diverse class of kids, with widely mixed "ability" levels, assorted cultural and ethnic identities, even lots of mainstreamed special education children, and still have an exciting, challenging, orderly, and caring atmosphere for everyone. In other words, literature circles—along with reading and writing workshops—are a key structure for detracking schools, which is one of the greatest unsolved issues of educational justice in our country.

Researchers like Jeannie Oakes (1985), Anne Wheelock (1992), and George Wood (1992) have voluminously documented the fact that ability grouping in American schools harms the achievement of kids in low and middle groups while providing few if any benefits for the kids in top groups. Further, Richard Allington (1983) has shown that the quality of instruction in low-track reading groups is consistently poorer than that offered to kids ranked as "higher" readers. There is simply no educational justification—and there is great social harm—in segregating kids into "Bluebirds," "Chickadees," and "Buzzards" groups, based on tested or perceived ability levels.

However, given that teachers and parents alike are deeply influenced by the "normal" ability-grouped model of instruction, how can we escape this destructive tradition? Literature circles are a natural substitution. Kids can still read at their own level, but they now do so by grouping *themselves*—not as externally labeled "Buzzards" but as people who are choosing one book at a time. Because the class includes students who are reading at all levels, a student can spend some time with skilled, above-grade-level readers—people who model the next step up—and at other times can "take a break," reading at his or her own comfort level with some other friends. The different discussion roles used in groups invite different learning styles to shine—kids who may not offer glib plot summaries can offer moving read-alouds or unique illustrations. Indeed, effective reading discussion groups tend to see diversity as an asset—the more people talk about books, the more they want to have a *range* of responses, ideas, and connections in the group. It's not as much fun if everyone has the same experiences, stories, connections to share; discussions are richer if people *aren't* all alike.

In a literature circles classroom, there are so many ways to succeed, to find your niche as a reader. The teacher, of course, plays an important role, kid-watching with care, balancing between challenging each child and sustaining, above all, the love of reading, writing, and talking about books. And, of course, because the role of presenter/taskmaster of round-robin reading has been renounced, the teacher is now *available* to take a facilitative role and, if kids are struggling, to give individual attention while the rest of the students work along in their kid-led groups.

Reader Response Literary Criticism

One of the most inspiring stories in American education is that of Louise Rosenblatt, who had a great idea in 1938 and stuck with it. Rosenblatt, of course, is the developer of the "reader response" school of literary criticism. It was her fundamental insight in *Literature as Exploration* that a text is just ink on a page until a reader comes along and gives it life. Debunking the old school of the so-called New Critics, she insisted that there is no one correct interpretation of a literary work, but multiple interpretations, each of them profoundly dependent on the prior experience brought to the text by each reader. Rosenblatt clung to, elucidated, and reexplained this simple, powerful idea for more than fifty years, until it finally began winning widening acceptance in the 1980s.

In recent years, Robert Probst, of Georgia State University, has emerged as a helpful interpreter of Rosenblatt's ideas for K–12 teachers. In his book *Response and Analysis* (1988), Probst lays out a concise description of reader response theory, applying it to the real situation in public schools. He explains how American teachers, in their hunger to push students up the cognitive ladder to the *analysis* of literature, forget or refuse to begin with students' *response* to their reading. Probst explains that in good teaching, the response always comes first. As he reminds us:

> The pleasures that drew us first to literature were not those of the literary scholar. When our parents read us *Mother Goose,* we enjoyed the rhythms of the language without analyzing the political or social significance of nursery rhymes. Later, we listened to "Little Red Riding Hood," not to identify characteristics of the fairy tale, but to find out

whether or not the wolf had the little girl for dinner. And still later, we read *Catcher in the Rye,* not to investigate Salinger's style and trace the literary influences of his book, but to see how Holden Caulfield copes. (p. 3)

In other words, the pathway to analysis, to more sophisticated and defensible interpretations of literature, must go through personal response, not around it. While Probst and Rosenblatt both agree that there are better and worse readings of texts, there are not "wrong" ones. Any work of literature is always a confrontation, a collaboration, between a reader's prior experience and the words of an author.

Ellin Keene and Susan Zimmerman's *Mosaic of Thought* (1997) has deepened our understanding of this delicate cognitive process by looking at reader response in light of current research on reading comprehension. Today we know a lot more, Keene and Zimmerman argue, about how proficient adult readers actually think: while reading, they make personal connections with the text, they ask questions, they look for important elements or themes, they create sensory images, they make inferences and judgments, and they create ongoing summaries or syntheses as they read. In other words, a skillful reader's "response" includes several kinds of active, ongoing thinking. They may do this thinking largely unconsciously, but somewhere along the line, mature readers acquire this set of powerful mental tools for interacting with text.

This comprehension research may be powerful and potentially practical, but reading pedagogy hasn't quite caught up. As Keene and Zimmerman acknowledge, in most classrooms kids are not yet learning these key ways of thinking. We teachers need to open up our heads and show exactly how effective readers think, naming and demonstrating each of these major cognitive tools. Then, we need to give kids plenty of time to practice applying these strategies, not in drills or worksheets, but in real conversations about real books. And what's the best format for this practice? Keene and Zimmerman recommend: "We have found that the most authentic, and therefore, successful application of the strategies is in the context of book clubs—small groups of children talking regularly about books and the strategies they use to understand them." They further suggest that when children join in these book clubs and other reading conversations, their responses can be scaffolded with written and artistic tools like letters, journals, and Post-it notes.

So, from a theoretical point of view, we can say that literature circles are a form of independent reading, structured as collaborative small groups, and guided by reader response principles in light of current comprehension research. As a classroom structure, literature circles can welcome, build on, and gradually broaden students' responses to what they read. As Keene and Zimmerman put it, "If reading is about mind journeys, teaching reading is outfitting the travelers, modeling how to use the map, demonstrating the key and legend, supporting the travelers as they lose their way and take circuitous routes, until, ultimately, it's the child and the map together and they are off on their own."

Now let's go into some real classrooms (at last!) and see how these travelers are doing and how these theories look in action.

4

Looking into Literature Circles

Nᴏᴡ ᴛʜᴀᴛ ᴡᴇ have defined literature circles, looked at their history, and reviewed the research, you may be wondering: What are they supposed to look like? How are kids arranged? What does the teacher do? How loud does it get? What happens when things go wrong?

Good questions. In this chapter we'll visit three teachers who have three quite different versions of book clubs circles happening in their rooms. We'll try to catch the feel and flavor of what literature circles can be like, for both kids and teachers.

Marianne Flanagan

ꜰɪꜰᴛʜ ɢʀᴀᴅᴇ, ᴍᴇᴛᴄᴀʟꜰᴇ ᴍᴀɢɴᴇᴛ ꜱᴄʜᴏᴏʟ, ᴄʜɪᴄᴀɢᴏ

You hear the noise long before you reach the door to room 213 in Metcalfe School: the buzz of literature circles echoes halfway down the stairwell. When you first enter the room, you may not believe that any reliable communication can happen amid the din in this too-small room; indeed, that's exactly what Marianne's colleagues, long bred to equate silence with effective teaching, seem to think as they walk past her doorway, shaking their heads. And yet as you get acclimated to the noise level, join a few student groups, and tune in to the ongoing conversations, the sophisticated quality of these literary discussions becomes apparent.

Children are tucked up close to one another, ten-year-olds talking with animation, seriousness, and sometimes passion about the novels they have chosen to read. They have come to class with notes and drawings reflecting their ideas about the day's reading. They toss searching and open-ended questions into their groups, read aloud favorite passages, stop to talk about difficult or powerful words. They are constantly flipping back through their books, using specific passages to prove points or settle disagreements. They laugh a lot, argue some, often touch one another to stress a point, and keep one eye on the clock to make sure they all get their fair share of "airtime."

Among the titles being discussed today are Katherine Paterson's *Bridge to Terabithia,* H. G. Wells's *War of the Worlds,* Beverly Cleary's *Dear Mr. Henshaw,* and Sid Fleischmann's *The Whipping Boy.* Because Marianne's class is just beginning with literature circles, they are using a set of simple, rotating roles. The roles help students bring up and independently discuss important topics of their own, rather than march through typical teacher-supplied study questions. Among the roles Marianne's kids are using today are questioner, literary luminary, connector, illustrator, and vocabulary enricher.

Over in the corner, Brian, Wilbert, and Roy are completely engrossed in their discussion of Elizabeth Speare's *Sign of the Beaver.* The colonial family in the story has been forced to move to the remote Penobscot region because the parents could not find work in the city of Boston. Wilbert, acting as today's "connector," shares a personal experience: "My Dad lost his job. We're not poor like the kid in the book, but he did lose his job." The kids talk quietly for a few minutes about family economic problems. Roy, who is today's questioner, wonders aloud whether a twelve-year-old boy should be left alone like this, in the woods for six weeks with only a rifle and some food. The boys enter a lively debate, centering around the possibility of Indian attacks. Roy doesn't think the one-shot, muzzle-loading gun would be much help: "Man, they'd send lots of Indians with lots of arrows," he says. "They'd shoot you before you could get them." Wilbert suggests that maybe if Matt got really good with the gun, he might "grow up to be a cop or something." Roy laughs and Brian chimes in: "Not in 1768! This isn't *now,* you know." They all have good laugh at Wilbert's anachronism.

The conversation returns to Indian attacks. Roy argues that because Matt has already met and talked to one member of the local tribe, such attacks are unlikely. "If you make friends with one Indian, then you're friends with them all," he asserts positively. Brian and Wilbert insist that Matt is still in danger. Suddenly, Roy's face lights up. "It's like what's-her-name," he says. "You know—that girl. . . ." And with that, he springs out of his chair and starts poking around in people's desks, looking for something. He rummages through half the room before he finds what he's looking for. Meanwhile, Brian and Wilbert just shake their heads and continue talking about whether or not their fathers would let them have a gun. Finally, Roy returns to the circle in triumph, carrying a thick U.S. history textbook. Flipping through the pages, he slaps the book down, open to an illustration of Captain John Smith and Pocahontas. "See," Roy announces, "if you were friends with one Indian, you were friends with them all!"

Marianne skirts around the edges, dipping briefly into the groups. Often, she gets drawn into the conversation if the book is one she has read herself—

indeed, Marianne enjoys the books so much that she often gets stuck in one group when she had planned to circulate through several. She hasn't preread every book kids are discussing, but she doesn't worry about whether she is "really teaching." There are other scheduled times during the school day when Marianne is very much in charge of the material and the process, selecting readings, offering interpretations, modeling strategies, and drawing kids' attention to an author's craft. Perhaps if she were conducting a teacher-directed lesson on *Sign of the Beaver,* Marianne might have gently challenged Roy's still-stereotypic thinking about Indians and their friendships. But this is not the time.

This chunk of the day—literature circle time—is separate and different and special. This is time for kids to pick, read, and discuss their own books. Marianne is happy to see the kids connecting with books, taking responsibility as readers and group members, constructing meaning together, and beginning to debate and challenge one another. She knows that in running literature circles, the teacher's main job is not to translate or interpret the books but to facilitate the work of the groups.

Theresa Kubasak

THIRD GRADE, BAKER DEMONSTRATION SCHOOL, EVANSTON, IL

"I've noticed that one of our literature circle groups has already started meeting," Theresa Kubasak calls out to her third graders. "Maybe that's our cue to put the math stuff away in our cubbies and move into our book clubs." Without any further prodding from Theresa or student teacher Erin McCarthy, the kids shift gears smoothly. They gather up the materials from their math work and stack them away, taking out their novels and journals and regrouping into five book clubs in different corners of the classroom. They set to work, talking about the self-assigned chapters they have read for today, comparing notes from their journals, and running their own lively literary discussions for more than thirty minutes. There are jokes, disagreements, connections, and lots of explicit self-assessment. Kids are using language like "I disagree with that because," "If you look at page 43, you'll see," "This reminded me of the time when I," and "Following up on what Trevor just said."

Of course, the kids didn't achieve this degree of autonomy and focus spontaneously. Their ability to operate in peer-led book discussion groups is rooted in two things: the warm community that Theresa has been cultivating since the beginning of the year, and about twenty days of specific literature circle training.

The community is a special one. There are 1,800 picture and chapter books here, grouped by theme and author. Scarves and hats from all over the world hang from the ceiling. There are several work areas: hand-built bleachers for class meetings, assorted worktables, and sawed-off tree stumps as stools.

Displayed around the room are large, beautiful albums for kids to write in, including

The Book of Dreams
The Book of Feelings
Our Friends
Our Parents
The Trip Book
Siblings
Pets
Phony Pets (for kids who don't really own any pets)

A place of special honor is reserved for the book of People Who Died, where kids have recorded the losses of grandparents, uncles and aunts, siblings, and even parents, over the past six years in Theresa's class. There is a constant stream of helpful, interesting adults dropping by, some of whom bake and bring the "bread of the day" for kids to taste.

Theresa's school encourages teacher autonomy and creativity, and she takes full advantage. She has built this year's whole third-grade curriculum around the theme "Ain't Got Nothin' But the Blues." On a huge cluster chart, she's mapped out a vast and ambitious exploration of everything related to the blues. The kids will study African cultures, the middle passage, slavery, abolition, the Great Migration, and the Harlem Renaissance. They'll undertake author studies of Walter Dean Myers, Faith Ringgold, Javaka Steptow, and Jerry Pinckney. They'll enjoy the music of Elmore James, Muddy Waters, Robert Johnson, and dozens more. They'll learn the structure and lingo of blues music, and write some themselves. They'll take field trips to a blues club, to an African art exhibition, to the blues archives at the Harold Washington Library. And more and more and more.

Built into the center of Theresa's elegant curriculum are literature circles, kid-led book clubs that meet all year long. Let's listen as Theresa tells how she got kids started, how she used those twenty days of training back in September and October. Then we'll come back to this spring day and listen in on a day's worth of meetings.

It seemed that for third graders with limited or no experience with lit circles, summarizing was the core skill we needed to teach. We don't use role sheets, so it's important to start out slowly and deliberately until the children internalize their roles, knowing them by heart like a cherished poem. With the whole class gathered on two L-shaped bleachers in a corner of the room, Erin and I modeled summarizing, drawing from a vast collection of picture books with which the children were familiar. After many examples, I read aloud to the whole class and asked them to summarize the story. When the kids went on too long, I said, "I'm sorry. This is supposed to be a summary. You're telling us too much. Can you try it again? Can you just touch on the most important part?"

With some children I made the sound of a game show buzzer with my mouth, saying, "Bzzzzzzzz. . . . I'm sorry. Your time is up. You were asked to give a summary, not tell the whole story."

The next day children chose a picture book from our class collection to read on their own, knowing they would be expected to come forward and summarize it. In the whole group, kids gave their summaries and received explicit directions for improving the summary as well as praise for what went well. Critiquing and praising in front of the class requires trust and the building up of emotional resiliency. If we are truly a "community of learners," we can guide children to this place of trust.

On day 3, the children were ready to choose their own book to read, breaking into lit circles to summarize their particular story. We took instant photos of each lit circle and posted them on the bulletin board, affirming their identity as part of a group. We continued this activity for several days, content that students had mastered the role of summarizer.

About a week and a half later, we introduced the role of word wizard by reading aloud Brian Pinckney's *Faithful Friend*. This rich tale of friendship features magic, zombies, and a lush vocabulary. As a class we listened for words to write on our word wizard chart (interesting, challenging, or beautiful words). We didn't interrupt the flow of the story while reading it, but I paused thoughtfully at a Creole word or at a particularly beautiful word or phrase. The children fleshed out the chart, noticing similes, giving me a chance for a quick mini-lesson on this device.

The next day we repeated the whole-class word wizard activity with Pinckney's *In the Time of Drums*. We discussed questions the word wizard may use and put them on a long skinny chart to be tacked up for all to refer to when needed. We modeled how to record words and continue conversation.

On day 3 of word wizarding, each child received a fat stack of Post-its and a response sheet on which to write their summary, word wizard choices, favorite part, characters, and things they were wondering about. Using *The Drinking Gourd* as a read-aloud, they all listened and wrote, later meeting in groups to share their ideas. The children were experiencing what it feels like to be a full, active participant in a literature circle. The next day, the students chose a book independently, again using the response sheet to jog ideas. They met in groups to share. It took us until the twentieth day of all this preparation to finally sign up for books and move into traditional lit circles!

Now it is April, and Theresa's third-grade literature circles are humming along. Near the door, one book club starts its meeting with a process issue. As Brenda points out forthrightly, Tony is always getting the group off-task by joking around. He's really amusing, but it's just not useful for the book-talk. Tony listens to all this undefensively; he seems to know that his jokester tendencies can be a problem. The other kids nod as Brenda challenges him to really do the job.

"You won't get out of hand?" she asks.

"I'm okay," Tony replies.

"'Cause we gotta stay on the book."

"I feel fine," he asserts.

Ms. Kubasak comes by and gets the kids to state the problem. She asks Tony to make a commitment. "What are two things you can do to be a funny guy and still be a good discussion member?"

"I'll be the questioner," Tony says, showing a list of notes jotted in his journal.

"Let's all be passage masters," suggests Beth.

After Ms. K. moves on, leaving them to settle their own group issues, Tony suggests that the group begin its work by considering some especially important words from today's reading selection, starting with *scowling*.

Another group is discussing E. B. White's *Stuart Little,* and they notice a pattern of problem/solution, something that Ms. K. has talked about during a previous whole-class mini-lesson. They decide to make a list of the problems and solutions:

Problem	Solution
Mom was washing and lost her ring.	Stuart's dad had to lower him down the chain and Stuart got the ring.
Stuart got locked in the refrigerator.	Mrs. Little finally opened the refrigerator.
One key in the piano that stuck drives George crazy.	Stuart goes in the piano to make the stuck key go down.

Across the room, another group is reading *Hope's Crossing,* a novel set during the Revolutionary War. There's some initial discussion about the reading assignment. Some members think they are reading too few pages each day. The book is interesting and easy, so why not step up the pace and finish the book sooner than they had originally planned? But then they realize Eva has been absent for few days and is already behind on the reading. Just when they want to jump ahead, it seems they are pulled back. But Eva looks at the calendar and realizes there's a school holiday coming up. "Don't worry, I'll catch up," she promises good-naturedly, and the schedule is readjusted. Now, before plunging into the day's discussion, the kids give Eva a quick summary of the events in today's chapters so she can join the conversation.

Pretty soon a lively debate breaks out about a British attack on the colonists.

Meiko: It was just the mom, the two girls, the baby, and the dogs.

Rachel: I hated it when she got captured and they shot the dogs.

Anna: That was the worst.

Eva: Think about it—dogs? The mom might get killed, the house might get on fire, they might starve. Compare those things to the dogs' getting shot. You wouldn't be . . .

Rachel: My dogs are like people to me.

Keegan: Do you think in wartime—you wouldn't be concentrating on dogs.

Eva: They're like my best friends. We play all the time. They do make mistakes.

Anna: I would take my dog with me.

Eva: Dogs to me . . . it would be like if you shot my mom and dad. Anne and Carla in the book . . .

Anna: Both people and dogs can help you. If something really horrible . . .

Meiko: Even though they can't talk, you can communicate.

Eva: I'm not saying you're wrong.

Keegan: Last year my dog, Milton, was out with my dad. My dog protects me a lot. A guy came in our house at nine at night. He was a burglar. My dad is a rowing coach and he leaves the dog home when he's gone. My dog is really faithful.

Eva: I'm not saying . . .

Meiko: We're just saying our opinion.

Anna: I worry about fire in our apartment house, what could happen to our dogs. I get so scared.

Rachel: We had fires in our neighborhood.

Anna: We had a tornado!

Rachel: Okay, let's talk about something else.

Eva: Can we get back to the book? No tornados, please!

Meiko: Well, I would stand up to [the British].

Keegan: You might get a whuppin'. If you stood up to the British, they have ways of killing you.

Meiko: I'd rather die than have someone . . .

Rachel: It's like that song we sang in the all-school show: "Before I'd be a slave, I'd be buried in my grave."

Meiko: I'd rather die than have someone controlling my life completely.

Today's literature circles session didn't have much of an introduction, and certainly no formal mini-lesson from Theresa. The kids sort of slipped into it spontaneously. But now, as Theresa calls the kids back to the wooden bleachers in the corner of the room, the sharing time is highly structured—and it lasts more than fifteen minutes. Into this stretch of the literature circle meeting, Theresa gracefully slides mini-lessons on vocabulary building, book selection, and solving group problems; she and Erin also demonstrate how book club members can disagree respectfully.

Some kids are dawdling, so the ones already on the bleachers start singing, to the tune of "Frère Jacques,"

> We are waiting,
> We are waiting,
> Just for you,
> Just for you.
> Please come over,
> Please come over.
> Tha-ank you,
> Tha-ank you.

They keep singing as classmates straggle in. The singers really get into it, turning it into a round, a quite melodious one at that. Even the latecomers are singing as they arrive and slip into their seats.

Theresa has brought a rolled-up poster to the group. "I found something really interesting," she says. "I discovered that many of the books you have been reading have something in common. Do you know what that might be?"

"Which books?" the kids ask.

"*Frog and Toad Together, Little House, Maniac McGee, Sarah, Plain and Tall, Strawberry Girl, Charlotte's Web, Julie of the Wolves.*"

As the kids puzzle, Theresa unfurls the poster. "They all won the Newbery Medal," she explains. "It's the biggest prize for kids' books, kind of like the Academy Awards."

One boy points to the cover of *The Bridge to Terabithia* on the poster. "My brother read that one," he announces.

"What a good place to get ideas for books to read," Theresa exclaims, "our big brothers and sisters. I do that in my own family. I get book recommendations from my brothers and sisters."

The kids spend a few minutes thinking of books their siblings or parents have read, and promise to nose around their families for future ideas.

Next, Theresa simply asks, "Okay, what went well today?" And then ensues a whole series of embedded mini-lessons. Some of them come up spontaneously from the kids' comments, and some are drawn from the page of notes Theresa has made while wandering the room for the past half hour, watchful for teachable points and next steps. The lessons go by pretty fast, but these are among today's highlights:

"How'd it go?" Theresa asks the group with the jokester problem. "Was Tony too funny?"

"I think it went perfect," says Joe. "He didn't goof off. It was great."

Tony is happy with his performance, too. He comments sagely, "Well, we did argue a little bit over some words. But eventually we worked it out."

"I noticed two ways that different people were using to figure out words that you didn't know. Like this group came upon the word *Hamlin*. And you read the sentence over to see if you could figure it out. Somebody said, 'It sounds like a place.' Which made sense. Then you also looked it up in the dictionary and found it really is a place. Those are two really good strategies—try to figure the word out from the sentence, or if that doesn't work, look it up."

"I was worried about Alex a little bit today. He was sitting with some people who really yak a lot, and I was thinking he might not get a word in. You know, some people are just quiet. Like Ms. McCarthy. Did you know that she was nominated as Illinois Student Teacher of the Year? Isn't that great? But she never talked about it, because she's kind of quiet and there are so many other people talking in here."

Alex pipes up, "But I got one, I got a word in today."

Theresa laughs. "Yes, I loved it. You just butted in, and it was so perfect."

"I noticed that sometimes it's hard to disagree with someone when they are your friend. Like Ms. McCarthy and I really disagree about this one character in Harry Potter, don't we?"

"We sure do."

"It's not like we really argue. It's not like we aren't going to hang out together, but we do argue about the book."

"Yeah. I think that this character, Professor Trelawney, is a big hoax. I can't believe Professor Dumbledore was shocked."

"Well, I'm never giving up on this character. I'm going to read some more so I can find some things to change your mind about her."

"Well, you can try."

"Chrissa and Bobby were working on a song about Maniac McGee and Martin Luther King, which they are going to sing for us in a minute. Can you tell us how you made this comparison? It kind of surprised me at first. What do those two people have in common?" While Chrissa and Bobby confer, Theresa quickly sketches a Venn diagram on the flip chart.

"They both got blacks and white together," Chrissa offers.

"They were not respected," says Bobby.

Theresa jots these words in the overlapping section of the Venn diagram. "I guess you've got something there. They did want to get everyone together." Theresa ponders for a minute. "Can we hear the song?"

The kids perform their song about Maniac McGee, all six verses, to the tune of a folk song about Martin Luther King called "Once there Was a Gentle Man." In fact, this is the same song that came up earlier in today's *Hope's Crossing* literature circle, the one the kids had performed in the recent all-school show.

Theresa's classroom is a very special place, and literature circles are not the only special feature. Here, abundance is offered to children, and much is expected of them. In this admittedly advantageous situation, Theresa Kubasak is practicing what I'd call "second wave" literature circles. It starts with tons of really good books, available in multiple copies. Many but not all of the books are coordinated with curriculum themes, so that kids can naturally extend their burgeoning interests. There are no role sheets, but Theresa starts the year by teaching the roles, with explicit lessons on visualizing, questioning, predicting, attending to authors' craft. The classroom culture is highly reflective; everyone understands that certain social and thinking skills are needed for small groups to operate well and knows how to debrief, hone, and refine these skills every day. The groups set their own schedules, including starting and ending dates. Kids have developed a broad repertoire of response strategies; they can analyze plot structures, make emotional connections, study the words in the text, or take a variety of other approaches. There are no mandated artificial projects at the end of the book but instead occasional book advertisements like the Maniac McGee song.

And, like the original version, these "second wave" literature circles are really, really fun. As one of the kids in the *Homer Price* group put it, shaking his head with a grin, "You think you're going to the Amazon, and then you go to Guatemala. You never know what to expect with books!"

Nancy Steineke

VICTOR J. ANDREW HIGH SCHOOL, TINLEY PARK, IL

It is 8:54, almost time for second period, and things are going to move really fast in Nancy's Steineke's class today. As the freshmen stroll in, there's already a note on the board that says, "Get out book, notes & illustrations, membership grid, processing sheets, table cards."

As kids are unpacking, even before the second bell rings to officially start the period, Nancy declares, "You are a movie star. Decide what movie you are going to cast yourself in and who will be your costars. This can be a remake of an old movie, starring you—or a brand new movie, maybe based on one of the books you are reading."

Nancy is cuing a warm-up activity that she always has students do in their literature circle groups before starting the book-talk. As a graduate of many cooperative learning training sessions, Nancy deeply believes that an initial warm-up activity is important to good book club discussions. Grown-ups do this all the time in their reading groups, she argues, when they snack and gossip at the start of meetings. Nancy doesn't want her freshmen to omit this necessary step, so for each meeting she offers a new, often goofy prompt for kids to use in getting started.

So today, the kids are pondering movie stardom while the school's daily announcements blare through the loudspeaker. As soon as all the badminton scores and pep club meetings have been announced, the kids move quickly into their six literature circle groups. They make sure their desks are touching, with everyone knee to knee. In case they need a reminder, there is a poster hanging on the wall describing "12-inch voices," reminding everyone to adjust their volume. Beside it hangs a thirty-nine-item list of Good Partner Skills, developed collaboratively by the class, which begins with "pay attention" and ends with "shower regularly."

The kids spend the first five minutes of their group meeting responding to the day's "membership" question.

"Romance movies are my favorite. I'd have to be in something with Mel Gibson or one of those Australian guys."

"I'd like to be on the *VIP* TV show, because there's a lot of hot action all the time. I mean, those girls are hot."

"I'd be in the next *X-Files* movie, costarring with David Ducovny. How do you spell his name?"

"Well, for me it would have to be something musical, with lots of dancing in it, like *Center Stage*."

At 9:00, Nancy shouts over the din of movie star talk: "You should be halfway through the grid. Keep moving!" The kids speed up, jotting their classmates' responses on a grid form, which has been gradually accumulating interesting, slightly random information about fellow members for three weeks now.

At 9:03, Nancy calls a halt to the warm-up and directs: "Time for the books. Go!" Today is the final discussion of some books the kids chose following a whole-class study of *To Kill a Mockingbird*. Three weeks ago, Nancy offered the kids an assortment of books grouped around the theme of prejudice, representing a wide range of reading levels and authorial styles, and including both fiction and nonfiction. Among the titles the kids picked were *Tobacco Sticks*, by William Hazelgrove; *Montana, 1941*, by Larry Watson; *There Are No Children Here*, by Alex Kotlowitz; and *The Water Is Wide*, by Pat Conroy. Now, as the groups begin twenty-five minutes of book-talk, the kids have lots to draw on. As always, everyone has brought three kinds of notes: a list of questions for discussion, some personal connections to the text, and an illustration suggested by today's reading.

Two groups have chosen *There Are No Children Here,* and right now they're going in two different directions. As the first *Children* group compares illustrations, they are surprised to find that three of the five members have independently drawn the very same scene from the book, a moment where the young inner-city kid, Pharoah, talks about rainbows and pots of gold. The students' pictures show several different versions of a rainbow arcing behind a dismal inner-city housing project, where the book is set.

"Oooh, you drew that, too."

"So did I."

"You, too? Hmmm."

"Why did we do that?"

"It's like, it's so sweet, he thinks that there is really a pot of gold at the end of the rainbow, behind a hot-dog stand."

"It reminds you that he's just a little kid."

"But his brother . . ."

"On page 285, it explains, he has all these responsibilities that none of us can even dream of."

"But Ricky tells him the rainbow isn't real."

"Yeah, but I don't think he is completely sure. He like, sort of tells him and sort of doesn't. Ricky acts tough, but he wants to chase rainbows, too."

"Even though he's old enough to know better."

"Ricky wants to have a dream."

"Like something good could happen to you even though you live in this terrible place. It's sad."

Across the room, the other *There Are No Children Here* group is taking a less empathic view of the welfare, crime, and violence depicted in the book.

"My mom is a single mom, and she wanted to get some help from the state, because my dad didn't get any health insurance on us. And the state said no, you can't have any welfare because you're in too big a tax bracket. And she said, if I had the money I wouldn't be asking! But in the book all these people get all the welfare they want."

"Why do the police even get involved in these housing projects?"

"What do you mean? When you're a cop, you put your life on the line. Your job is to serve and protect, just like it says on the car. You can't just decide who to protect and who not to."

"But the people who move into those projects know what they're getting into when they move in there."

"The police don't get to choose where they are assigned."

There's an uneasy silence as the kids ponder this disagreement. After looking down at his list of questions for a moment, James asks, "Well, what do you think Pharoah and Ricky would have amounted to by now?"

"They went to Catholic schools, right?"

"Yeah, so they're probably in college."

"Not Ricky—he'd be in jail."

"Wait a minute, when was this?" James thumbs to the front of the book, noting the 1994 copyright.

"Let's see, if Ricky was fifteen when this book was written, then he would be, uh, twenty-two today."

"Well, it's like 90 percent of parochial school kids go to college."

"How's the mother gonna send him to college? She didn't even have a hundred dollars to keep him out of jail, where's she gonna get fifty grand for college?"

"He could get a scholarship."

"I wonder where they are, really, today."

"How could you find out?"

As kids work, Nancy drags a chair around the room and sits in briefly in each group. While she mostly listens, she's not shy about asking a prodding question, offering her view of the book, sharing a laugh, or giving feedback on the group's process. She may also pipe up with directions for the whole class at any time. At 9:17 she hollers, "I'm not hearing very many follow-up questions!" At 9:28 she announces, "Only five minutes left—be sure you talk about what happens on the last page of the book."

Today, as always, Nancy saves the last ten minutes of class for reflection, half in literature circles, and half with the whole class. She asks the kids to quickly jot "three interesting ideas from the book" that came up during the discussion, followed by "three things you noticed about your group's process." In their circles, the kids compare notes and select a reporter. When the whole class gathers, each group reports in turn, noting pluses and minuses. Today's meetings yield a mix of self-assessments.

"We got off track some. But it was sort of about the book, but pretty far from it."

"We did okay on using names. We stopped doing it last time."

"People cared more about the whole discussion than making their individual points."

"The discussion didn't get boring. There weren't any awkward pauses."

"We made a lot of personal connections to this book today."

At the very end of every literature circle meeting in Ms. Steineke's class, after all the processing is done, the kids say to each other, "Thank you for the nice discussion." Of course, this little formality was originally Nancy's idea, one of a hundred lessons she has used to show her kids how productive small groups actually work. But now, when the kids say thank you, they smile broadly and really seem to mean it. It's 9:41, time for the next class.

Nancy has used many structures and tools to get her students to this point (she tells more about her own strategies in Chapter 10). But what is most striking today is that everyone has come prepared and everyone has participated. After months of practice and careful training, the kids can sustain long and focused conversations about books and the ideas in them. There is a balanced distribution of airtime in all groups. There are no wallflowers, so silent partners, no slackers, no nonparticipating members. If you sit in on any of the six groups for a couple of minutes, you will hear every student chime in about something. The groups know how to disagree respectfully, how to get out of conversational dead ends, how to put an end to digressions, how to draw one another out, and how to "bring it back to the book." Just about the only problem that arose today was when Bob decided to try on Jeanette's platform shoes, but his brief bid for attention fell flat; the other kids just rolled their eyes and turned back to their book discussions.

▼ ▼ ▼ ▼ ▼ ▼ ▼ ▼ ▼ ▼ ▼ ▼

5

Getting Started: Preparing and Orienting Students

Literature circles are really fun! Lit circles are very neat. They are very, very awesome. Lit circles are very, very complicated, though.
—Stacey, fifth grade

These kids are amazing! They really work at pulling everyone into the discussion, they're kind and thoughtful . . . I never have to get them back on task, they're so involved in what they're doing. . . . It just blows my mind that they can do so much when you just guide them and let them go.
—Kristen Overcash, fifth-grade teacher

THESE TWO animated comments nicely embody the realities of preparing students to do literature circles. Getting a basic version going is usually relatively simple, because the structure is self-teaching. What kids can do with just a little preparation can be truly amazing.

On the other hand, literature circles are inarguably complex, including as they do a decentralized classroom, lots of different books being read, lots of logs and materials circulating, the frequent reshuffling of groups, plenty of noise and movement, and a wide range of choices for the teacher. This means that while you can easily jump-start some "rough draft" literature circles, the longer-term process of fine-tuning and problem solving will take time, patience, creativity, artifice, and stick-to-itiveness. But it's worth it.

Four Ways of Starting Lit Circles

Chapters 8, 9, and 10 offer detailed stories of how many different teachers started and are now running their own versions of lit circles. Their classes range from kindergarten to intermediate grades to high school, and even to a college criminology course—so there's a model there for everyone. Since those classroom veterans have so many variations to share later on, this chapter will simply offer *four basic versions* of literature circle training that have served well in a variety of classrooms.

But first, a brief note on the word *training*. In some quarters, *training* is a politically incorrect term; it labels you as a Skinnerian behaviorist bent on dehumanizing children and atomizing the curriculum. Unfortunately, the English language has not yet supplied us with an alternative word that substitutes semantically for "an organized procedure for preparing a group of people for some experience." Therefore, over the next few pages, we use the term *training* as shorthand for a quite humanistic, sensitive, and respectful way of getting kids ready to run their own literature circles.

Here are four ways of getting started:

1. Quick training for experienced readers and collaborators (all grades).
2. Training using a whole-class novel and Post-it notes (elementary).
3. Training using a short story, novel sets, and response logs (high school).
4. Training using short stories, a novel, and role sheets (elementary).

Before you jump straight to a version that matches the age of your students, keep in mind that really good classroom ideas are not tied to the grade level at which they originated. In fact, the procedures in all four of these models are highly translatable to other grades. For example, Debbie Gurvitz has third graders teach literature circles to her kindergartners—there's no reason why older kids of any age can't teach lit circles to younger ones, or vice versa.

Whatever the grade level, good literature circle training has the same key steps:

1. Explain—let kids hear how this activity works and why it is important.
2. Demonstrate—provide live or videotaped examples, by kids or adults.
3. Practice—help kids try out a variety of approaches.
4. Debrief—ask kids to notice and catalog effective procedures.
5. Refine—provide ongoing training through mini-lessons and coaching.

There are about a zillion ways to provide kids with these experiences, and no one of them is correct. But each step is important, and we neglect any of them to the kids' disadvantage. For example, relatively few teachers actually show kids what a book club meeting looks like before expecting them to re-create one. Now we realize how important it is to bring in a group of older kids, or fellow teachers, or parents, or a homemade videotape from last year's class, to give the kids a living demonstration of book clubs in action before we expect them to run their own.

In the early days of literature circles, most teachers used role sheets as the chief tool for getting kids started with book clubs. Now, fewer of us take that route. Instead, we begin with open-ended reading response logs, the same kind that our kids already use in literature response and reading workshop activities. Logs fulfill the same cognitive and social tasks as the role sheets, but without narrowing kids' thinking to one kind of response at a time. Keeping a response log helps a reader notice and harvest reactions as she reads, and also provides a rich assortment of topics for group meetings. There are lots of journal formats: kids' ideas can be logged on notebook paper, in spiral notebooks, or on Post-it notes pasted right to the pages of the text. If early primary kids can't write words yet, we can have them respond in drawings, and we can get parents, older students, or other helpers to transcribe their words.

During the first wave of literature circles, we also tended to think of training as something you did *before* you got into the real reading groups. We would break preparation up into lots of steps and stages, covering a lot of "book club subskills" at the start. We wanted to be sure that kids knew how to do literature circles before they did literature circles. Now we are more inclined to plunge the kids into some good reading and teach the discussion skills as we go, working inductively. Instead of expecting the teacher to present comprehensive rules and guidelines for effective book clubs, we just do book clubs and ask the kids to notice, catalog, and practice the skills that help them have effective meetings.

Following these basic principles, here are four models of training, nested in different grade levels. The first one is for classes with a solid background in collaborative learning and response-centered literature study. The second two approaches use open-ended reading logs to support the reading and energize group interaction. The last model uses the "traditional" role sheet approach as a temporary step on the way to more open response.

Quick Training

With warmed-up, collaboration-wise students—or kids already accustomed to a literature-based classroom—an hour may be all it takes to introduce literature circles. One simple approach is described below. If you want to shorten the reading time and still retain a full demonstration, students can read a poem, article, short story, or picture book instead of a chunk of a real book. The great thing about using a whole book is that by the end of this demonstration, most people will be so hooked that they will finish reading the book, whether the lit circles continue or not—a powerful lesson.

1. Provide a wide choice of good books and invite everyone to "choose themselves into" a group of four or five people who want to read the same text. This will take a few minutes of informal negotiation.
2. Review the idea of open-ended response logs, where readers jot down feelings, connections, words, phrases, doodles, questions, comments, or any other "noticings" about what they read.

3. Give a set amount of time for some reading and some writing (twenty to thirty minutes is plenty). Tell the groups to look at the book and assign themselves a section that everyone feels can comfortably be finished in *five minutes less than* the allotted time. The extra five minutes will be used for writing notes in logs, either during or after the reading.

4. When everyone has done the reading and jotted some notes, invite groups to get together for ten or fifteen minutes. Simply explain that the goal is to have a natural conversation about the book (i.e., just talk informally, no raising hands, no one is the teacher). Encourage each person to "chip in" either spontaneously or from their notes, however the conversation unfolds.

5. During the conversations, visit each group unobtrusively for a few minutes, strictly as an observer. Be sure not to "steer" the discussion! Jot down specific examples and comments to make during the debriefing.

6. Call the class together to share and debrief. The first step—a sacred rule in all versions of lit circle training—is to *talk about the book*. Ask each group to give a sample, or "taste," of their conversation. Then shift to reflecting on the *process of the meeting*. Ask people to notice the specific behavior (eye contact, encouraging, etc.) that helped their groups work well and any that might have hindered them (digressing, interrupting). Make a list of these social skills and no-nos.

7. Have groups assign themselves another chunk of the book for a second meeting, to be held a day or two later. Remind people to jot notes in their response logs, during or after the reading. Turn the skills lists into a poster, and add items to it as you debrief future meetings. Hey, this isn't training any more; you are *doing* literature circles.

Training Using a Whole-Class Novel and Post-It Notes

Olga Marquez teaches third grade in a full-immersion dual-language program. In her colorful classroom, every object in sight is labeled in both English and Spanish, and she has a large collection of books in both languages, including multiple copies for literature circles. This year, she has decided to introduce book clubs in a new way—using a whole-class book, *Charlotte's Web,* by E. B. White. While Olga's ultimate goal is for student groups to read different books, she thinks it will be helpful to read the same book the first time through. That way, she can offer mini-lessons that will be relevant to everyone, and the kids will be able to compare notes across groups. For a few days, Olga previews literature circles for the kids, describing how they will work. One group of six kids, mostly new arrivals from Mexico, will have the Spanish translation of *Charlotte's Web*; the rest will have the English version.

Olga wants to add another wrinkle to the training this time. Last year, she used the role sheets, and the results weren't too good. For her nine-year-olds, the sheets seemed to be too much work, too overwhelming, and kids struggled to finish them. Olga still wants to teach the response roles, so kids are aware of the different kinds of thinking they reflect. But now she invites kids to capture their thinking with a simpler, more congenial response tool: little one-and-a-half-inch Post-it notes, put right in the pages of the book where they find ideas worth discussing in their groups.

Just before she hands out the books and Post-its to everyone, Olga offers a mini-lesson about the different ways readers can respond to what they read: connecting the story to their own life, asking questions, picking a favorite part, making mental pictures, noticing tricks that the author uses, wondering about words, and more. This isn't the first time kids have heard this stuff. Since the start of the year, every time that they read a story or talk about a book in Ms. Marquez's class, the same repertoire of thinking strategies has been modeled and used.

"We're going to do the same thinking," Olga explains, "but instead of saving it on regular paper, we're going write our thoughts on these Post-it notes." And with that, she passes out packs of Post-its, to kids' immense delight. "The good thing about these," she explains, as kids clutch their unexpected goodies, "is that you can stick this right on the page where an idea occurred to you, so when you come to your group meeting it's marked for you, and you can see right away what you wanted to share. You can stop and write notes while you're reading, or you can read all the way through and then go back and put some in later. It depends on your style of reading."

Now it is time for *Charlotte's Web,* and Olga announces a half hour of reading time. She cautions kids to make sure each Post-it hangs out of the edge of the book where they can find it easily. As the kids read and start jotting notes, the novelty of this approach is immediately apparent. They love it, and write note after note.

Pg. 1 Fern's father is going to kill a little pig just because it is smaller than the others. It's unfair because it is just a little pig.

Pg. 3 I think the dad was being injustice because he was going to kill a pig for nothing.

Pg. 5 I think the brother was real mean because he talks grumpy.

Pg. 13 I think that if the barn is very old, they supposed to fix it.

Pg. 15 I think that the pig was happy because Fern was always there.

Pg. 16 I think that is so sad for Wilbur that he is tired of living. That part is so sad.

Pg. 18 Wath dose rooting means?

Pg. 21 I think it was funny. And it remind me when I sliped and fell in mud.

Pg. 21 I think that this picture is funny. It made me remind me of my little brother.

Pg. 40 Spiders realy help us they eat insects.

Pg. 43 I think it was grose tha a green worm comes out of spit.

Pg. 64 I think that is very nice of Charlotte to help Wilbur. If I was Charlotte I would do the same thing with my family and my friends.

After a half hour of reading and Post-it frenzy, Olga has a bit of a hard time getting them to stop.

Now she quickly polls students to see how far they have gotten in the book, and forms kids into groups based on how many pages they have read. This way, students will be talking about the same chunk of the book, and no one can spoil the rest of the story by talking ahead. The kids who've read less than ten pages make one group; the ones who've read twelve to fifteen make up another, and so on. This process yields seven groups ranging in size from two (the kids who have read just a few pages) to seven, the kids who've read the farthest.

"Okay. Now just have a nice talk about the story. You can use your Post-its however they help you." Once the conversation starts, there's a din in the room that doesn't stop until Olga gavels literature circles to a close at 11:00, a few minutes late. As it has for fifty years, *Charlotte's Web* has given kids plenty to talk about. For many of these children, from rural Mexico, stories about pigs have special resonance.

"We had pigs at our house. Big pigs!"

"I used to have a pig, too, a pet pig. And I came home one Saturday night and they already cooked him."

"Yuk."

"No!"

"Cooked him. He had a apple in his mouth and everything."

"Oooh."

It is amazing how far Olga's kids have come with such simple training. These eight- and nine-year-olds are already running their own book clubs, having spirited and pointed conversations that are almost 100 percent on task, without needing any significant adult supervision or complex tools. The Post-its seem to feed the discussions with more than enough material to talk about. The kids are especially eager to find out who else picked the same spots in the story to discuss. There's a lot of pointing at pages, going back to the text for evidence and support.

Of course, they're not finished yet. These groups, initially based on reading speed, will mostly stay together for the rest of the book. Olga gives them the plan for the rest of *Charlotte's Web*. "Every day we'll have an hour for literature circles. You'll probably want to have some reading time and some meeting time every day. It will be up to each group to decide how much to read, when to read, and when to meet. I'll be here to help you."

As groups work their way through the book, there are some interesting wrinkles. The fastest readers finish the book quickly and hold several meetings that range over the whole book; meanwhile, the kids reading more slowly have the same number of meetings, but each one covers just the sections of the book completed so far. Olga allows kids to change groups freely, if they can catch up to the other group's place in the book. To make sure that the speedier groups have plenty to think about, she offers them choices of extra response activities to try, like researching spiders or pigs, writing letters to characters, and making new illustrations for sections of the book.

Every day, Olga keeps shaping and refining the process. In opening mini-lessons, she reiterates the different kinds of thinking that you can catch on a Post-it note. In sharing sessions after each meeting, she helps the kids critique their meetings. Sometimes she will raise an issue that she has noticed while visiting groups and wants to offer as a mini-lesson. More often, she simply opens the discussion by saying, "What went well in our literature circles today and what went badly?" The kids can be insightful—and frank. Once, Angelo raises his hand and says, "Today in our group, Juan and Jesus and them kept getting off the subject." Olga lets this start a brief discussion on ways that groups can keep themselves on task. Another time, Julia confides that "some people talk too much," leaving others with no chance to speak. But as Julia goes on and on and on about this topic, it becomes apparent that she is the big talker herself. Realizing that Julia is basically self-critiquing, Olga is gentle. "You're right," she nods, "it's very important to share time in our groups. We want to hear what everyone has to say."

Now, many other teachers come to visit Olga's class and watch her kids operate in book clubs. Visitors are impressed by the kids' autonomy, their responsibility, their focus—and the passel of Post-its hanging out of all their books. This particular day, a literature circle is discussing Gordon Korman's comical novel *Liar, Liar, Pants on Fire*. Not surprisingly, the book text has opened up the eternal childhood problem of lying versus telling the truth.

Angelo: If you were Zoe, what would you have done?

Carrie: You know, I would have told the truth, because it's like when I do something bad and I tell a lie to get out of it or something—I have like this big bubble in here somewhere—that I want to tell the truth. But when I tell the truth, my mom does tell me she is very upset or something, but I don't have the bubble in here anymore because I feel relieved that I don't have that guilt in there about lying.

Luis: I think she's right, because you don't gotta lie to be popular or an honest guy—you just gotta say the truth and not lie to people.

Jane: I think it is very good to tell the truth, because if you lie, then they will never believe you.

When people ask Olga the key to getting third graders to have conversations like these, she always laughs and says, "It's the book. It's such a great book." Well, yes. But it's also a great teacher, who has found a simple and direct way to get kids talking about all kinds of books.

Training Using a Short Story, Novel Sets, and Response Logs

Everyone who has taught school for more than five minutes has mumbled the following sentence at one time or other, usually after a particularly painful encounter with educational bureaucracy: "I wish I could just take my friends and start my own damn school." Well, that's what five of us did, back in 1996. We started something called Best Practice High School. Ever since we started dreaming up this school, literature circles were always supposed to be one of its signature activities. Now, several years later, BPHS English teachers like Tina Peano and Jenny Cornbleet continue to investigate and refine the model.

Last fall, Tina and Jenny started another year of lit circles, and this is how they got the kids going. Drawing examples from both of their classrooms, we'll start with an overview and then cover the details day by day.

Day 1
Introduce literature circles
Discuss response logs
Read short story and write a response
Write another type of response and discuss
Copy list of response types into reading logs

Day 2
Book selection and group formation
Groups make reading schedule
Read first chapter/25 pages
Write responses

Day 3
Meet to discuss first reading
Discuss and list key social skills
Copy skills to journal

Day 4
View classmates in video
Revise social skills list
Meet to discuss next reading/Chapter 2

Days 5, 6, 7 (meeting every other day)
Daily mini-lesson
Groups read and discuss remainder of book, in thirds
Daily debriefing of management issues

Day 1

Jenny's first-period sophomores gradually saunter in around 8:30, give or take a few minutes. Except for a few transfer students, these kids have done literature circles before, either as freshmen at BPHS or in their elementary schools, or both. "This time we'll be making some changes," Jenny says. "No more role sheets. We're going to use our reading response logs instead." For a quick review, she asks, "What can you put in a response log?" Though they are still half asleep, the kids manage to lob out some viable suggestions:

your connections	questions about the story
opinions	a drawing
criticism	something it reminds you of
questions for the author	

"Okay," Jenny says. "You know this, you use these all the time. So let's go right to work." She hands out the story "This Is How I Remember It," by Betsy Kemper, from the very useful collection *Microfiction,* edited by Jerome Stern. She tells the kids to jot down a few responses either while reading or after reading the story.

"This Is How I Remember It"
Betsy Kemper
Watching Joey pop the red berries into his mouth like Ju-Ju Bees and Mags only licking them at first, then chewing, so both of their smiles look bloody and I laugh though I don't eat even one . . . then suddenly our moms are all around us (although mine doesn't panic until she looks at the others and screams along with them things like *God dammit did you eat these?* And shakes me so my "No" sounds like "oh-oh-oh" and then we're being yanked toward the house, me for once not resisting as my mother scoops me up into her arms, and inside the moms shove medicine, thick and purple, down our throats in the bathroom; Joey in the toilet, Mags in the sink, me staring at the hair in the tub drain as my mom pushes my head down and there is red vomit everywhere, splashing on the mirror and powder-blue rugs, everywhere except the tub where mine is coming out yellow, the color of corn muffins from lunch, not a speck of red, *I told you,* I want to scream and then it is over and I turn to my mother for a touch or a stroke on the head like the other moms (but she has moved to the doorway and lights a cigarette, pushes her hair out of her eyes) and there is only her smeared lips saying, *This will teach you anyway.*

The kids are immediately engaged, and a little puzzled with this tale. Jenny gives them a good ten minutes to reread and jot notes. The kids have a variety of reactions:

Sometimes I hate reading short stories, because if you read it and like it you're left wanting more and you want to read the rest of the book if there is one. On the opposite, you hate the story and you're glad it's over now. With this story, my opinion is that I'm on the median with it. I now want to know what else happens with the boy. Where did the berries come from? In my life how I can connect with it is that sometimes when my mother questioned me about something, she would shake me as if trying to get the answer out.

—*Kyle*

This was a really unbelievable story but it happens in everyday in real life. Once my brother and I were playing with the "poisonous" berries off the tree and he accidentally swallowed one. We had to rush him to the hospital. They said that their moms put medicine down their throats. My mom tried the Heimlic manuever. So I don't know how but it happens. All the time.

—*Arielle*

I can relate to this story because I was at a picnic in Detroit with my family when I was about eight years. I got my lip bit off by an angry dog and my mother said I shouldn't have played with it.

—*Jeremy*

The story is not hard to understand because the mom is givin her child tuff love. It's when a parent acts like they don't give a damn but in their hearts there thankin the lord for not takin you and the other moms must like to show there love up front.

—*Sammie*

The author gave great details it was like a good visualization just how the mothers were responding to the reaction of their kids eating the berries. It was like I was there sitting there watching them.

—*Deavona*

There was a quote that said, "*I told you,* I wanted to scream." I think that quote explains how the girl want to be believed but how she didn't hold it over her mom for making her throw up. If it was me I would have been mad at my mother for a while but if she would have explained why she did it, then I would've understood.

—*Antoine*

The reminds me of the time I cut my arm. My mother panic scream and stuff. She didn't know what to do, she ask people or my step dad what we was going to do, why it wont stop bleeding but after I had my arm bandaged up she told me to watch my self and stop being so wild.

—*Virginia*

This story sort of related to me because my mother always yells at me for things that I didn't do and when she finds out she's wrong she still won't apologize. She'll find some reason to say that she's right even though she's not.

—*Danielle*

Jenny puts everyone in groups of three or four and lets the groups talk freely for about ten minutes, using their notes however they help.

Next, Jenny pulls them back together. She asks a spokesperson from each group to share one thread of the story, one topic their group got interested in, disagreed about, laughed over. There's pretty widespread condemnation of the mother, and many recollections about being falsely accused are shared. Now Jenny directs the kids back to the earlier list of reading log possibilities on the flip chart. "Did anyone in your group make a kind of response that wasn't on our list?" she wonders.

"Well," laughs one student, "I told the mom how to be a better mom."

"Great," Jenny says. "That's something good readers do, they talk to the characters in stories. So how can we put that on the list?" She adds "Advising a character" to the list. "What else?"

One group reacted to the story's being all one sentence, says it made them uncomfortable and confused the first time through. Another group reports that they had talked about the title a lot; it seemed weird that an author would imply right in the title that the story might not be completely true. Within a couple of minutes, the students realize they have been reacting to issues of style and craft, and this too goes up on the list as something good readers can attend to.

Now that the list of response choices has grown, Jenny asks kids to go back to the story and try a different kind of reading log response, just for practice. "Pick something off the list; if you connected last time, then pose some questions this time. Go ahead, give it a try." After about three minutes, she asks a few kids to share their samples.

I think she should have told her daughter how sorry she was for thinking she was disobeying her, because that's how children get outrageous and become problems for their parents, because parents sometimes take their job of being grown and a parent for granted. There is also somethings I can't understand like how can she possibly think she had ate any when the others mouths were red. Why didn't she just look at her mouth?

—*Lakiesha*

This story makes me feel angry because that one child didn't do anything but he still got punished for it. It makes me angry that the mother doesn't even comfort her child or apologize after the whole thing was over. It's sort of ironic the way the mom gets so upset when she thinks her child has done something that could kill him but in the end she causually lights a cigarette which will kill her too.

—*Jihan*

I think the kid is starved for attention and is raised by a bad mother, one who doesn't really care about her son. He might have been an accident unwanted pregnancy. The kid notices that the other mothers care about their kids and show affection and his mom does not.

—*Cai*

I can relate to this story because when I was little, I was at my cousin's house and his mom just went shopping and we had some cupcakes and she told us to wait till after dinner and the phone ring. My grandmother call her to bring her newspaper down to her house and she did so that was our chance. We took a little bit but it was good and we couldn't stop eating it. Then his mom came back and saw us, we got a whipping, then we ate.

—*Jason*

This person remembers everything by color. I thought it was sickening because it was too graphic for me. This person says that Joey had red berries and her smile look bloody. Then this person describes what the vomit looks like.

—*Tamara*

Time is running out, and Jenny asks kids to copy the amended list of response log options right into the front of their journals. "That way, you'll always have a reminder if you can't think of what to write about," she promises.

Day 2

This is book selection day, and Jenny uses a "book pass" to aid the process. In her scrupulously locked book cabinet, Jenny keeps multicopy sets of thirty-five different titles, and she wants the kids to be able to pick from the whole range. The titles include

Alicia, My Story by Alicia Appleman-Jurman

Always Running by Luis J. Rodriguez

The Autobiography of Malcom X with Alex Haley

The Avenger by Howard Rigsby

Bless Me Ultima by Rudolfo A. Anaya

The Bluest Eye by Toni Morrison

Cages by Peg Kehret

Cantora by Sylvia López-Medina

The Chocolate War by Robert Cormier

Clover by Dori Sanders

Contact by Carl Sagan

The Contender by Robert Lipsyte

Darkest Hour by V. C. Andrews

The Diary of Anne Frank by Anne Frank

Forever by Judy Blume

Friedrich by Hans Peter Richter

The Giver by Lois Lowry

Go Ask Alice by Anonymous

The House on Mango Street by Sandra Cisneros

How the Garcia Girls Lost Their Accents by Julia Alvarez

Adventures of Huckleberry Finn by Mark Twain

Interview with a Vampire by Anne Rice

Journey of the Sparrows by Fran Leeper Buss

The Joy Luck Club by Amy Tan

Living Up the Street by Gary Soto

The Martian Chronicles by Ray Bradbury

The Miracle Worker by William Gibson

Night by Elie Wiesel

Number the Stars by Lois Lowry

The Outsiders by S. E. Hinton

The Pigman by Paul Zindel

Scorpions by Walter Dean Myers

Slam! by Walter Dean Myers

A Summer Life by Gary Soto

Their Eyes Were Watching God by Zora Neal Hurston

First, Jenny pushes all the desks into groups of five. She puts a stack of six or seven different titles in each group, one copy each. When the kids come in, their job is to browse several of the books in their group, jot some notes about each one, and then switch to the next "table" when she gives the signal. They have done this before, skimming books to gauge their potential interest, so Jenny just reminds them about reading the first page or two or scanning the summary and blurbs on the back cover for clues about whether this book is for you. After a half hour of this table hopping and book tasting, the kids will have been exposed to a good bunch of books. Finally, they can select their favorite by putting their name on the sign-up lists Jenny has hung on the wall, one for each book.

The process is either energetic or chaotic, depending on your point of view. Some kids fixate on the very first book they pick up and don't want to try any others. A few get so hooked that they remain behind, causing seating short-falls for the next batch coming in. Other kids cut side deals with friends to get in the same group together regardless of what book they will read. Jenny really has to mush things along. But by 9:00 the sign-up lists are full. There are groups for *The Bluest Eye, Go Ask Alice, Clover, Contact,* and *Always Running.* Only two people signed up for *Scorpions* and so they have to join other groups.

Now it is time to build a schedule of reading time and meeting time. Jenny has just three weeks for this cycle of LCs, since a schoolwide integrated unit begins three weeks hence. Jenny wants the kids to meet a couple of times early in their book, to make sure that everyone is on track and well hooked. Then the schedule can spread out, with kids reading bigger chunks of the book and meeting a few days apart. She makes a basic plan and hands a math problem to the kids. Each group must decide for itself how many chapters to read for each meeting.

Meetings	Pages
Friday, September 6	
Monday, September 9	
Friday, September 13	
Friday, September 20	
Friday, September 27	

The rest of today is given over to starting their book and jotting some notes in reading logs. Tomorrow, Friday, the kids will meet to discuss the first chapter (or about twenty five pages, whichever is longer).

Day 3

Today is the first real meeting in the book groups, and to keep things simple and ensure that the reading gets done, Jenny has limited the reading to about twenty-five pages—usually the first chapter or two of each book. Kids go directly to their groups, and using their notes to help them, talk for about fifteen minutes. Then Jenny pulls them together to see how things are going.

"Take a minute and write in your reading log about two things. What one prediction can you make about the rest of the book, based on this first twenty-five pages? And then, what are some things you noticed people doing in the last few minutes that helped your group to work? Also, you can write about things that didn't work. Did anyone notice any behavior that messed up your groups?" She knows kids will be a little more hesitant on this one; nobody wants to rat out their friends. So Jenny adds, "Or maybe you were in another group somewhere else that had problems?" With their discussions fresh, kids have lots to write.

Kyle
1. Luis is probably going to cause trouble with his new gang.
2. Besides me, the meeting was great. I'll speak more next time.

Ian
1. I think Alice is going to run away again and start doing drugs again.
2. It was fun today but Andel and Kevin kept interrupting me, which I ain't appreciate.

Mario
1. I think that them 2 guys that beat up Alfredo are probably gonna do it a couple of more times before they get caught.
2. I think that the discussion went pretty well. Everybody contributed and shared something about what they read.

Lashawndra
1. I think the story will confuse me again. This book is confusing when you first read it but then things start to make sense.
2. My group discussion went well. It led off by us asking each other questions and everyone answering them. Our discussion is always fun. Yes, everyone participated. One or two are shy, because they always talk but they can't look at the person while talking. But other than that everything was ok.

Now Jenny asks volunteers to share their thoughts, and she rapidly records them on the flip chart. Once they have amassed a list of helps and hindrances to small-group work, she asks the kids to copy it in the front of their logs, alongside the earlier list of response log options. Now kids have their own self-generated lists of the thinking skills and the social skills needed in literature circles. The assignment for the next class is to read another chapter—twenty-five pages or so. This will be the last "training day" before kids start reading much longer chunks of text and meeting weekly, instead of daily, the long-term pattern at BPHS.

Day 4

Today's session starts with the kids viewing a videotape of BPHS students meeting in a literature circle last year. The tapes shows a quite mature, effective group and there is a lot to see, so Jenny shows it twice, the first time through without instructions. Then she directs their attention to their own list of social skills, still displayed on the flip chart from the last session. "This time, I want you to watch and see which of our social skills these guys are using. Make notes!" The kids are glued to the screen as they tally the many social skills the older kids are using. In the following discussion, the kids are amazed to see almost their whole list of skills displayed, from eye contact to supporting ideas with pages in the book. Jenny checks each skill off as it is enumerated. About the only problem the kids can find on the tape is that one student doesn't say very much, and they roundly critique him for not speaking up and the group for not drawing him out. Jenny just smiles. "So that would never happen in your groups, right?"

Now it's time for the literature circles. As they get into groups, Jenny encourages them to consciously use the social skills on their list and the ones in the video to keep their discussions productive. As they meet, she circulates, stopping briefly at each group. Jenny makes a few notes as she moves around, of what's working and what needs work. These cues will feed her mini-lessons on the next three Fridays, as the kids read and discuss the remaining thirds of their book.

Days 5, 6, and 7 (Three Successive Fridays)

After reading shorter chunks the first couple of days, each group now divides the remainder of its book roughly into thirds, looking for sensible stopping spots at the end of chapters. Groups will meet on three successive Fridays, for the whole class period. Each Friday meeting will follow the same pattern: there will be a five- or ten-minute mini-lesson from Jenny; then there will be a good chunk of meeting time, thirty minutes or so; and finally, there will be sharing time, used for debriefing the groups, sharing favorite passages or books, and taking care of logistics.

What will these daily mini-lessons look like? Thus far, Jenny's mini-lessons have been mainly procedural, because the kids are immersed in their initial training. (The lessons have also been more maxi than mini, since the groups are in start-up mode.) But later on, as groups get running on a normal schedule, there will be plenty of other mini-lesson topics. These will come not from a preset list, but from Jenny's observation of kids' needs as she floats between groups during literature circle meetings. Some of the time the mini-lessons will consist of Jenny directly presenting an idea or strategy; other times, the mini-lesson will be collaborative, with Jenny and the students brainstorming practical solutions together.

For example, during the third round of meetings Jenny notices that many kids are voicing vociferous opinions, but mainly using volume rather than the actual text to prove their points. So she plans a mini-lesson around the idea of "taking it back to the book." The mini-lesson structure is simple; like many, it begins with Jenny sharing her observation with the class. "I've noticed that a lot of you guys have strong opinions about the books, but that hardly anyone ever disputes them. You are so loud and dogmatic that no one dares to disagree. But I've heard some really loud opinions that I would definitely disagree with. In other words, you're not always right. So what can we do about this? What can we do to make sure that people really back up what they say?"

The kids immediately agree that opinions should fit with the facts of the book, that you should be able to point to a passage in the text to support your position. Randolph suggests, "You gotta just say prove it!" and a slogan is born. "Okay," Jenny says. "Let's try that in your meetings today. If someone makes an interpretation of the book, you can challenge them by saying, 'Prove it,' and then they would have to show you a place in the book that supports their interpretation. Okay? Let's go to work."

After this three- or four-minute mini-lesson, the students re-form into their book clubs. As Jenny ranges through the room she is amused by the predictable phenomenon: Cries of "Prove it!" abound, as everyone challenges everyone else to prove everything. In group dynamics terms, the kids are at the "mechanical stage" of implementation. After overusing the strategy for a while, they will settle into a more natural pattern. "Prove it" will become a useful and modulated part of their discussion repertoire.

As all this training moves along, kids start having some really good meetings. Here's one that emerged in a group reading *Journey of the Sparrows,* a novel about Hispanic immigration by Fran Leeper Buss.

Jermaine (*showing illustration in his journal*): See, that's her. And that's the border.
John: Uh-huh. And this is the immigration?
Jermaine: Right.
Darris: Let me tell you something that tripped me out in the book. When she was talking about "a brown Jesus" hanging over the wall over the thing, and she described him as having other characteristics. And doesn't she seem a little bit racist now?
Karem: You see like a lot of pictures of Jesus but they are not brownish.
Darris: Yeah.
Karem: It made her feel weird seeing a white Jesus.
Darris: The guy, right, they talk like, is he in the crate with them?
Santoro: Well, no, they like talking about them—she's like remembering things about her father.
Darris: Boy, that got me so confused. Okay, so is he in the car with them or not?
Santoro: What I want to know is, are they going to go back to El Salvador or aren't they?
Jermaine: They can't. I think it said on page 15 that they would get killed if they go back.
Santoro: And if they do they can get caught—the immigration people can catch them.
Jermaine: It's better than getting killed going back to Mexico.
Darris: If they send you back there they kill you anyway, Jermaine.
Jermaine: That is a risk I had to take. . . . So what does everyone think about the crossing the border part? Where her and her brother and her older sister and her friend Thomas, probably some kind of love friend, cross?
Santoro: To me it was scary because they could have gotten caught, and at one time they could get caught, but I don't know, it was scary to me.
Darris: Karem?
Karem: Well, it was kind of scary, but having family members and friends having gone through that. So it's like, I don't know. A lot of my friends . . .
Jermaine: Had to leave Mexico and come here?

Karem: Yeah. It's messed up over there, you know.

Darris: Actually, I don't know.

Karem: Well, if you watch the news, yeah, it's kind of messed up.

Jermaine: It's one thing to pick up and leave and go somewhere and another to be running away from somewhere.

Karem: Yeah.

Jermaine: I mean, Mexico's they home. Even though there some crazy stuff going on there, that's always going to be where their roots are traced back to.

Karem (*nods*): Yeah.

Training Using Short Stories, a Novel, and Role Sheets

Some teachers prefer to begin literature circles using a set of the role sheets on pages 107–132. They feel that some kind of transitional device like this is needed when kids venture from familiar teacher-directed, whole-class activities to decentralized small-group work that requires much more student responsibility. Especially for kids who haven't had much experience with collaborative learning or small-group work, some temporary scaffolding feels necessary. Role sheets are some simple tools designed to ease this shift, supporting students both while they are reading and while they are talking with each other in peer-led groups. In a sense, the role sheets act as a kind of surrogate teacher, introducing suggestions and structure into kids' groups without dictating anyone's ideas or feelings.

To find a model for training kids with role sheets, we could do no better than follow Barbara Dress into a classroom. Barbara is a former teacher and reading consultant for Palatine School District 15. She retired early so that she could consult on lit circles with teachers in Chicago and suburban schools. Barbara worked with Sandy King's third graders, at Marion Jordan School, for two weeks, about forty-five minutes a day. Sandy's kids were in great shape to start literature circles—their reading and language arts program is rich and literature-based. Sandy reads aloud to her students daily, the kids have an active writing workshop, and they think of themselves as real authors. (While this story comes from third grade, the same process and schedule have been used to train many middle and high school kids, simply by changing the short stories and the novel to age-appropriate literature.) With Sandy and me observing and occasionally helping, here's what Barbara did, first in a quick overview and then in detail.

Overview

Day 1

- kids read a good story and discuss it; the idea of literature circles is introduced

Days 2–5
- kids learn *one role per day* using short stories
- groups of four students *in the same role* meet daily to discuss
- whole class meets to *debrief and clarify* the day's target role

Days 6–10
- kids put the roles together while reading a short novel
- groups of four students in *different roles* meet to discuss; roles rotate daily
- whole class meets daily to *debrief and share*

Day 1

Barbara greets the kids, who are wearing name tags so that she can quickly learn their names. Graciously, she asks if anyone has ever heard of literature circles. No one has any actual experience, but this doesn't stop third graders from speculating on the definition. Barbara welcomes everything and jots key words on the overhead. She then incorporates kids' ideas and language into an overview of the activity.

She tells the kids that they will be working for two weeks on this project, taking one step at a time. She also tells them they will be reading several great stories this week and a good book next week. The rest of this session is given over to the story "The Flying Patchwork Quilt," by Barbara Brenner. Barbara reads the story out loud, slowly and dramatically, stopping a couple of times to invite kids' predictions and clarifications. When she's finished, she invites students' comments and responses, and a lively whole-class discussion ensues. Barbara has done her job for this day, which was simply to get acquainted, build some trust, share a good story, and model for the kids the delight of rich discussion topics.

Day 2

Today, Barbara wants to help kids learn the role of *question asker* (see page 121) as she's adapted it especially for this class. Before handing out that role sheet, she talks to kids about open-ended questions. Referring to the story from yesterday, she asks kids to remember or think of some possible questions about the story. As kids offer suggestions, Barbara makes a distinction between "fat" and "skinny" questions. Skinny ones can be answered in a word or two, she explains, leaving nothing more to say. "Fat" questions, on the other hand, you can say lots and lots about. There aren't necessarily right answers to these questions, Barbara says, and everyone can have different things to say about a *really* fat question.

Now she hands out copies of the question asker role sheet and another short story. She invites kids to read the story, think of two or three really "fat" questions about it, and jot them on their role sheet. This time, kids can read the story several different ways. Ms. King is reading it aloud in one corner, so those who want (or need) to have the story read to them can go there. Alternately, groups can pick one of their own members to read it to the others, and one group elects this option. Other kids read silently. A couple of partners sit on the floor reading alternate pages to each other. As kids begin to finish, Barbara reminds them to jot some fat questions on their QA sheets.

Next, kids go into their groups and meet for ten minutes or so, sharing and discussing their fat questions. Barbara, Sandy, and I circulate, available to help but not really needed. The kids have plenty to say. For the last few minutes, we gather as a whole group again and Barbara takes sample questions from each group. As always, she skillfully praises and shapes, making sure kids understand what kinds of questions a good asker brings to a group.

Day 3

Today, Barbara teaches kids the role of *passage picker*. Using a third story, she follows the same pattern as yesterday, first explaining the basic idea of the role and then helping kids brainstorm good examples. One important skill for passage picker (and *word wizards,* coming up tomorrow) is being able to locate things quickly in the text, so Barbara spends a good deal of time showing kids how to mark on their sheet the page and paragraph of passages they want to share.

Now the kids read a story as passage pickers. When they're finished, they meet in their same homogeneous, four-member groups to try out the role. There's plenty of noise, of course, as kids read aloud their favorite sections. When they finish meeting, volunteers from different groups share examples of what passages they picked and tell why. There is further discussion about the problem of locating your passages. Tomorrow's session will provide more practice on this. Again, Barbara gently and subtly shapes kids' responses, reinforcing contributions that genuinely fulfill the passage picker role.

Day 4

Today, Barbara teaches kids the role of *word wizard.* She follows the same pattern, first explaining the role, then helping kids practice it by thinking of noteworthy words from yesterday's story. Finally, she sets them to reading another new story with the WW sheet in hand. The kids then meet in their groups and try out the role. When they finish, Barbara asks volunteers from different groups to share examples of the words they focused on.

Day 5

Today, Barbara teaches kids the fourth (and most popular!) role in this set: the *artful artist* (or illustrator). She talks about responding to the reading with a picture instead of with words, and gets kids talking about the importance of the illustrations in favorite books. She stresses that whatever pictures they choose to draw as illustrators do not have to depict actual events or scenes in the story, but can represent personal thoughts, feelings, or connections—even abstractions or designs. Then she goes over the official artful artist role sheet, gives kids one last story to read, and they go to work. Because of kids' pride and care in their artwork, this role sheet takes a little longer than the others to prepare, and Barbara has to work to get them back to their groups. Gradually, kids return to their groups and take turns sharing their graphic responses to the reading. When they are finished, Barbara asks volunteers from different groups to show examples of their illustrations. Barbara asks kids to tell what conversations sprang up around the pictures, so they get the message that the drawings are to extend the discussion, not just for decoration.

Days 6–10

Now it's time to put the literature circles together. So this week Ms. King's third graders will read a whole novel, meeting daily in their groups—the same four-member groups that trained together, role by role, last week. The book, selected by Barbara for its wide appeal, is *The Chocolate Touch,* by Melanie Chatoff. A takeoff on the King Midas tale, this is a genuinely funny story about a young boy who suddenly develops . . . well, the title says it.

Each day's session is divided into two roughly twenty-minute parts: reading time and group meetings. During the reading time, kids are free to read the assigned chapters (about fifteen big-type pages per day), work on their role sheets, or (if they have already finished both, which is rare) read something else. Kids who are slower readers need all the reading time they can get; some are doing part of the reading at home, a few with help from a parent or sibling. All kids have to budget their time so that they will be ready to play their assigned role.

When groups meet, Barbara and Sandy circulate to observe, assist, and help solve problems. Since it is a good, involving book, kids have plenty to say, and the discussions go well. The kids discuss about one fifth of the book each day, and on Friday, there is a general whole-class conversation when everyone reflects back over the two-week learning process. The kids are pleased and proud of themselves, and a bit sad to say good-bye to this dynamic white-haired lady who has brought such a special treat into their classroom each morning.

Barbara, who is an inveterate educational tinkerer, is already talking about all the things she will change the *next* time she models literature circles in a classroom. She's thinking maybe she should introduce the artist role first, since it is the kids' favorite, and it helps the students who aren't fluent writers to enter their group on an equal footing. But for Ms. King's kids, the job is well done. They "get it." They understand the system and—most important—they love it.

Ms. King is impressed, too. As the year goes on, she uses literature circles steadily, as a regular and recurrent part of her classroom schedule. Since the training period is now over, kids pick their own books and move among constantly re-forming groups, and much less teacher intervention is needed. A few months later, Sandy looks back and writes: "There is a lot of discussion going on and kids love the freedom they have to choose. The kids are more accountable for what they read, they know what to look for while they read (they monitor their comprehension, so to speak) and they really enjoy it!"

Training Variations and Suggestions

Teachers in our lit circles network have shared a number of other tips about orienting and training students, especially when things don't go smoothly and troubleshooting is needed.

- Have older kids teacher younger ones.
- Have experienced lit circle kids train other kids, regardless of age (younger ones can teach older ones).
- Make a videotape of lit circles in your or someone else's classroom; you can use it to train kids next year. (Colleagues can also borrow the tape.) These tapes work best when the students plan, write, and perform the narrative.
- Have kids *visit* a classroom in which lit circles are working well—a few at a time, of course.
- Use fishbowl demonstrations for training and problem solving. Ask one lit circle to hold its discussion in the middle of the room while everyone else observes, perhaps taking notes for later debriefing. If you want to demonstrate a certain problem, or model a helpful strategy, you can "cook" the membership of the group. Or, to be absolutely sure, you can become a member of the fishbowl group yourself. A helpful addition is the "freeze" feature—a rule that allows anyone observing the fishbowl to stop the action to ask a participant to explain a comment, suggest another course of action, or make an observation. When the freeze discussion is over, the group continues talking about the book until the next freeze is called. Yes, it sounds artificial, but students in fishbowls usually seem perfectly able to carry on despite the interruptions.

6

Forming, Scheduling, and Managing Groups

PROBABLY THE number one question teachers have when they start thinking about introducing their kids to literature circles is, Where in the world am I gonna get all those books? That's why much of Chapter 7 is devoted to getting books and other lit circle materials into your classroom.

Meanwhile, don't wait. While a huge classroom library is a nice thing to develop over time, you don't *need* one to begin lit circles. All it takes is thirty books—five copies each of six different books—to get started. You can even use a class set of the *same* novel to start things off, following Olga Marquez's model on page 57. Or ask the librarian to dig up some multiple-copy sets, or rummage through the bookroom. If you keep on scrounging, in no time you'll have enough books to keep kids going.

Group Size and Formation

What size groups work best for literature circles? In the ideal classroom, group size would be determined by the number of kids who freely choose a particular book or article. The factor moderating pure choice, of course, is that we want to form *small, functional* discussion groups of people *reading the same stuff* (except for intentionally heterogeneous groups, discussed in Chapter 10). That means teachers must balance offering real choice against massaging kids into groups containing a reasonable number of members. Among our Chicago-area literature circle teachers, the favorite group size seems to be four or five, at least for kids in the intermediate grades and up. This allows a good variety of voices and perspectives without the group's getting so big that distractions and inefficiencies take over. This size is also realistic for schools where lots of kids are absent every day, for one reason or another. With at least three remaining members, a circle can go along fine. For younger kids, some teachers like to keep the group size smaller—three or four, perhaps even using pairs in the early primary grades (see Chapter 8 for more details on primary-grade applications).

In practice, many factors force teachers to have groups larger or smaller than the optimal four or five. When six kids want to read the same book, you have to decide whether two groups of three or one group of six will be more productive—balancing active participation against diversity of ideas. When only two kids are interested in a book, the teacher has to ponder whether the pair in question can really feed each other or whether each should move along to a second-choice title that will pull them into a larger group. Obviously, in order to get groups of decent size, teachers will have to do more than massage—they may have to negotiate, cajole, finagle, bargain, logroll, or bribe. Literature circle teachers are often heard saying things like, Okay, if you'll read *Monster* now, and be the fourth member of this group, I'll help you get a group together for *Holes* next cycle.

In the everyday practice of literature circles, most students in the room *won't* be reading their absolute-number-one-choice-in-the-whole-world book—many people will have compromised to make the system work. But we notice in working with kids at all grade levels that even just adding the smallest degree of control—like deciding whether you're going to read a certain book now instead of later, or getting your third choice instead of no choice at all—feels welcome and makes a big difference in motivation. And as teachers get more books in their room, as kids develop more skill with their roles, as the norms of student-centered learning are built and reinforced, more and more true choices become available.

Helping Kids Pick Books

In the baseline version of literature circles, the teacher typically offers kids a choice of at least six or eight different titles, representing a wide range of reading levels and interests. Sometimes, these titles will be thematically related, novels of westward expansion, coming-of-age stories, or dystopic futures. Before the kids make their choices, the teacher will display the books for several days, encouraging kids to check them out by scanning the back cover blurb, reading the first few pages, or talking to other kids who have read the book. Perhaps the teacher will give a book-talk on each title or conduct a book pass like the one Jenny Cornbleet uses (p. 65). Then, at an appropriate moment, the teacher asks kids to list their top three choices on a written ballot and hand it in. The final group formation rests with the teacher; she is free to take the ballots home and, in the privacy and serenity of her own study, form promising groups. Yes, later on, when kids get good at literature circles, we can let them form their own groups more directly, with less teacher intervention. But right now, we want things to work well the first time around.

Here's how Nancy Steineke forms her literature circle groups, excerpted from her forthcoming book, *Reading and Writing Together: Collaborative Literacy in Action* (2002). This example talks about high school kids, but the same process works in classrooms from primary on up.

On the day scheduled for students to make their selections, I have a ballot already prepared, listing the books, asking for a ranking (#1 is first choice, #2 is second choice, etc.), and also providing designated blanks to write the ever necessary name, date, and hour. After passing out the ballots, I tell the students that I want them to make informed choices so they need to go through two steps before they rank their selections.

First, I do a quick book-talk on each book so that students have some idea of the plot, its connection to whatever theme is being studied, and also any caveats or previous readers' opinions (i.e., "slow start, but then it really gets going").

Next, I group the kids in the rows or circles so that the number in the row or circle matches the number of choices: eight books equals eight kids. Then we do a quick book pass; each student gets to look at each book for one minute, and then the book gets passed. One minute is enough time to look at the cover, skim the summary on the back, check how long it is, and maybe read a bit of the first page. Before we do the pass, we have a quick discussion listing what they might look for in a book during the minute's worth of examination. During the book pass, I emphasize that this activity is solo; that means no talking! Once the book pass is completed, then everyone can rank his selections. I always tell them to rank their top four choices out of the eight or nine titles available. After collecting the ballots, I warn everyone that there are limited numbers of copies, so everyone will not automatically get her first choice; however, in the past I have never had a student who didn't get one of the top three choices.

I always try to give myself a cushion of at least two days between the voting and actually passing out the books. That gives me a chance to catch anyone who was absent on voting day. It also gives me a little time to form the groups and organize the books. Once I've got the ballots, I sort them out by first choices. Any book that doesn't have at least three people choosing it gets dropped and those students are reclassified by their second or third selection.

Next, I look at numbers. The best lit circle is a group of four. If one member is absent, a fine discussion can still be had with three. When someone is absent from a group of three, having a full-blown lit circle discussion with only two is difficult for most students. On the other hand, five is the ideal number when you have one student who has a high rate of absence or one who might end up sitting out because he doesn't come prepared. Since these students will be gone most of the time anyway, it's still essentially a group of four. However, a group of five is not ideal when everyone is usually there. Try as I may to reinforce the processing and discussion skills after each discussion, a group of five always has one member who is a shadow, letting the other four do the talking.

Finally, I look at the faces in the current groupings and try to tweak the groups for optimal success based on personality, discussion skill level, and homework habits. If the high achiever's first choice puts him with the kids who seldom do their homework, I'll move him to his second choice. It would be nice to fantasize about him being just the role model these less motivated kids need, but, being a pragmatist, my gut tells me that he'll probably be the only one prepared, quickly get frustrated, and then have his angry parents call me about the punishment these lit circles are inflicting upon their child. On the other hand, if I can put a less motivated student with several stronger ones, that often can push that student in a positive way. I also look for gender and personality balance. If a group consists of one girl and three guys, I think about whether the guys will be skilled enough to include her, and I'll also think about whether the girl is going to be comfortable in that situation. All of these are individual judgment calls, but if you've been working with a class for a while you can make them pretty quickly.

By now you are probably wondering if anyone gets any book they even wanted to read. The answer is yes. I'd say that 90 percent end up getting their first choice and close to 100 percent have gotten their first or second choice. With all my meddling, how can that be? One reason is when the kids have already read at least a half-dozen novels on their own, they've become book connoisseurs, so to speak. They know what they like and don't like. Choosing books based on who else wants to read a particular title or which one has the fewest pages takes a backseat to choosing a book based on potential reading enjoyment. This fact hit home just recently. One of the choices from our Holocaust text set is *The Giver,* by Lois Lowry. Since I put this list together several years ago, the middle schools that feed into the high school have also put this book on their reading lists, so many of the ninth graders have already read it. If students were looking for the easiest way out, they'd opt for a book they'd already read, right? When I looked at the most recent ballots, hardly any students listed *The Giver* as a top choice, instead opting for books they hadn't read before. I repeat: readers know what they want.

The other reason the groups seem to fall into place is that the selection is an absolutely silent, individual process. It is completely solo. I purposely do not give them the opportunity to negotiate with their friends, because I want them to choose the book that interests them versus the book that "Suzy" wants them to read. I know this sounds controlling, but groups of friends do not necessarily create the best lit circles. They have too many other agendas and common experiences to share, discuss, plan, or review. If these kids really want to read a book together, they can start a junior chapter of Oprah's book club! Also, there are always one or two kids in class who don't have a lot of friends, whatever the reason. Still suffering the pain of being chosen next to last for high school P.E. teams, I am highly sensitive to avoiding the replication of that experience in my own classroom. In the end, I am always aiming for heterogeneous groups made up of people with diverse experiences and opinions, since these are the ingredients necessary for lively discussion.

The Teacher's Role in Student Choice

All this student choice is great, but teachers often worry, What if a kid picks a book that's too hard or too easy? Well, maybe we should call it modified student choice. Yes, we do want the teacher to actively oversee, guide, and steer the book selection process for literature circles, just as Nancy Steineke does. That's one reason we ask kids for three top choices instead of just one, so the teacher has room to maneuver, to make a skillful intervention if the number-one choice is way too hard or too easy. With younger students a face-to-face conference can be a helpful adjunct to the balloting process, if a choice seems questionable. If the problem is a too-hard book, many of our primary teachers just ask the kid to read a page or two aloud. If the child doesn't know ten words per page, the teacher can suggest another choice.

If a student has picked a suspiciously easy book, the teacher can probe the decision. Maybe the kid is just interested in the topic, regardless of reading level. Maybe he just needs a break, just like adult readers do when we cleanse our palate with a "beach book." And maybe having this kid join a group of slower readers will be a boon to the others, in spite of Nancy's skepticism. But the key thing to remember with book choice for literature circles is that kids need to be reading books they can read. Book clubs are for independent pleasure reading, not skills lessons.

So there's plenty of teacher artistry left in the book selection process for literature circles. Yes, student choice is the foundation. But you want your kids to succeed when they join in these groups, especially for the first few times. So you will use your most graceful and subtle interventions to make sure kids and books are well matched.

Scheduling

Literature circles are *not* a spontaneous activity. You cannot suddenly arrive in your classroom and announce, Hey kids, let's try doing literature circles today!

Chaos—or maybe entropy—will ensue. No, by definition literature circles require planning, preparation, and readiness. They need to meet on a regular, frequent, predictable schedule. To get book clubs started, we need *two to three hours a week*—time for reading, for writing in reading logs, for meeting in small book clubs, and for gathering as a whole class to share responses and monitor the development of our conversations. The time demands will be greatest at the beginning, when kids need lots of class time to learn the process and get help.

If this sounds like a big chunk of time, remember three things:

1. We are trying to replace less effective reading activities with a *more effective* one. Literature circles build kids' comprehension, thinking, and engagement with literature, as well as their achievement as readers. There will be no regrets about reallocating this much time.
2. We are making a *long-term investment* in a fundamental, recurrent activity that can continue throughout the year.
3. Once kids really have fully internalized the norms and procedures of literature circles, we can "recapture" some class time by spinning off some reading as homework. Then we use class time only for group meetings, mini-lessons, and sharing.

Time can be tough to find in today's overstuffed school days. Especially for departmentalized middle and high school teachers, who must often deliver a huge mandated English curriculum in forty- or fifty-minute daily periods, two or three hours a week for literature circle work may not be reasonable. However, even for high school classes, an intensive and regular schedule is absolutely required for the initial preparation. You cannot learn lit circles effectively if you do them only one day a week at the beginning—later on, maybe. At Best Practice High School, when we take kids through the initial training, we meet several times a week, doing much of the reading and note taking right in class, stopping for relatively frequent meetings and debriefings. But once the kids have internalized the process, the reading becomes a homework assignment, and we shift to once-a-week meetings, gathering only on Fridays for about forty minutes.

So whatever your grade level, you'll enjoy the greatest certainty of success if you schedule in-class time for all the literature circle activities, at least at the start. Prematurely sending kids off to read and do their logs or role sheets as homework invites problems. You can count on a few kids coming to their group without the book or with an empty journal or just "spacing out" the whole thing. You are then guaranteed management problems that, though not overwhelming, decrease the energy in the room. Better to start by doing the whole cycle in class, where you can make sure everyone is ready and can provide immediate help.

So how does this scheduling puzzle play out in real schools? Many teachers divide their literature circle week into reading days and meeting days. Here's how Marianne Flanagan fit literature circles into her week in fifth grade:

Self-Contained Elementary Classroom

Monday	Tuesday	Wednesday	Thursday	Friday
10:15–11:00	10:15–11:00	10:15–11:00	10:15–11:00	10:15–11:00
Groups meet	Read & logs	Groups meet	Read & logs	Groups meet

Using this plan, kids have two sessions a week for reading and note writing and three for meeting. When Marianne wants kids to read longer chunks of books between meetings, she can schedule two or only one meeting a week, with more reading time in between.

If the kids are younger—say, *primary* level—teachers often divide each book club session into reading time and talking time, like this:

Monday	Tuesday	Wednesday	Thursday	Friday
10:15–10:30	10:15–10:30	10:15–10:30	10:15–10:30	10:15–10:30
Read	Read	Read	Read	Read
10:30–10:45	10:30–10:45	10:30–10:45	10:30–10:45	10:30–10:45
Groups meet	Groups meet	Groups meet	Groups meet	Groups meet

In this schedule, the teacher may read a picture book aloud to kids during the first few minutes, and then the kids fan out into small-group discussions (with or without an adult or older kid helper) for the second section.

When the kids get older and school becomes departmentalized, innovation gets tougher and time gets tighter. Sometimes it feels as though our secondary schools were designed to *prevent* coherent, ongoing, student-centered activities. Teachers are under such enormous time and curriculum "coverage" pressure that they feel guilty about spending even a few minutes of class time on something not officially mandated—or something not certain to succeed. Nevertheless, creative middle and high school teachers have solved this problem aptly, and here are a couple of the most common schedules:

Middle School with Double-Period Language Arts/Reading

	Monday	Tuesday	Wednesday	Thursday	Friday
8:15–9:00 *Period A*	English*	English	English	English	English
9:00–9:45 *Period B***	LC Groups meet	LC Read & notes	LC Groups meet	LC Read & notes	LC Groups meet

*   "English" stands for the mandated curriculum, including teacher-guided lessons on required books, writing, etc.
** Once the lit circles are well established, the period B schedule can alternate in two- or three-week *cycles* with writing workshop or other activities that require long, regular chunks of time.

High School Language Arts (Single Period)
Phase One: Training
Temporarily allocates *all* class time to literature circles for training. This means daily for two or three weeks, alternating between group meetings and reading sessions, the same as the middle school period B above.

	Monday	Tuesday	Wednesday	Thursday	Friday
1:00–1:45	LC	LC	LC	LC	LC
	Groups meet	Read & notes	Groups meet	Read & notes	Groups meet

Phase Two: Long-Term Implementation
Now lit circles can be spun off as a once-a-week activity, with reading and logs done as homework.

	Monday	Tuesday	Wednesday	Thursday	Friday
8:15–9:00	English*	English	English	English	LC Groups

* "English" stands for the rest of the mandated curriculum, including teacher-guided lessons on required books, writing, etc.

Each of these schedules assumes that the whole class works on literature circles at once, in perhaps five or six groups. Of course, it is also possible to have only *one circle meet at a time,* while other students read, write, conduct peer conferences, do some math, visit centers, or are otherwise productively engaged. However, when only one lit circle meets at a time, it is usually because *the teachers are running the groups.* They cannot comfortably let all the groups meet simultaneously. Such teachers may feel a need to be present in each group, to supervise, and all too often, to take over. They clearly aren't yet attuned to the dynamics—or trusting of the power—of genuine kid-led collaborative learning.

The problem here—as in many classrooms where lit circles are being tried—is confusion between time devoted to teacher-directed and student-sponsored reading. In teasing apart this puzzle, let's look back at a classroom we visited earlier in this book—Karen Smith's fifth grade, in Phoenix. After working with her emergent literature studies for a few years, Karen settled on a pattern whereby students worked in kid-run groups for three weeks per month and then joined in a group with her for one week per month, to read a book together. In this teacher-and-kid-directed literature study, Karen was a fellow reader, but she also prepared carefully and dug deep to help individual kids excavate meaning and connect with the author's craft. This meant that during this stretch of Karen's school day, kids were guided by her about one fourth of the time, while during the other three fourths they pursued their reading as individuals in kid-run groups. Karen's is the essence of a balanced curriculum—and the process of structuring that student-sponsored time is what this book is mainly about.

Setting a Meeting Calendar and Ending Date

In primary-grade literature circles, the kids usually read (or listen to) a book at one sitting, and then have one meeting about it. Not too many scheduling wrinkles there. When kids get bigger, though, things get more complicated. We have to ask, How long does it take to read a book, and how many times on the way through it should kids stop and meet with their group?

Our best answers come from the hundreds of teachers who have experimented with various schedules and reported their results. For kids from about fourth grade up, who are reading real chapter books, most teachers allow two to three weeks to finish a book. Anything longer and the books drag out. Shorter spans can be even better, if the books are pretty short or the students are on a reading "tear," burning their way through books. As for the frequency of meetings, the younger kids (third through sixth grade) need to meet with their groups every two or three days, while the middle and high schoolers might meet a bit less often, maybe once or twice a week. This means about six or seven meetings per book for the younger kids and three, four, or five meetings for the bigger ones.

At least in the early days of doing literature circles, you'll do the kids (and yourself) a favor by establishing a common ending date for everyone. Indeed, if you want to have some time for sharing between groups when books are finished, and if you want groups to be able to swap members after each book, then common ending dates are almost necessary. There's nothing complicated about this: at the start of the cycle, you and the kids estimate how long it will take for everyone to finish the books and then establish a common completion date. The length of time needed will depend on many things: How long are the books? How fast are the readers? How much class time can we allocate to reading? What other homework do kids have? Once established, the finishing date provides natural pressure for groups to budget their reading assignments and discussion schedule carefully, making sure the book is divided evenly and will be done on time. Another handy side effect is that the faster readers (who will generally choose longer, harder books) will be reading more pages per day, and the slower readers (who typically pick shorter, easier books) will be reading fewer. Still, in this kind of unobtrusive, "natural individualization," *everyone* reads and discusses a whole book each cycle.

▼ V A R I A T I O N : **Allow Rolling Ending Dates**
To keep things simple at the start, and to ensure the maximum reshuffling of group membership, we usually advise common ending dates. That means every group finishes their book on the same day, whatever its length. This is a handy management policy, but it can distort things if kids try to meet impossible deadlines, are reluctant to read ahead even though hooked, or stretch thin books out for too long. So let go of the

common ending date and go with the flow. If a group completes a book on a day when no other groups are finishing, what's the worst that can happen? They can pick another book and stay together. Or they can wait a few days until another batch of kids becomes free, reading some short fiction or nonfiction in the meantime to keep warmed up. Maybe they'll even negotiate with some other kids about starting a new book group next week and begin reading that book. In Maggie Forst's class, kids are often reading two and three books at a time as they finish up with one group and get ready to jump into one or two more. One great side benefit of open ending dates: when different groups finish at different times, there is a naturally balanced flow of book projects and book-talks—one every day or so instead of a "project season" chock-full of one report after another.

Have the kids make their own reading and meeting schedule at the first literature circle meeting, right after they receive their chosen books. You can offer them a premade calendar of the next three weeks, with school holidays, assemblies, and other irregularities indicated. Their job is to divide the book up into natural chunks for their meetings, which could be mandated by you or left to them to decide. In any case, the kids must submit their provisional reading and meeting schedule for your approval.

How Many Literature Circles Per Year?

Teachers often ask, Should my kids be doing literature circles all year, one book after another? Hmmm. Sounds good to me. But there are a few other valuable activities in school and such immense pressure on teachers to accomplish other goals. So, yes, when other demands or opportunities arise, you can "mothball" literature circles for a week or a month, bringing them back later with confidence that kids will get right back in the groove. Some teachers call these two- or three-week patterns "cycles"—they'll do a cycle of lit circles, then a cycle of a curriculum unit, then lit circles again, or perhaps a cycle of writing workshop.

▼ V A R I A T I O N : **Let Kids Schedule Their Whole Reading Workshop, Not Just Their Book Clubs**
We used to think we were pretty student-centered when we let kids pick their own books and then assign themselves chapters so that the book would be finished three weeks later. Then we visited some of Lucy Calkins's classrooms in New York, where kids schedule not only their book clubs but also all their independent reading. They have more than

an hour a day to schedule—and because many of these kids are reading a whole-class book, a book of their own, and a book club book all at the same time, their choices expand exponentially: Do I meet with my book club? How long? How many chapters of my independent book do I want to read? What can I do at home and what do I need to do here in class? Every day, these kids are making hard and complicated choices and taking lots of responsibility.

In some of our Chicago schools, lit circles alternate back and forth with solo independent reading. In other words, half the time kids are doing *individual* independent reading (picking their own books and dialogue-journaling with student and teacher partners, à la Nancie Atwell), and half the time they are engaged in *group* independent reading, picking books as a club, reading and discussing them with a few friends. Under this plan, kids are always reading an independent book, along with whatever class novel is being studied, textbooks are being read, and all the rest. And just in case this sounds like too much reading for a third grader or eighth grader to keep straight, you should visit some of the schools in New York, where Lucy Calkins's team often has kids reading three books at a time.

Using Time Within Literature Circle Meetings

Once you know how often lit circles will meet, at what time, and for how long, you need to develop a structure within that span. Many teachers see literature circle sessions as unfolding in three steps. First, they gather all the kids together for a short mini-lesson, to officially mark the start of lit circles and to work explicitly on one element of effective book-talk. Then the class scatters into its five or six or seven groups, to meet and discuss books and perhaps to do some reading. Finally, the teacher regathers the class at the end of the session to share highlights and debrief the day's discussion. Typical time distributions might be

> 5 minutes—mini-lesson
> 20–30 minutes—group meetings (and/or reading time)
> 5–10 minutes—sharing/debriefing

These three phases pretty accurately mirror the steps that occur in adult book clubs; there's a "greeting and getting organized" step (often including a bit of eating and gossiping), then a long stretch of focused book-talk, followed by a few minutes of wrapping up and laying plans for the next session. Not all teachers follow these steps every day, nor do they need to. You'll remember in Chapter 2 that Theresa Kubasak's kids slid right into their book clubs without any formal opening, and all the mini-lessons were delivered in a longer chunk of sharing time afterward. You'll find your own balance between teaching skills and facilitating groups.

Mini-Lessons

We generally use two main kinds of mini-lessons in literature circles: procedural and literary. In procedural mini-lessons, we are teaching kids the routines, norms, and procedures that make book clubs work. We cover topics like

How to select books that are right for you
How to divide up a book for multiple meetings
Things that can be included in a reading log
Knowing the signs of active listening
How to share "airtime" in a group
Ways of disagreeing constructively
How to create a self-assessment rubric

In literary mini-lessons, we draw students' attention to elements of authors' craft, usually focusing on broad elements that reach across the different books that kids are reading. We might raise issues like

How do authors hook us on the first page?
What are some ways that authors reveal character?
What are the main ingredients of a mystery?
What does "believable" dialogue sound like?
How does an author's time period affect her work?
What makes a good book title?
How much detail is too much?

Some literary mini-lessons can be quite simple. One worth repeating frequently is when the teacher simply talks about whatever she herself is reading, whether an adult or children's book. She can tell how she chose the book, explain how the beginning worked for her, speculate where the story seems to be going, tell how she's responding to the book so far, explain how she connects it to others she's read, and so on. Perhaps she'll read a passage aloud to share the author's style, humor, or language. This is simply modeling in its purest form, with a veteran book person "opening up her head" and showing kids how life-long readers think and act.

What topics get taken up in mini-lessons depends on the stage of development of the groups. When lit circles are just getting started in a classroom, there tend to be a lot of procedural mini-lessons, focused on the norms and mechanics of becoming functional book clubs. Indeed, at these early stages, the mini-lessons sometimes get a bit maxi, even exceeding the five-minute limit. Later on, when groups are humming, the mini-lessons can focus on fine-tuning, adding variations, and problem solving.

▼ VARIATION : **Hold Mini-lessons After, Not Before, Book Club Meetings**

Many teachers habitually kick off book club meetings by gathering the whole class for an initial five- or ten-minute mini-lesson on some aspect of literature or some procedure of book clubbing. Theresa Kabasak does it the other way around, saving most of her mini-lessons for after the group meetings. While teachers always observe kids' lit circle meetings in order to come up with mini-lesson topics, opening mini-lessons at best draw on yesterday's meetings. Doing mini-lessons during sharing time based on a just-completed round of lit circles pretty much guarantees fresh problems, topics, and examples.

There is no fixed or correct sequence of mini-lessons; on the contrary, smart teachers develop their mini-lessons by observing the kids at work. They notice common problems, things that a number of groups are struggling with. They try to figure out what the next step is for these kids. Then they shape these insights into mini-lessons. For example, if a teacher notices that many groups are drifting off their books into general conversation, she might plan a mini-lesson that begins, Over the past few days, I have noticed that many groups are having trouble staying close to their books. Can anyone suggest ways we could deal with this? As kids offer suggestions, the teacher makes a list:

Remind each other
Videotape ourselves and watch how we are doing
Put a note on the table in front of us: "Stick to the book!"
Use the egg timer and check ourselves every three minutes
Invite in a guest moderator
Have one person be the on-task-master

The list itself becomes a visible reminder of the problem and some solutions, and the teacher may simply send kids off to their group, encouraging them to select one or more of these strategies for testing.

Many helpful mini-lessons are embedded in the teacher stories throughout this book. For more ideas, be sure to visit the teachers in Chapters 8, 9, and 10, as well as our old friends Theresa Kubasak (p. 42), Olga Marquez (p. 57), Nancy Steineke (p. 49), and Jenny Cornbleet (p. 61).

Sharing Time

As we learned from Theresa Kubasak, a class gathering after book clubs can be used for mini-lessons of almost any type. But perhaps the simplest and the most natural kind of sharing time is for the teacher to ask, What were you talking about in your groups today? What was a hot topic? What did you spend time on, wonder about, or argue about? In our Chicago schools, we say, What were the "threads" of the discussion? And then we let each group get a bit of air-time, telling about their books and the ideas they've sparked. Of course, hearing people talk too long about a book you haven't read can get old, so we are sure to keep these reports short and focused.

A closing session like this lends itself especially well to debriefing the *process* of the day's book discussions while they are fresh in our minds. Particularly in the early days of book clubs, many teachers use the sharing time to help kids notice what's happening in their groups, to make decisions about what is useful and not-so-useful behavior, and to make plans for future improvement. Theresa Kubasak calls these "what-went-well meetings," even though there is just as much talk about what didn't as what did.

Nancy Steineke asks each student to write down three "noticings" about their group's process that day, things that worked and things that need work. Then the kids in each group are supposed to share ideas and formally adopt a specific goal for improvement in their next meeting. At that time, they'll post a graphic reminder of the goal, in the form of a table card reading "Ask more fol-lowup questions" or "Prove it with the book."

Once groups have matured and don't need such frequent processing, shar-ing time can be used for many other activities. This is a natural time for kids to offer short book projects and presentations, especially if they are presented on a staggered schedule, with only one or two per day. Some teachers use sharing time for reading aloud, from one of the books being read in the room, or from another one by the same author, or from a book with related content. Sometimes literature circle books raise informational questions that need inves-tigating and reporting back. When one group of Phyllis Smith's kids read *Bunnicula,* it made them wonder about the diet and reproduction of rabbits. So Phyllis invited an expert from the House Rabbit Society to visit the following week, during sharing time, to answer kids' questions about bunnies.

Earlier, when we reviewed various approaches to getting started with litera-ture circles, we noted that this is an unfolding, long-term process. The mini-les-sons and sharing time that we organize before and after literature circle meetings are powerful. They provide us with brief but regular opportunities to patiently fine-tune, shape, and nurture kids' book clubs. This is a labor of months and even years, and a most pleasant one if we maintain developmentally appropriate expectations and a sense of fun. This is our opportunity to solidify, by small steps, day by day, our students' grounding in the culture of books.

Book Projects

Author and educator Yetta Goodman tells a pithy story about the phenomenon of school book projects, which goes roughly like this: "I am coming to the end of a really great book, lying in bed under my reading light, next to my husband, who is also reading under his own light. As I turn the last page of my book, enjoy the ending, and then close the cover, I don't generally turn to Ken and say, 'Honey, will you pass me that shoe box so I can make my diorama now?'"

The moral is clear. Real, lifelong readers don't generally make dioramas; they don't sit down and draft "missing scenes" from a freshly finished book; they don't make posters or put on puppet shows. What real readers actually do is find someone to talk to, ASAP. We need to enthuse about the book, to grieve the lost characters, revisit the funniest lines, savor the beautiful language. This sharing impulse, of course, is where book clubs come from in the first place.

The other thing that real readers do after finishing a great book is *start another one.* As educators, we have to question anything that interrupts this healthful impulse. If a kid is reaching out his hand to grab another book, do we really want to pull it back and say, Wait! First, before you read another book, you need to spend six days sewing a quilt of key scenes from the last one!

Let's face it. Sometimes, the book projects that follow literature circles are not natural, relevant, or energizing activities. Instead, they are something we teachers assign just to evoke a tangible product, something that can be graded. We may not know how to evaluate something as slippery and subjective as a live book discussion, but we can sure as heck slap a grade on a project. Been there, marked that!

All those cautions having been issued, the fact remains that sharing responses to books can be a great social activity if done in the right spirit: to connect with other readers and potential readers of our books, to advertise (or condemn) important books. At the end of a reading cycle, each group can figure out a way to share their books with others in the classroom. At one level, this is a way for readers to pull together their own thinking about a book, to celebrate and culminate their reading. But this is also a vital form of "advertising" in the classroom; these reports are one of the main ways that students hear about books they might like to read—or avoid—when the next cycle begins. The sharing, which might last for one or two days every couple of weeks, can also provide a nice change of pace, a coming together, an opportunity for students to discuss, perform, or connect their readings.

The scope and formality of this sharing, as well as the time devoted to it, can vary. Many teachers advise groups to finish their book a day or two before the end of the cycle so they'll have time to plan and prepare their product or presentation. If more days are allocated and the cycle is stretched accordingly, then kids can create more formal, polished reports—but they will ultimately be doing less reading. Evaluating students' sharing presents similar choices. Depending on the teacher's judgment (or the grading policies of the school), kids can create projects as a group, prepare a multipart product or performance in which each student is responsible for one component, or do individual projects. Although regular book reports are possible outcomes, they certainly violate the playful spirit of literature circles. Among the sharing devices used by kids in our literature circle network are

Posters advertising the book.

TV movie critic–style reviews.

Readers theater performances.

Performances of a "lost scene" from the book.

A sequel to the story.

Read-alouds of key passages (with discussion and commentaries).

Videotaped dramatizations.

A time line of the story.

Panel debates.

Reader-on-the-street interviews (live or videotaped).

Report on the author's life.

A new ending for the book.

A new character for the book.

Collages representing different characters.

A piece of artwork—painting, sculpture, poem, mobile, collage, diorama—interpreting the book.

An original skit based on the book.

A new cover for the book.

An advertising campaign for the book.

Diary of a character.

Letter recommending the book to the acquisitions librarian.

Impersonation of a character (in costume, with props).

Interview with the author (real or fictionalized).

Interview with a character.

Letters to (or from) a character.

The story rewritten for younger kids as a picture book.

Plans for a party for all the characters in the book.

A song or a dance about the book.

News broadcast reporting events from the book.

Family tree of a key character.

Gravestone and eulogy for a character.

A puppet show about the book.

A board game based on the book.

Background/research on the setting or period.

A diorama of a key scene (just kidding!)

▼ ▼ ▼ ▼ ▼ ▼ ▼ ▼ ▼ ▼ ▼

7

Books and Materials

WHILE LITERATURE circles are a quite elegant classroom activity, they are not dependent on equipment. Teachers who want to get started won't require any exotic, high-tech materials. What they will need is lots of *books*—fiction and nonfiction—as well as articles, magazines, and other printed materials. Because *choice* is such a key element of literature circles, teachers must provide plenty of real reading alternatives in the classroom (or quickly available outside). And those choices need to be available in sets of four, five, or six copies of the same text, so that groups can be formed around kids' preferences.

Sometimes, of course, the teacher will prefer literature circles where all groups read the same book or pick from a small set of preselected choices. This may be done either for training purposes or to hook literature circles into a chunk of required curriculum. These variations are, with certain cautions, perfectly valid, and we will address each of them later. For now, however, we're going to concentrate on "basic," student-directed literature circles, mainly used in language arts classes, structured around wide, genuine student choice.

Books

Quantity of Books

Very few teachers begin literature circles with a huge classroom library already in place. Traditional American schools provide teachers with quite a different assortment of reading resources: typically, book money goes for classroom sets of thick, costly textbooks and anthologies, and single copies of "real" literature are then ordered for the library. So the first challenge for would-be literature circlers is to get a few sets of attractive titles into the classroom, so kids will have something to pick from. Still, you don't need a five-thousand-volume classroom library to *begin* using literature circles. Though it obviously limits kids' choices in an absolute sense, most teachers actually start with four to six copies of a handful of titles—perhaps only enough to total the number of kids in class. What this essentially says to the kids is, You gotta pick *one* of these six books to read. But isn't that better than getting only one choice?

Most teachers should be able to assemble this kind of rudimentary library, at least temporarily, through several sources. First, they can work with their *school or public librarian,* checking out multiple copies of promising titles. They can also borrow sets of books from *other teachers* or from the school *bookroom,* where leftover/unused copies of novels often accumulate. Enterprising teachers can also look outside the building for sets of books. Marianne Flanagan, whom we met earlier, wrote and won a $300 *grant* during her first year of literature circles, which brought more than twenty-five sets into her room in one purchase. Some progressive school districts are beginning to spend their *book budgets* in new ways. In Orland Park, Illinois, with the active support of the superintendent and curriculum director, the district stopped purchasing most of the workbooks, black-line masters, activity kits, and other assorted "consumables" that accompany the adopted basal series—and then shifted the leftover money to classroom libraries selected by teachers. Indeed, committed teachers need not wait for their own districts to follow suit—they should officially request new budget allocations, sending memos and proposals through the appropriate channels, so that kids get the books they really need.

Until book-buying priorities shift in American schools, however, it is likely that most lit circle teachers will continue to be part-time scavengers, prowling garage sales (where ten cents a copy is not an uncommon price), saving up book-club points, soliciting donations from the PTA/PTO, running bake-a-book sales, and otherwise building their collections. As a classroom library grows, however, it starts exerting a magical magnetic power on other books in the area. Books just seem to flow to the classroom. As other people— parents, friends, community members, ex-students—become aware that a beloved teacher is collecting books, donations happen. It turns out, quite happily, that the world is full of books that need a new home and new readers.

Special sources of books for elementary teachers are the children's book clubs—Tab, Trumpet, Scholastic, and others—which sell their wares through monthly newsletters distributed to school kids. Teachers' payoff for abetting this crafty capitalist caper is "points," credits that can be spent for free books for the classroom. And since the prices charged by most clubs are very, very low, teachers can get lots of books for a few points. Copies of out-of-copyright classics (*Huckleberry Finn, War of the Worlds,* etc.) often go for as little as $1.50. While these flimsy paperback editions are only good for perhaps a half-dozen readings, they're still a cheap way to build a library fast. Shrewd teachers heartily support the children's book clubs: they encourage their kids' parents to buy plenty of books when each order form comes out—or even to buy a book or two for the whole class, not just their own child.

Quality of Books

I recently visited a third-grade classroom where one lit circle group was doing very poorly. I could see as I walked in the door that this group, which was usually on-task and animated, was bored and distracted. I slid into the group, trying to figure out what the problem was. The kids had their logs dutifully filled out, and every once in a while someone would pitch a question into the silence, but there were no conversational takers. They couldn't seem to get anything going. I asked the kids to summarize the book for me. "It's about a kid who does a science experiment," they explained patiently, "and it gets all smelly." "Uh-huh. And what else?" I ask. "Ummm. Nothing, really. It's just stinky."

I took the hint and read the book. The kids were right. It was about a student whose science experiment gets smelly. I mean, so what? What were the kids supposed to talk about? "It reminds me of the time when my science experiment got stinky"? There was no character development, no conflict, no clash of people or values, no risk, no growth—basically, no story. With all due respect to the author, this particular title just didn't make a very good literature circle book.

So what does make a good book for literature circles, and how are we to judge? You don't have to be an expert in children's or young adult literature to make some good book selections and get started with literature circles. The starting point can always be children's books that you love yourself. If someone read you *Goodnight Moon* or *Mother Goose* as a child, they should be in your classroom library, too. If you loved *Charlotte's Web* as a kid, many of your students probably will, too. If you gobbled up Nancy Drews by the dozen, stock up. If you read Mark Twain or Sherlock Holmes tales as a teenager, they will undoubtedly hook some of your students, too.

Then what? How do we grow our repertoire of great books for kids? Of course, we should be reading books aimed at the age we teach, watching the reviews in journals like *The Horn Book, The New Advocate, Language Arts, Journal of Adolescent Literature, English Journal,* and *Reading Teacher.* We listen for titles recommended by colleagues or discussed at conferences; then we track them down and read them.

When it comes to putting in book orders for your literature circles, selecting titles for multiple-copy sets, it's easy to panic. If you are trying to get started and don't yet feel expert about the current offerings, it's fine to trust the major prize committees. If you look back over a few decades of Newbery and Caldecott winners, the majority of the selections have had lasting merit. The major book distributors like Scholastic and Troll will make it easy for you, providing prepackaged sets of prize-winning books, often arranged in themes and by grade-level ranges.

This business of becoming an expert in children's or young adult literature is the work of a whole career, even a lifetime. It takes years to get "caught up" with the classics, and steady reading to stay current. But what a lovely job! No professional development we can sign up for can match the deep practicality and pleasure of reading kids' books for ourselves. We do not have to read every book our kids ever read, but what a delight it is to have an "inside" chat, a private joke, a shared reference with a student who has read the same book we have. The more kids' books we read, the more such energizing teaching moments we will enjoy.

People always ask our consulting team for a list of recommended books. Many of our favorites are mentioned throughout the chapters of this book, and we gather them all (plus a few other titles) in Appendix C. For more comprehensive guidance, we are lucky to have some wise and trustworthy colleagues who make book lists their specialty. Among our favorites is the list in *Literature Circles and Response,* by Bonnie Campbell Hill, Nancy Johnson, and Katherine Schlick-Noe, and the even more current CD-ROM version found in *Literature Circles Resource Guide,* by the same authors. Stephanie Harvey and Anne Goudvis have a very useful list of nonfiction resources in *Strategies That Work* (2000).

Levels of Books

As teachers select sets of books for literature circles, they consider not just topics, authors, and interests but also the *reading levels* of their students. After all, one of the wonderful built-in features of literature circles is that they can provide for some temporary, kid-driven grouping in the classroom. When a student selects a book, she is putting herself into a temporary, appropriately leveled reading group.

This means that whatever grade you teach, you need multiple-copy sets of books at a wide range of reading levels—from relatively thinner, easy books, to thicker, harder ones. If you are giving kids limited book choices within themes, this is especially critical. For example, if you want your eighth graders to select a novel of survival, you'll need to offer a graduated range of titles running from quick reads like *Hatchet* to medium-hard titles like *Into Thin Air* to genuine toughies like *Kon-Tiki.*

As we order these books and create these choices, we may have to remind ourselves that literature circles are independent or recreational reading. During this special part of the day, we are not working at kids' instructional level but their fluency level. Simply: in literature circles kids must be reading books they can read. Research by Richard Allington (2000) shows that when only 5 percent of the words in a text are unknown to a reader, meaning begins to break down and engagement is risked. Yes, there may be other times of the day when we purposely put more kids into more challenging text, in the interest of teaching a reading strategy. But now, during book clubs, kids need comfortable books to choose from.

Of course, all this book choosing works best when kids have plenty of chances to peruse a book before they commit to it: having books on display for flip-throughs, hearing the teacher give a brief "book chat," or reading the posters or book reviews prepared by circles who've previously read the book. Given a good assortment of subjects, authors, and difficulty levels, kids will usually group themselves wisely: in general, they'll pick books they can read comfortably and want to read. But sometimes, if the subject matter—or the other kids in the group—are really appealing, students may pick a title that's tougher than their usual comfort level. At other times, kids may also pick down, enjoying a really easy book on a topic of special interest. Literature circles automatically mix kids up in constantly shifting groupings, so that everyone gets to know and work with everyone, without the usual rigid classifications of high, low, or middle. The structure invites safe, comfortable experimenting and risk taking among developing readers.

Reading Response Logs

In the old days of literature circles (back in the late 1980s and early 1990s), we used to start kids off with the role sheets described later in this chapter. Now, we have more options. The open-ended reading response log has become the bread-and-butter tool of literature circles. The physical form of response logs differs from classroom to classroom: it can be a spiral notebook, composition book, loose-leaf paper, or Post-it notes inserted right in the book. But what these logs have in common is their function: they are a place where kids can capture and save responses while they read—or immediately after they read. When students bring these logs to their literature circle meetings, the ideas feed the discussion, reminding members of feelings, connections, questions, visions, hypotheses, or predictions that occurred to them while they were reading.

Of course, reading logs aren't the invention of literature circle teachers. They have been around for ages, and are in constant use in most classrooms where thoughtful reading of good literature is an everyday activity. The variety of reading log models and the richness of their outcomes has been extensively documented in the professional literature. Among the most prominent and generative journaling models are those described by Nancie Atwell, Ralph Fletcher, and Lucy Calkins. Already in this book, you have seen how reading logs fit into literature circles for teachers like Theresa Kubasak, Nancy Steineke, and Jenny Cornbleet and Tina Peano. More examples are coming in Chapters 8, 9, and 10, where teachers from kindergarten through college share their variations and adaptations.

▼ V A R I A T I O N : **Pursue a Line of Thought**

Once you get into the meat of a really good book, maybe a third or halfway in, there's almost always at least one thing that you find yourself noticing, something that you will want to keep track of as the rest of the book unfolds. Maybe it's the zigzagging journey of a particular character you wonder about, maybe it's the way the author piles up powerful sensory details, maybe it's the parallel between this story and another one. Some people call this systematic noticing a line of thought. Both Karen Smith, whom we met in Chapter 3, and Lucy Calkins, whose New York classrooms we admire, ask kids in book clubs to identify at least one line of thought in the first part of a book and then actively track it as they finish the book. A line of thought is a powerful and sophisticated organizing question for kids' reading logs and their discussions.

Post-It Notes

By now, the 3-M company should have given literature circle teachers some kind of reward—or a piece of their profits. We must use more of those little yellow squares than any other customer in the country.

It seems funny looking back, but when the first edition of this book came out, teachers didn't use Post-its very much in the classroom. They were still very expensive, and no cheap knock-offs had yet appeared on the market. The first of our colleagues to dig into his own pocket for Post-it notes was Eric Paulsen, who was teaching fourth grade in Highland Park, Illinois. He got excited about literature circles the first time he heard about them, so he printed up some role sheets and plunged in. While his kids liked the activity immediately, they experienced some problems. These nine-year-olds were having a hard time relocating important items they had found during their reading, things they had planned to share with their groups. While the preprinted role sheets did include blanks that reminded kids to record the location of chosen items, filling in these blanks became a tangle and a bore.

Wanting a simpler and more concrete solution, Eric tried Post-it notes. Giving kids a supply of the smallest (one-inch-square) variety, he asked them to flag the items, placing the note so it "underlined" the item they wanted to mark and leaving an edge sticking out of the book as an easy marker. He also reminded kids that they could write on the Post-it note—either an arrow pointing directly at a given word or phrase in the text, or a few words to remind themselves what they wanted to say to their group. Now, Eric says, his kids' discussions run much more smoothly—fewer of those awkward, energy-sapping moments when group members paw through their books trying to find lost ideas.

Today, most of the teachers in our network schools use Post-it notes, alternating with or along with some kind of reading log, as the primary mechanism for helping kids harvest their responses as they read. Post-its have the advantage of being locatable right in the text, next to each item you want to remember and share with your group later on. When you hang those notes right out of the edge of the book, they act like index tabs to your reader response; you can flip immediately to each page or idea you want to discuss. No journal can match this geographical advantage. Of course, if you are in kindergarten (or high school) there may still be times when you look at your own Post-it note and wonder, "Now, what did I mean by this?" On the other hand, the small size of Post-its has some downsides. Even if you buy the bigger ones, like the three-by-three-inch variety, you're still offering kids a pretty tiny writing surface. Especially younger writers are not going to get many words on a Post-it; for everybody, they inherently work against any extended response that might burst forth. And drawings, well, forget it—we almost always need more space for the visualizations we get from books.

Assessment Tools

Teachers often devise special tools for managing and assessing the work of literature groups. These may include forms, checklists, observation guides, grading formulas, binders, and portfolios. We'll talk about these record-keeping and assessment materials in Chapter 12. A number of other tools, especially ones used for training students, are scattered through the teacher stories in the book, especially in Chapters 5, 6, 8, 9, and 10.

Clipboards

When it's 9:30 in Sandy King's third-grade class, that means it's lit circle time. Without a cue from Sandy, all the children start pulling their novels and clipboards out of their desks. Grinning and looking quite official, these twenty-six eight-year-olds march off to their current groups, happily toting the tools of their new trade.

One of the simplest ways of concretizing some key norms of literature circles is to issue students a clipboard, which they bring to each circle meeting with their notes for the day and some blank paper attached. This means that kids go off to their group with two things—the book they're reading and their prepared ideas for the discussion, ready to go. The clipboard also has some nice symbolic properties—it implies an organized, businesslike approach that the younger ones especially seem to enjoy. On a more practical note, having a clipboard makes it possible to jot notes no matter where you're sitting—in a circle of chairs, on the reading rug, on the hallway floor. Because literature circles are a fairly noisy activity and groups need to get some separation from one another, it becomes operationally quite helpful if, wherever groups form, kids are able to write. Clipboards solve that problem.

Role Sheets

Role sheets are designed to be "book club training wheels," a *temporary*, getting-started tool. Many teachers have found that when students are first learning to operate in peer-led discussion groups, it is helpful to offer them an intermediate support structure that makes the transition more comfortable and successful. In this regard, literature circles are no different from any other small-group activity that teachers might implement in the classroom. Whenever you introduce a decentralized, student-centered small-group structure, you are giving up some degree of direct guidance over the kids—and teachers often want some surrogate mechanism to help the groups know what to do, to use their independence well. Of course, we want kids to internalize these procedures rather than depend forever on these training wheels; the goal of these support tools is to make the tools obsolete.

That's where we came up with the various role sheets for literature circles, each of which gives a different, rotating task to each group member—setting a cognitive purpose for the reading and an interactive one for the group discussion. All of these roles are designed to create positive interdependence by giving group members clearly defined and interlocking but very open-ended tasks. The job sheets also enact some key assumptions about reading. They recognize that readers who approach a text with their prior knowledge activated and with some conscious purposes will understand better and remember more. Each role sheet embodies a specific kind of thinking that real readers do: visualizing, questioning, connecting to one's own experience, evaluating and making judgments, noticing elements of the author's craft, and so forth. So the role sheets have both cognitive and social purposes: they help kids read better *and* discuss better.

Success with role sheets depends very heavily on the teacher's instructions and timing. Smart teachers know that students can mistake the roles for a business-as-usual worksheet in disguise, so they emphasize that a literature circle is a natural, friendly, spontaneous, and free-flowing conversation. You don't have to raise your hand to speak, you don't go around the circle in order, one person at a time. The discussion may be started by anyone, may take off in any direction, and needn't return to any mandatory theme. Everyone is invited to bring up anything that struck them about the reading, whether it was in their notes or not. Group members are not restricted to the category of responses that happens to be their role for the day. There's no obligation to "work through" any or all of the notes on people's role sheets.

We explain to students that role sheets are really just a backup, an insurance policy, a source of topics in case the conversation lags. Often, in a successful lit circle meeting, people *never* refer to their role sheets. After all, if everyone comes to the group with lots to talk about, who needs a sheet? To dramatize this, we tell kids to start their literature circle meeting with the role sheets *face-down on the table,* and to flip them over only if they completely run out of things to talk about.

▼ VARIATION: **Use the Roles but Not the Role Sheets**

The different kinds of thinking embodied in the basic set of role sheets (connecting, questioning, visualizing, and analyzing) are validated by reading comprehension research as keys to successfully interacting with text. When kids use these cognitive lenses, they engage with, understand, and remember what they read. But teachers also find that when they use the sheets for very long, the discussions become rote and mechanical. So early in the year they teach the kinds of thinking embodied in the roles, and have kids practice them with short pieces of literature or nonfiction, but never hand out the actual sheets. To help kids remember the inventory of responses, they list them on a poster hung in the room or have kids copy them into their reading logs.

Depending on what approach to training you are using, kids should not use role sheets for more than three or four weeks, perhaps for an initial set of short stories, short informational text, or a single novel. This allows students to rotate through each role two or three times, adopting these different cognitive angles on their reading, internalizing the repertoire of group discussion roles, and practicing within a safe structure until less guidance is needed. Once they have experimented with this assortment of roles and had a few successful group meetings, you can phase the role sheets out, replacing them with a reading log. After all, the goal of literature circles is to have natural and sophisticated discussions of literature—and once that is happening, you want to remove any artificial elements immediately. My editor and I have joked that perhaps in this new edition, we should add a special notation on the bottom of the role sheet pages, in a microscopic typeface, far too small for aging teacher eyes to decipher: "Dear Student: If your teacher uses these sheets for more than three weeks, please report this violation by calling 1-800-NO-ROLES."

But the problem isn't just that teachers cling to the sheets for too long; there are some deeper difficulties. No matter how you try to redesign them, the role sheets still look a lot like worksheets. Oh, sure, we know they are not meant that way. We can protest that the roles are really very open-ended, that they merely ask kids to do the same kinds of thinking that proficient readers do (visualizing, connecting, questioning, etc.). And we can show how we warn kids not to rely on the sheets too much. "Use these only in a conversational emergency," we tell them, "if everyone in the group has completely run out of things to discuss." But it doesn't matter. Too often, when kids pick up one of these things—role sheets, job sheets, whatever we call them—they construe them as just another worksheet. They subconsciously shift into that Standard Busywork Mode they've acquired over many years of paper pushing in school: do the minimum, get it done as fast as possible so you can talk to a friend or do something fun.

Even more troubling to some teachers is that the role sheets segment kids' responses to reading. That is, they restrict the reader to a single kind of cognitive response per day. If you take the illustrator role today, it makes you feel you are mainly supposed to be visualizing while you read. But real readers don't work this way. They think about all elements of the text and use all their cognitive lenses, jumping around, noticing a key word, visualizing a scene, questioning a character's motives, and so forth. Though teachers can moderate this restricted thinking by assuring kids that all responses are welcome, the criticism is both valid and serious. Some educators believe that we should always have kids engaging in whole, real activities, at their developmental level, rather than trying to split complex activities into component parts. Others argue that kids cannot always jump into complete activities, and that separating out and practicing subparts is not only permissible but necessary. Many in the former group, whether they label themselves as whole language teachers, constructivists, or progressive educators, tend to be uncomfortable with the idea of breaking down kids' response to literature even for brief, temporary practice.

Luckily, this debate needn't matter. You can have literature circles just fine, with or without role sheets. Here in our Chicago network, after ten years of feedback from students and swapping ideas with colleagues, we use the role sheets much less, though we do teach kids the thinking skills behind them. We simply find that reading logs are a more natural and open place to record responses, that they are just as effective for training kids, and that they don't risk the burnout phenomenon that plagues the role sheets. But every time we are ready to discard the sheets forever, we visit (or receive an e-mail from a colleague somewhere describing) a classroom where they are being used in a constructive and creative way.

One final role sheet tale. On a recent visit to San Diego, I ran into a member of a local adult book club. She told me that another woman in the group was a schoolteacher who brought a set of literature circle role sheets to one meeting, just for fun. I braced myself for the inevitable story of how the book-club members scoffed at these mechanical, literature-debasing handouts. "They were fabulous!" my new friend enthused. "The group thought these were the most fun thing we ever did. Everyone really enjoyed preparing their roles and using them in the discussion. It was such a refreshing change from just general conversation." The moral of this story: role sheets may actually be more valuable to experienced book clubs, instead of the beginning ones where we have traditionally used them.

On the pages that follow are some of the roles that teachers in our network have used successfully. All of these role sheets are designed to support purposeful reading, to enact the key principles of collaborative learning, and to initiate a genuine, kid-led, self-sustaining discussion. If your students are already accustomed to discussing rich, open-ended questions about their reading and/or are veterans at keeping reading response logs, they probably won't need any role sheets to get going on lit circles. If not, no matter. Many teachers have started lit circles and reading logs at the same time—introducing the idea of recording one's thoughts, questions, and doodles, during and after reading, and then using the kids' fledgling journals as the basis for small-group talk.

The four sets of role sheets presented here have been developed and used by some of the contributing teachers you've met in this book. The "big kid" versions that work well for students in about fourth grade through college are listed first, followed by a section of role sheets especially designed for primary kids, and then by a variety of other sheets keyed to particular students or types of reading. The order is

Set A   Eight all-purpose, basic roles for fiction
Set B   Five basic roles for nonfiction (these may be supplemented with others from Set A)
Set C   Five roles for primary students
Set D   Eight Spanish role sheets for primary/intermediate students, prepared by Bonnie Barelli, of Tioga Elementary School

While readers of this book are entirely welcome to copy these role sheets for classroom use, teachers may find it even more helpful to design their own job sheets, with help from their students.

▼ VARIATION : **Design New Role Sheets for Specific Reading Material**

We keep saying that literature circles are really nothing but solid collaborative learning tied to reading. So it isn't surprising that teachers keep thinking up new collaborative tools for different genres. In Lafayette, Louisiana, Bill Chiquelin wanted to use lit circles with poetry, so he created four new roles: the alliterative alchemist (who watches for poetic devices having to do with the way words sound), the figurative language fanatic (a metaphor/simile hunter), the form forager (who looks for structure in poems), and the theme theorist (who looks for meaning in the poem). In New Market, Maryland, Eric Bokinsy liked the basic lit circle roles just fine but wanted more, so he came up with the cartoonist (who recounts the day's reading in four panels), the cartographer (who maps the physical movement of the day's reading), and the prognosticator (who predicts events that might happen in the rest of the story). In Ann Arbor, Michigan, Karen Schulte helps teachers deliver social studies content within the rigid guidelines of the Michigan Curriculum Framework, which mandates certain technical language. So Karen incorporated the official framework language into special role sheets designed for students to use while reading and discussing social science texts in small groups: geographer, historian, lawyer, economist, and vocabularian. In Nanuet, New York, Sonata Smith wanted to adapt literature circles to a unit on body systems. So she developed new job sheets called biosystem investigator, biosystem leader, biosystem illustrator, vocabulary analyst, and biosystem summarizer.

Although these roles can be used in almost any combination, some are more universal than others. We generally use the four "basic" ones, then fill in with optional roles, depending on the kind of literature being studied.

Basic Roles	Optional Roles
Connector	Summarizer
Questioner	Researcher
Literary luminary/passage master	Vocabulary enricher/word wizard
Illustrator	Travel tracer/scene setter

The four "basic" roles reflect fundamental kinds of thinking that real readers habitually use, whether consciously or unconsciously:

The *connector* role embodies what skillful readers most often do—they connect what they read to their own lives, their feelings, their experiences, to the day's headlines, to other books and authors.

The *questioner* is always wondering and analyzing: Where is this text going? Why do these characters act as they do? How did the author evoke this feeling? Is this a plausible outcome? Sometimes questioners seek to clarify or understand; at other moments, they may challenge or critique.

When we take the *literary luminary/passage master* role, we return to memorable, special, important sections of the text, to savor, reread, analyze, or share them aloud.

The *illustrator* role reminds us that skillful reading requires visualizing, and it invites a graphic, nonlinguistic response to the text.

These roles ensure four different "takes" on the text: the analytical (questioner), the oral/dramatic (literary luminary), the associative (connector), and the graphic/artistic (illustrator). Using these four roles as a base, the teacher or kids can select roles to fill out the group, depending on the nature of the book and the reading goals at hand. For self-selected fiction titles, many of our colleagues have drawn from the optional roles listed above for assigning roles to various-size groups. In a pinch, of course, a large group can have *two* of almost any role without difficulty.

These roles are meant to *rotate* each time the groups meet, so that as students work through a book, they are also exercising varied purposes for reading. Sometimes kids (and even adult teachers) feel insecure about a certain role and will avoid it unless an arbitrary rotation forces it on them periodically. To explore this, some of our Chicago-area teachers experimented with having kids stay with just one role for a longer time, even throughout a book—but the results weren't great. Kids didn't get a chance to internalize different roles, people got typecast in one job, staleness was especially pronounced, and disputes arose about perceived differences in the workload attached to each role. Not exactly the kind of lively, productive climate we want to develop. For the brief time that we use the roles, random rotation seems to work best.

▼ V A R I A T I O N : **Use Group Role Logs Instead of Individual Role Sheets**

Instead of training kids with role sheets, Judith Epcke gives out a spiral notebook for each role in each group. That means there is one connector notebook, one questioner notebook, and so forth, per group. When kids jot notes for their assigned role in the next LC meeting, they write in the official notebook for that role. Later, they come to the group and talk from their notes. After the discussion, the kids swap notebooks and take home the one for their next role, and so on. One neat result of this procedure is that all previous connectors' or discussion directors' comments are collected in one volume. This also makes it very simple for the teacher to track the work of a group by correlating the entries in just four notebooks.

In the previous edition, the questioner was called the "discussion director." The job was essentially the same: to list two or three questions that members of the group might want to discuss when they met. But in the old version, this director person was also given the task of convening the group—along with whatever else the moniker "director" might imply. After about ten years of using this role (we are a little slow here in Chicago), we noticed that the discussion director role was asymmetrical and often problematic. Not only did it give an extra task to one group member, it also implied that one person was the boss. The problems that routinely cropped up around this were, in hindsight, entirely predictable. Often, group members would depend too much on the discussion director to bring good ideas, to get things going, and to run the conversation. Further, this role could be an inadvertent license for kids who liked to dominate a conversation. In short, the discussion director role was not in sync with the kind of "leaderless" literature discussion groups we really wanted, where responsibility was shared equally and concurrently among all students.

For all these reasons, the questioner has replaced the discussion director in the basic set. Again, the questioner role carries the same reading and thinking tasks as the former role; we have mainly subtracted the extra leadership aspect and the weird dynamics it often spawned. Calling the role *questioner* also better labels this job's purpose. The essential job is to ask questions about the events, the characters, the author, the artistry, the story, just as skillful readers consistently do, both consciously and unconsciously.

Discarded Roles

While I do encourage readers to develop their own new roles, I also want to warn against some of the role sheets circulating widely in the teachers' underground handout exchange. One is the "process checker" or "peer evaluator" (and variants), roles that are widely used in any number of collaborative learning models. This person's job is to monitor and rate the other members of the group on the quality of their participation at each day's meeting. The teacher can collect this sheet as a way, among other things, of evaluating the kids' performance in circles on any given day.

When we tried the process checker role in literature circles, it was a loser right from the start. To begin with, it made one group member into more of a cop than a kid; it lent a kind of authoritarian tone to the proceedings. More important, the process checker role *does not set purposes for reading*. All the other roles offer guidance for students *while* they are reading and making notes for an upcoming session. Process checkers don't go to work until the meeting begins. In real classrooms, kids often translate this role into a "day off." We noticed that kids getting the process checker sheet were less likely than others to do their reading in advance.

Given all these drawbacks, plus the burst of better role ideas we were receiving from colleagues, many of the teachers around here threw the process checker role out. Kids don't need a turncoat in their midst to ensure that they work: they need a good assortment of real roles that give them different purposes for preparing and different ways of beginning a conversation. Then—and only then—do they need official and constructive ways to self-evaluate their work. Marline Pearson took another approach (p. 214), turning the process checker role into an extra, separate sheet that *everyone* periodically fills out, as a way of reflecting back on the group's process.

There are zillions of other literature circle role sheets and other aids floating around the school world. We all encounter these handouts, black-line masters, and magazine helpers every day. Some of them are meaningful and engaging tools created by brilliant and innovative colleagues. Others are the very embodiment of the terminology drift and pedagogical infidelity I talked about earlier. As we try to differentiate between the adaptations and the degradations, here would be my test: does this role represent something that real readers do, either during the reading process or during a discussion—or better yet, both? Do real readers ask *questions* while they read and while they discuss books? You bet they do. Do real readers make *synonym strips* and bring them to their book clubs? Uh, not really. Do they turn books into *recipes*? (Take one of these, add a pinch of that, stir in some you-know-what, add a cup of x, and mix it up, to make a something-or-other.) Probably not. Maybe telling the good stuff from the junk isn't so hard after all; if you think a role is artificial and gimmicky, so will the kids.

CONNECTOR

Name

Group

Book

Assignment p _____ – p _____

Connector: Your job is to find connections between the book and you, and between the book and the wider world. This means connecting the reading to your own past experiences, to happenings at school or in the community, to stories in the news, to similar events at other times and places, to other people or problems that you are reminded of. You may also see connections between this book and other writings on the same topic, or by the same author.

Some connections I made between this reading and my own experiences, the wider world, and other texts or authors:

SET A

QUESTIONER

Name

Group

Book

Assignment p _____ – p _____

Questioner: Your job is to write down a few questions that you have about this part of the book. What were you wondering about while you were reading? Did you have questions about what was happening? What a word meant? What a character did? What was going to happen next? Why the author used a certain style? Or what the whole thing meant? Just try to notice what you are wondering while you read, and jot down some of those questions either along the way or after you're finished.

Questions about today's reading:

LITERARY LUMINARY

Name

Group

Book

Assignment p _____ – p _____

Literary Luminary: Your job is to locate a few special sections or quotations in the text for your group to talk over. The idea is to help people go back to some especially interesting, powerful, funny, puzzling, or important sections of the reading and think about them more carefully. As you decide which passages or paragraphs are worth going back to, make a note why you picked each one. Then jot down some plans for how they should be shared. You can read passages aloud yourself, ask someone else to read them, or have people read them silently and then discuss.

Page No. & Paragraph	Reason for Picking	Plan for Discussion

ILLUSTRATOR

Name

Group

Book

Assignment p _____ **– p** _____

Illustrator: Good readers make pictures in their minds as they read. This is a chance to share some of your own images and visions. Draw some kind of picture related to the reading you have just done. It can be a sketch, cartoon, diagram, flowchart, or stick-figure scene. You can draw a picture of something that happened in your book, or something that the reading reminded you of, or a picture that conveys any idea or feeling you got from the reading. Any kind of drawing or graphic is okay—you can even label things with words if that helps. *Make your drawing on the other side of this sheet or on a separate sheet.*

Presentation plan: Whenever it fits in the conversation, show your drawing to your group. You don't necessarily have to explain it. You can let people speculate what your picture means, so they can connect your drawing to their own ideas about the reading. After everyone has had a say, you can always have the last word: tell them what your picture means, where it came from, or what it represents to you.

SUMMARIZER

Name

Group

Book

Assignment p _____ – p _____

Summarizer: Your job is to prepare a brief summary of today's reading. The other members of your group will be counting on you to give a quick (one- or two-minute) statement that conveys the gist—the key points, the main highlights, the essence—of today's reading assignment. If there are several main ideas or events to remember, you can use the bullets below.

Summary:

Key points or events:

-

-

-

-

-

SET
A

RESEARCHER

Name

Group

Book

Assignment p _____ **– p** _____

Researcher: Your job is to dig up some background information on any topic related to your book. This might include

the geography, weather, culture, or history of the book's setting.
information about the author, her/his life, and other works.
information about the time period portrayed in the book.
pictures, objects, or materials that illustrate elements of the book.
the history and derivation of words or names used in the book.
music that reflects the book or the time.

This is *not* a formal research report. The idea is to find some information or material that helps your group understand the book better. Investigate something that really interests you—something that struck you as puzzling or curious while you were reading.

Ways of gathering information:

the introduction, preface, or "about the author" section of the book
library books and magazines
on-line computer search or encyclopedia
interviews with people who know the topic
other novels, nonfiction, or textbooks you've read

From *Literature Circles: Voice and Choice in Book Clubs and Reading Groups,* 2d edition, by Harvey Daniels.
Copyright © 2002. Stenhouse Publishers.

WORD WIZARD

Name

Group

Book

Assignment p _____ – p _____

Word Wizard: The words a writer chooses are an important ingredient of the author's craft. Your job is to be on the lookout for a few words that have special meaning in today's reading selection. If you find words that are puzzling or unfamiliar, mark them while you are reading, and then later jot down their definition, either from a dictionary or some other source. You may also run across words that stand out somehow in the reading—words that are repeated a lot, used in an unusual way, or key to the meaning of the text. Mark these special words, too, and be ready to point them out to the group. When your circle meets, help members find and discuss the words that seem most important in this text.

Word	Page No. & Paragraph	Definition	Plan for Discussion

SET A

SCENE SETTER

Name

Group

Book

Assignment p _____ – p _____

Scene Setter: When you are reading a book where characters move around a lot and the scene changes frequently, it is important for everyone in your group to know *where* things are happening and how the setting may have changed. So that's your job: to track carefully where the action takes place during today's reading. Describe each setting in detail, either in words or with an action map or diagram you can show to your group. Be sure to give the pages where the scene is described.

Describe or sketch the setting (you may also use the back of this sheet or another sheet):

Where today's action *begins*:   Page where it is described

Where *key events* happen today: Pages where they are described

Where today's events *end*:   Page where it is described

CONNECTOR (NONFICTION)

Name

Group

Book

Assignment p _____ **– p** _____

Connector: Your job is to find connections between the material your group is reading and the world outside. This means connecting the reading to your own life, to happenings at school or in the community, to stories in the news, to similar events at other times and places, to other people or problems that you are reminded of. You might also see connections between this material and other writings on the same topic, or by the same author. There are no right answers here—whatever the reading connects you with is worth sharing!

Some connections I found between this reading and other people, places, events, authors . . .

From *Literature Circles: Voice and Choice in Book Clubs and Reading Groups,* 2d edition, by Harvey Daniels. Copyright © 2002. Stenhouse Publishers.

SET B

QUESTIONER (NONFICTION)

Name

Group

Book

Assignment p _____ **– p** _____

Questioner: Your job is to write down a few questions that you had about this selection. What were you wondering about while you were reading? Did you have questions about what was being described? What a word meant? Why the author used a certain style? How things fit together? What the whole thing meant? Just try to notice what questions popped into your mind while you read, and jot them down, either while you read or after you're finished.

Questions I had about this reading:

PASSAGE MASTER (NONFICTION)

Name

Group

Book

Assignment p _____ – p _____

Passage Master: Your job is to locate a few special sections of the reading that the group should look back on. The idea is to help people notice the most interesting, funny, puzzling, or important sections of the text. You decide which passages or paragraphs are worth reviewing and then jot down plans for how they should be shared with the group. You can read passages aloud yourself, ask someone else to read them, or have people read them silently and then discuss.

Page No. & Paragraph	**Reason for Picking**	**Plan for Discussion**

SET B

VOCABULARY ENRICHER (NONFICTION)

Name

Group

Book

Assignment p _____ – p _____

Vocabulary Enricher: Your job is to be on the lookout for a few especially important words—new, interesting, strange, important, puzzling, or unfamiliar words—words that members of the group need to notice and understand. Mark some of these key words while you are reading, and then later jot down their definitions, either from the text or from a dictionary or other source. In the group, help members find and discuss these words.

Word	Page No. & Paragraph	Definition	Plan for Discussion

ILLUSTRATOR (NONFICTION)

Name

Group

Book

Assignment p _____ **– p** _____

Illustrator: Your job is to draw some kind of picture related to the reading. It can be a sketch, cartoon, diagram, flowchart, or stick-figure scene. You can draw a picture of something that's discussed specifically in the text, or something that the reading reminded you of, or a picture that conveys any idea or feeling you got from the reading. Any sort of drawing or graphic representation is okay—you can even label things with words if that helps. *Make your drawing on the other side of this sheet or on a separate sheet.*

Presentation plan: Whenever it fits in the conversation, show your picture without comment to the others in the group. One at a time, they get to speculate what your picture means, to connect the drawing to their own ideas about the reading and the subject at hand. After everyone has had a say, you get the last word: you get to tell them what your picture means, where it came from, or what it represents to you.

CONNECTOR

Name

Group

Book

Assignment p _____ – p _____

Connector: Your job is to find connections between the book and the world outside. This means connecting the reading to

your own life.
happenings at school or in the neighborhood.
similar events at other times and places.
stories in the news.
other people or problems.
other books or stories.
other writings on the same topic.

Some things today's reading reminded me of were

QUESTION ASKER

Name

Group

Book

Assignment p _____ **– p** _____

Question Asker: Your job is to write down some good questions for your group to talk about. These could be questions

you had while you were reading.
about a character.
about the story.
about a word.
you'd like to ask the author.

Write your questions here:

SET C

PASSAGE PICKER

Name

Group

Book

Assignment p _____ **– p** _____

Passage Picker: Your job is to pick parts of the story that you want to read aloud and talk about in your group. These can be

a good part.	a scary part.
an interesting part.	some good writing.
a funny part.	a good description.

Be sure to mark the parts you want to share with a Post-it note or bookmark. Or you can write on this sheet the parts you want to share.

Parts to read out loud:

Page No. &   **Why I picked it**
Paragraph

ARTFUL ARTIST

Name

Group

Book

Assignment p _____ – p _____

Artful Artist: Your job is to draw anything about the story that you liked:

a character
the setting
a problem
an exciting part
a surprise
a prediction of what will happen next
anything else

Draw on the back of this page or on a bigger piece of paper if you need it. Do any kind of drawing or picture you like. When your group meets, don't tell what your drawing is. Let them guess and talk about it first. Then you can tell them about it.

SET C

WORD WIZARD

Name

Group

Book

Assignment p _____ – **p** _____

Word Wizard: Your job is to look for special words in the story. Words that are

| new | funny | important |
| strange | interesting | hard |

When you find a word that you want to talk about, mark it with a Post-it note or write it down here:

| Word | Page No. &
Paragraph | Why I picked it |

When your group meets, help your friends talk about the words you have chosen. Things you can discuss:

How does this word fit in the story?
Does anyone know what this word means?
Shall we look it up in the dictionary?
How does this word make you feel?
Can you draw the word?

INTERROGADOR

Nombre

Grupo

Título

He leído de la página _____ **a la página** _____

Interrogador: Tu trabajo es de escribir algunas preguntas que tuviste mientras leías esta parte del libro. ¿De qué estabas pensando mientras que estabas leyendo? ¿Tenías preguntas sobre lo que sucedía? ¿La definición de una palabra? ¿Lo que hizo un personaje? ¿Lo que iba a suceder después? ¿Por qué el autor usó un cierto estilo? ¿O lo que todo significo? Al menos, trata de notar lo que estas pensando cuando lees, y escribe algunas preguntas que tengas mientras estas leyendo o cuando acabas de leer.

Preguntas sobre la lectura hoy:

Preguntas para hoy:

**SET
D**

ARTISTA TALENTOSO

Nombre

Grupo

Título

He leído de la página _____ a la página _____

Artista Talentoso: Dibuja una parte del cuento que le gustó mucho.

los personajes
el lugar (donde ocurre el cuento)
el problema
la solución
tu parte favorita

No habla de tu dibujo hasta que el resto del grupo esté preparado para compartir. Los otros compañeros tienen que adivinar lo que dibujaste.

CONECTOR

Nombre

Grupo

Título

He leído de la página _____ **a la página** _____

Conector: Tu trabajo es encontrar los enlaces entre el libro lo que está a tu alrededor. Este libro me hace pensar en . . .

otro libro que he leído
otro lugar que he visto
algo que pasó a mí, a mi familia, u a mis amigos
unos personajes de otros libros
unas películas que he visto
otras cosas que pasaron en la escuela, en casa, o en el vecindario

CAPITÁN DE LOS PERSONAJES

Nombre

Grupo

Título

He leído de la página _____ **a la página** _____

Capitán de los Personajes: Tienes que conocer y entender a los personajes del libro. Describe las personalidades—como se comportan. Describe como se sienten. ¿De qué piensan?

¿Se parecen los personajes a tí, a alguien de tu familia, o a algunas personas a quienes conoces?

Yo pienso que . . .
El personaje principal (¿Quién es el personaje más importante del cuento?) es . . .
Haz un dibujo del personaje.
Otro personaje que me gustó es . . .
Haz un dibujo de este personaje.

SABELOTODO DE LAS PALABRAS

Nombre

Grupo

Título

He leído de la página _____ **a la página** _____

Sabelotodo de las Palabras: Busca diferentes partes del cuento que quisieras leer en voz alta al grupo. Busca alguna parte que . . .

te hizo reír
te puso triste
relata una conversación interesante entre los personajes
usa descripciones vívidas
te hizo pensar en otras ideas, libros, o cosas que te pasaron
te causa curiousidad o te hizo maravillar

TRAZADOR DEL CAMINO DE LA LITERATURA

SET D

Nombre

Grupo

Título

He leído de la página _____ **a la página** _____

Trazador del Camino de la Literatura: Cuando se lee un libro, los personajes se cambian mucho de lugar y el ambiente cambia frecuentemente. Es importante que el grupo sepa dónde suceden las cosas y cómo cambia el ambiente. Éste es tu trabajo: trazar por dónde pasa la acción de la lectura de hoy. Describe cada lugar en detalle con palabras o en forma de un mapa para enseñarlo al grupo. Indica las páginas donde se describe los lugares.

Describe o dibuja el lugar donde ocurre la acción:

Donde empieza la acción: La página

Donde pasó algo importante hoy: La página

Donde terminó la acción de hoy: La página

INVESTIGATOR DE LA LITERATURA

Nombre

Grupo

Título

He leído de la página _____ **a la página** _____

Investigator de la Literatura: Tu trabajo es buscar información sobre cualquier tema que tenga algo que ver con el libro. Esto puede ser

la geografía, el clima, la cultura, la historia del lugar donde ocurre el cuento.
información sobre el autor/la autora, su vida, y otros libros que escribió.
información sobre el período representado en el cuento.

Lo importante de esta investigación es buscar información o materiales que ayuden al grupo a comprender mejor el libro. Investiga algo muy interesante (algo que te pareció curioso o interesante mientras lo leías).

Maneras de investigar:

Leer la introducción, cualquier información sobre el autor
Leer otros libros de la biblioteca o revistas
Hacer investigaciónes en las computadoras o en la enciclopedia
Entrevistar a personas que sepan mucho del tema
Consultar otros libros de ficción, libros de información, u otros libros de texto

SET D

ILUMINADOR DE LA LITERATURA

Nombre

Grupo

Título

He leído de la página _____ a la página _____

Experto: Tu tarea es localizar unas cuantas secciones especiales del texto que al grupo le gustaría escuchar. El propósito es ayudarles a recordar algunas secciones interesantes, profundas, divertidas, confusas, o importantes. Decide cuales pasajes o párrafos del texto valen la pena de ser escuchados, y luego escribe sus planes para compartirlos. Podrías leer los pasajes en voz alta, otra persona podría leerlos, o miembros del grupo podrían leer en silencio, y luego hablan sobre la lectura.

Localización	**Razón por la cual fue escogido**	**Plan de lectura**

Página
Párrafo

Posibles razones por las cuales un pasaje ha sido escogido para ser compartido:

Importante
Sorprendente
Divertido
Confuso
Informativo
Polémico
Bien escrito
Provoca discusión

Otras:

▼ ▼ ▼ ▼ ▼ ▼ ▼ ▼ ▼ ▼ ▼ ▼

8

Primary-Grade Applications

When I heard we were going to do lit circles I was really excited. Best of all, I learned how to make friends from a book.
        —*Eva Coleman, Baker Demonstration School*

IN THIS CHAPTER and the next two, classroom teachers tell how they have adopted and adapted literature circles for different ages of students. These innovators come from a wide range of city and suburban schools and work at grade levels from kindergarten through college. Each of these teachers has had to refine, replan, and rearrange their student-led discussion groups many times—and some have had to compromise under the pressure of curriculum mandates and standardized testing. None of these models is "pure," and none of us has perfected their use. In fact, many of the accounts just ahead focus on those imperfect early days when literature circles were just getting started. But all of these different models do have a few things in common: they give kids more time to read, more choice in what they read, more opportunities to pose and pursue their own questions, more responsibility in making meaning for themselves, and more freedom to conduct their own inquiry.

Literature Circles in Primary Grades

Teachers often ask whether literature circles need to be structured differently for primary-grade children. Well, unless you have five-year-olds who can run their own peer-led book discussions for thirty minutes, you bet they do! In the schools where we work, we see a dividing line around third grade. That is, we use a set of special procedures to adapt literature circles for kindergarten, first grade, and second grade—and then, from about third grade up (all the way through high school and adult book clubs) we use essentially the same basic structure described elsewhere in this book.

As we make these few key adaptations, though, we want to carefully preserve most of the defining features of true literature circles:

1. Students *choose* their own reading materials.
2. *Small temporary groups* are formed, based on book choice.
3. Different groups read *different books*.
4. Groups meet on a *regular, predictable schedule* to discuss their reading.
5. Kids use written or drawn *notes* to guide both their reading and discussion.
6. Discussion *topics come from the students*.
7. Group meetings aim to be *open, natural conversations about books,* so personal connections, digressions, and open-ended questions are welcome.
8. The teacher serves as a *facilitator,* not a group member or instructor.
9. Evaluation is by *teacher observation and student self-evaluation*.
10. A spirit of *playfulness and fun* pervades the room.
11. When books are finished, *readers share with their classmates,* and then *new groups form* around new reading choices.

So what are the main differences when literature circles come to the primary grades?

- The *books are appropriate for emergent readers*—which means picture books, wordless books, big books, kid-made books. Like all other primary-grade reading activities, literature circles require lots of books, because the little ones burn through books fast!
- To make sure that everyone understands the story, the *books are often read aloud* to the children, either by the teacher, by other kids, by upper-grade children, by parents at home, or through tape recordings in the listening center. Obviously, the teacher needs to do some careful orchestrating to make sure everyone in a circle is ready to meet but not let responses go "stale" while kids are waiting for a meeting.
- The *children typically read the whole book* before coming to a group discussion, rather than reading sections of the text and having several meetings like the older kids reading chapter books. This is mainly because of the nature of the books, which are designed to be one-sitting reads.
- During or after reading, kids record their *responses in drawing or writing at their own level.* For the youngest kids this often means simply drawing a picture of "something they thought of" during the reading and bringing this drawing with them to the group as one cue for sharing. Or they may dictate their response to the teacher, aide, parent helper, or another child. For older primary children, a *reading log,* perhaps

mixing writing and drawing, can be used to record impressions and ideas for sharing.

- Even if they have drawn a picture or jotted in a log, young children often need *extra help remembering what they want to share* in the literature circle. So some teachers provide large Post-it notes for kids to mark their favorite parts of a book, encouraging them to put some words or pictures on the note to represent the response they wanted to share. Marianne Kroll and Ann Paziotopoulos provide children with sets of illustrated *bookmarks* keyed to the kind of books they are reading (the fairy tale set includes Beginning, King, Queen, Good/Evil, Ending, Magic, and Message). Kids are invited to pick just one of these bookmarks to mark a special spot in the story that they want to discuss in their group. Ann and Marianne also offer children blank bookmarks so they can illustrate their own reasons for selecting a passage to share. Putting this all together: if after reading a book, kids do some drawing or writing and mark some favorite spots in the text, they should be well prepared to join in a group discussion.

- Though it is not necessary, many primary teachers organize literature circles in which *kids read different books* instead of the same titles. This way, the job of a group member is to give others a taste of the flavor of his or her book, perhaps helping them decide whether they would enjoy reading it.

- *Children all have the same role* in these groups. Everyone has basically the same two-part job: to share something from their book using their log, drawings, or bookmarks as cues, and then to join an open discussion of ideas in the books.

- When heterogeneous readings are being used, the *group meeting has two phases: sharing and discussion.* Imagine, for example, that each child in a group has been read a different picture book at home the night before. When the literature circle convenes, kids first need to take turns offering some kind of summary, retelling, or read-aloud highlights from their book. Then discussion can open up in which kids ask one another questions, compare books, and just talk about authors, illustrators, characters, problems, connections, feelings, and ideas.

- Because books (and attention spans) at this level are short, primary literature circles are typically *single meetings*: a group of kids gathering together on a single occasion to talk about one set of books. The new groups are then formed around another set of readings.

- The *teacher may be present* in primary literature circles. While young children can supervise themselves just fine in well-structured *pair* activities (buddy and partner reading, peer response to writing), some teachers find that more elaborate, larger-group activities like literature circles require more guidance—especially when they are just beginning. If the teacher does elect to attend each group meeting, there are several consequences. First, the rest of the class must be engaged in some other, self-monitored activity (writing workshop, independent reading, etc.), so that the teacher can give her full attention to the circle she's in. As a corollary, making the teacher a group member means that literature circles will meet less often than they would if they were kid-run. Finally, teachers must be very careful not to turn the literature circles into a traditional reading group. The role here is to *facilitate* sharing and discussion, not just to teach skills. At other times of the day and week, the teacher has ample opportunities to offer guided instruction, but literature circles are the time for pure, kid-centered book-talk.

With the youngest kids, we tend to be pretty preoccupied with teaching them reading skills and skills of decoding and comprehension. But literature circles are different. They focus on talking about books—the events and people and ideas and feelings that are in stories. In fact, you don't even need to be able to read to be in a literature circle. Many primary teachers use common fairy tales as the content for proto–book clubs. Nobody needs to decode any print to wonder, *Why were Cinderella's stepsisters so mean to her?* or to speculate, *What would you have done if you had been in her slippers?* If we can get good stories into kids' heads, they can get started on literature circles right away. Sure, we hope they'll also move toward reading the books for themselves, which we'll work on during other parts of the day. But now, at lit circle time, nobody has to wait. Everyone can be "on grade level" in a book club.

A Kindergarten Model

People often wonder if the youngest kids in school can really join in a small, student-led book discussion group. The answer is yes. Even kindergartners can join successfully in literature circles if the conversation is grounded in good literature, well structured, and brief.

In Mary Ann Pegura's kindergarten classroom, proto–literature circles are part of the read-aloud on some days. It starts when Mary Ann gathers the kids on the rug, selecting a good, exciting picture book like *Wednesday Surprise* or *Owl Moon.* She reads through the beginning of the story with animation and excitement, stopping at the point where the climax or resolution of the story is looming. Then Mary Ann closes the book and invites kids to go to their tables for a five-minute "book club meeting."

The job of these mini–book clubs is to *predict* the end of the story. At their tables, the kids have a two-step conversation: first they go around the circle and each child has a chance to offer her or his own prediction, giving reasons why they expect a certain outcome, based on details in the story. Once everyone has weighed in, the group is then supposed to come to a *consensus,* a word that Mary Ann has carefully taught the kids earlier in the year. This means kids have to confer back and forth about whose hypothesis—or what combination of predictions—seems most likely to come true.

To support this two-step, peer-led conversation, Mary Ann uses a couple of key organizational structures. At each table of four, she places a single red beanbag in front of one child, who gets to moderate the discussion for that day (this job rotates daily). When the kids arrive at their book club, the beanbag functions as a kind of "talking stick." The kids know that you can talk only when you are holding the beanbag and that the person of the day gets to start and finish the meeting as well as report the consensus when the groups move back to the rug to share predictions and enjoy the climax of the book. Because the stories are exciting, the structure is clear, and the time is short, Mary Ann's kids move into and out of their lit circles with energy and focus.

One reason that Mary Ann's kindergarten lit circles work so well is that kids love to guess the outcome of interesting stories. But this predicting stuff isn't just fun; it is also cognitively rich. Mary Ann is encouraging her students to practice one of the key mental processes that skillful, mature readers rely on. While there is nothing wrong with asking young readers to share their "favorite part" of a story or to tell "what they liked," predicting an ending and giving reasons for those predictions that refer to details in the text evoke the kind of thinking that real readers do, laying a strong foundation for deep reading in the future. Of course Mary Ann doesn't do this every day or let it become a lockstep element of sharing a book with kids. After all, some stories just cannot be interrupted for predicting or anything else—we need to get to the ending!

First-Grade Models

Many first-grade teachers we work with grow literature circles out of their take-home reading program. We've learned much about this from Lynn Cherkasky's work at the Foundations School, in Chicago, as well as from the model developed by Christy Clausen in Seattle (Hill, Johnson, and Schlick-Noe 1995). The basic structure is simple. On Fridays, kids form into clubs based on a book choice and make plans to meet the following week for a discussion. Then the kids carry their chosen books home in a bag packed with a pad of Post-it notes and some instructions that help parents read the book club selection with their child. Over the weekend, kids and parents read the book together, flagging important (memorable, interesting, puzzling, funny) spots in the book with the Post-it notes.

On Monday, kids return to school with their flagged books, ready to join in book club meetings that have a more experienced reader as facilitator—

either the teacher, an older student, or a parent helper. Typically, these groups meet consecutively, not concurrently; one group at a time meets with the teacher while the rest of the kids work at some other activity (centers, writing workshop). Later in the year, as kids become more able to sustain peer-led meetings, the teacher can start spinning kids off into independent groups—first two groups going at once, then three, then a whole classroom. It helps tremendously if bigger kids from elsewhere in the school or other kinds of helpers can visit and act as guest facilitators in these groups. This allows the primary teachers to get kids into true literature circles earlier and provides wonderful models of big kids or adults who read.

When the book clubs gather for their Monday or Tuesday meeting, the teacher may begin by asking kids to quietly page through their books, reviewing their Post-it notes to decide on one highlight they'll share when the group starts talking. Then the teacher invites a first phase of discussion, during which each student gets a turn to share a highlight, a comment, or a favorite picture. Often kids like to begin by talking about a favorite part or showing a favorite illustration. Once around the circle, the facilitator invites a second, more interactive stage of the conversation: kids make connections with others' ideas, find common elements or contrasts, and pooling and jigsawing the information they've gleaned. The teacher usually sees two groups on Monday and another two on Tuesday, getting to all the groups before their memory of the weekend reading, Post-it notes notwithstanding, has faded.

This is indeed a simple structure, but there are a few underlying management details that help these early book clubs work well for young readers. First, teachers give careful thought to the book selection process. One simple way is for the teacher to pick four or five surefire titles (which must be available in multiple copies, of course), displaying these choices in the classroom for kids to browse and select from. Some teachers have kids fill out written book ballots, which the teacher can quickly review to ensure good choices and well-balanced groups. Others are more hands-off, letting kids simply grab books and form groups on the spot Friday afternoon. Because we know the teacher will be facilitating the group meeting the next week, we don't worry so much about the chemistry of the groups as we do later on, when the kids are running their own discussions. And because book clubs are recreational, not instructional, reading, we don't worry too much about reading level, either. Some kids will pick books they can read on their own; others will rely on their parents' reading. But no matter how they get the book into their head, all students will share a common experience: understanding, enjoying, responding to, and later, discussing a good story among friends.

Another option in primary book clubs is to have members read different books. While in the standard version of big-kid and grown-up literature circles, groups by definition read the same book, in primary classrooms teachers often offer more choices. Instead of having everyone in a group read Eric Carle's *The Very Hungry Caterpillar,* for example, the members might instead each read a different Eric Carle picture book, offering the possibility of a rich conversation about what Carle's books have in common in content, style, and illustration. Or the kids might read six different nonfiction books about a related topic—insects, dinosaurs, etc.—offering another great opportunity to connect and jigsaw ideas when the group meets. Sometimes, assembling these text sets can be a little extra work for the teacher; at other times, it can be a clever ad hoc solution when multiple copies of good titles are not available, but author or topical sets can be cobbled together.

Most of the first-grade book clubs we have visited range between five and eight members and meet for about fifteen minutes. This means that if the teacher is the only group facilitator available, she may need to schedule two or three book club groups Monday and another two or three Tuesday to get through the whole class. Obviously, if groups are a little larger (say seven or eight instead of four or five) there will be fewer groups to meet. Whatever the group size, the teacher or facilitator's job is to help all the kids get roughly equal airtime in the group and to help members make the shift from a first round of sharing individual ideas to the later job of connecting across the group, helping kids tackle questions like, How are Eric Carle's books alike and different? What have we learned about dinosaurs from all these books? What seem to be Jerry Pickney's favorite subjects to illustrate?

Family involvement is key to these book clubs, and so we take several steps to engage and orient parents. Many of our teachers introduce literature circles during the fall parents night, so everyone will know early in the year how important the book clubs are and how they work. Some of our teachers even do a quick literature discussion activity during parents night, using a short short story to illustrate the power and fun of peer-led literature discussions. In many of our Best Practice network schools, we also sponsor regular parent book clubs that meet monthly to share ideas and, not incidentally, to build deep understanding of and support for the kids' book clubs that meet in the classrooms.

Every time a book goes home, the teacher includes an instruction sheet explaining ways that the family can enjoy the book together and help get the child ready for the book club. One teacher's standard letter goes like this:

Dear Families,
It's book club time again! In this bag is the book your child has chosen for his/her book club selection for next week. On Monday she/he will be meeting with five or six other students who also chose the same book. When the kids and I meet in this group, we will spend 15–20 minutes sharing highlights from our books, connecting and comparing

what we have learned. Once again, we are asking you to help your child read the book and to get ready to contribute to their book club.

Your job should be a pleasant one: simply read this book with your child sometime over the weekend. It works best if you can find a quiet and special time to sit together without interruption and really savor the experience. It is important to sit beside each other in a comfortable spot (a comfy couch, in bed), so that you feel close and so you can both see the book easily. Who should do the actual reading? You two decide! Because we encourage kids to pick books from a wide range of difficulty and topics, this may or may not be a book your child can read on her/his own without help. You can read the book aloud, the child can read the book, or the two of you can take turns.

The idea is not just to "plow through" the book but to take your time, to stop and share reactions and feelings as you go, to puzzle over questions, to make predictions, notice the pictures, or tell stories about how this book reminds you of events or people you know. It's especially helpful if your child can read the book more than once over the course of the weekend (remember, to young children, "repetition is the spice of life"!). Perhaps you could arrange one reading with Mom or Dad, and another with a grandparent, sibling, friend, or neighbor.

Sometimes kids (and even grown-ups) can forget what they have read after a few days, and that's why we have included some Post-it notes with this book. While you are reading the book with your child, please help her/him select a few (2 or 3) sections to mark for sharing with the book club next week. These might be favorite parts, parts that were funny, silly, interesting, scary, confusing—or just parts that you and your child talked about for any reason. For each of these places in the book, have your child stick a note right on the spot they want to remember, letting it hang out from the edge of the page so it is easy to locate when the group meets. To help even more, you or your child can write a word or symbol on the Post-it note to label why this spot in the book is worth remembering and talking about.

Thanks for your efforts, and happy reading!

Teachers sometimes shy away from parent-child book activities for fear that disadvantaged kids won't be able to find a weekend reading partner. They assume that single-parent or stressed-out or poor families can't deliver the same help as advantaged suburban households. But our colleague Lynn Cherkasky, all of whose students are poor inner-city kids, never takes no for an answer. Having studied the abundant research on family literacy in poor communities, Lynn knows that reading is highly valued and that even when work schedules or family troubles get in the way, someone can almost always be found to serve as a partner. She tells her students, "If your mother or father can't read with you, find someone who will—your aunt, uncle, grandmother, neighbor, brother, sister, or friend." For those few kids who genuinely can't find anyone to read with them over the weekend (a very rare occasion) Lynn somehow finds time to read the story with the child herself before the book club meets—or she locates a student teacher, aide, or parent helper to do so.

Kid-Led Book Clubs in First Grade

At Seward School, Norma Rocha-Cardenas uses the same basic structure with her 100 percent Spanish-speaking kids, with a few important variations. The books, the notes to parents, and the other materials are in Spanish. On Fridays, the kids pick their books by written ballot, listing their top three choices from six alternatives. Looking ahead to the meetings on Monday, Norma forms them into groups, putting a balance of stronger and weaker readers in each. The books go home with kids over the weekend, with the request that parents help kids come up with *preguntas* about the stories. To help the parents develop good questions with their child, Norma offers stems like *donde, que, porque, que passaria si?*

On Monday morning, Norma's first-grade book clubs all meet at once, on their own, rather than staggering the schedule so Norma can attend each group. Norma says she doesn't want the kids to become dependent on her prodding but to rely on their own reactions instead. So she has taught them a three-step model to run their own literature circle meetings. First, everyone jots down the *titulo, illustrador, y autor.* Next, the kids *leer el cuento* (if the parents have done their job, this will be the third reading of the book). There are choices of how the kids can do the reading: *todos, solitus,* or *campaniero* (as a whole group, alone, or in pairs). Finally, it is time for *las preguntas,* an open conversation about the questions kids have brought in.

Norma's literature circle groups continue to work with their chosen books through the rest of the week. After the Monday meetings, she asks kids as homework to bring in one more really good discussion question, and these are used for another short meeting on Tuesday. On Wednesday, the kids do journal writing based on their reading and discussion. Thursdays, they do some kind of project or activity that celebrates the book. And on Friday, they return the old books and pick new ones, as the cycle starts again.

A Second-Grade Model

At Jenner School, in the heart of Chicago's Cabrini-Green housing project, Angie Bynum's thirty-two second graders meet in literature circles routinely. Angie has a large selection of picture books in multiple-copy sets that she received through a grant from the *Chicago Tribune,* and this tempting assortment of titles is displayed in face-up stacks on large tables at the back of the classroom. When it is lit circle time, Angie's kids browse through this horizontal library, gradually forming themselves into groups of four or five. This process takes a good ten minutes of searching, talking, and negotiating, and often results in kids rereading old favorites as well as venturing into new ones. As each group assembles and picks up its books, they check in at Angie's desk.

Next, the kids push together a set of desks and take turns reading the book aloud to one another. Often, each child simply reads two facing pages, and the reader changes with each turn of a page. When the story has been read and any initial comments shared, everyone takes a few minutes to silently make notes. After a while, they transition into a conversation, and individual kids pitch in ideas about the book. As with any other well-organized literature circle, the discussion is natural, spontaneous, and wide-ranging. Sometimes the kids draw directly from their written notes and sometimes they simply talk about their personal responses to the story or the comments of other circle members. The whole process, from book selection through reading aloud, note writing, and discussion, involves about forty-five minutes of highly student-directed activity, activity few adults realize that kids at this age—or kids at this particular school—are capable of.

Here's one more primary variation that reminds us of an important option. Debbie Gurvitz invites older kids to train the younger ones and to sit in on their discussions. This kind of cross-age coaching can be adapted to any grade level; at Best Practice we use videotapes of seniors' literature circles to train the freshmen.

Literature Circles in Kindergarten and Third Grade

Debbie Gurvitz

LYON SCHOOL, GLENVIEW, IL

Literature is the most important component of our curriculum. I read aloud to my students three times a day. Literature is presented for varying purposes, including enjoyment; awareness of story; literacy experiences in reading, writing, and language; awareness of author and illustrator; acquiring information; analyzing and comparing style; and most important, acquiring a disposition to become a lifelong learner.

Last summer I had the opportunity to attend the Walloon Institute, where I gathered additional information about the strategy and use of literature circles in the classroom. Knowing that this concept was originally developed for middle- and upper-level students, I pondered how to implement this strategy in kindergarten. Two questions came to mind as I approached the use of literature circles in the kindergarten classroom. How was I to use this strategy in a developmentally appropriate manner, and how was I to implement this strategy at the emergent-reader level?

Setting the Stage for Literature Circles

The first thing I did was to make sure that my students became familiar with terms that were going to be used in upcoming literature circles. So, in the whole group, we began using the terms *illustrator, connector, summarizer,* and *vocabulary enricher* (word wizard) as they came up in discussion following a story. This strategy was not applied during all read-alouds, but only to those I selected or as the terms came up naturally in discussion. In large-group or small-group discussions, or as individuals or pairs, I asked children to respond to a story by creating an illustration, by connecting it to a personal experience, or by summarizing it through dictation. If the children illustrated, connected, or summarized individually or in pairs, we would then compare and contrast illustrations, connections, or summaries in a large-group setting.

Next, I wanted to build kids' familiarity with the terms and processes of cooperative groups. For this practice, we developed an activity around the November presidential election. The children heard the platforms of three bears running for president. The platforms were presented as read-alouds of *Corduroy,* by Don Freeman, *Good as New,* by Barbara Douglas, and *Jamberry,* by Bruce Degen. The students were randomly placed in three groups. Each group (six students per group) heard one story (platform). The students worked in pairs and were given the following roles: connector (connect to personal experience), illustrator, and summarizer. The children were to present their work and persuade the rest of the classroom to vote for their candidate. All writing was dictated and all roles, whether illustrator, summarizer, or connector, included an illustration. Excellent discussion took place as a result of the use of this strategy. The students did sway some votes in favor of their candidate. All the final writings were placed in a rotating classroom book.

I found this to be a valuable experience but learned that additional helpers in the room were really necessary to facilitate the process. When we did the election activity, we luckily had the assistance of one parent volunteer and a student teacher. I was at a loss as to how I could move on to real literature circles without having help—more student teachers or parent volunteers—when the solution suddenly appeared.

Literature circles were also being used in several of our third-grade classrooms at Lyon School. As "staff developer," I had the opportunity to observe the implementation of some of these literature circles. While visiting one room, I proposed to the "big kids" that they teach the strategies that they were using in literature circles to my kindergartners.

The third-grade students took their role as "teacher" quite seriously as they conducted their first "inservice" on literature circles. Each kindergarten student was paired with a third grader. The groups consisted of six third-grade students and four kindergarten students. The classes were divided into four groups. Each group was assigned one book written by Mem Fox, our January–February featured author: group 1, *Hattie and the Fox;* group 2, *Possum Magic;* group 3, *Koala Lou;* group 4, *Shoes from Grandpa.*

Three sessions were needed to complete our first round of literature circles. Here's what we did at each meeting:

Session 1—The discussion director reintroduced the roles, the literary luminary read the text, and the group members got to know one another.

Session 2—Each group held a literature circle, with each member serving in his or her assigned role. The discussion director and literary luminary were facilitators.

Session 3—Small-group and large-group discussions. Evaluation by students and teachers. The goal was to encourage and spark interest for individuals to want to read the books that were presented.

The roles we used were

Questioner (third-grade student). Coordinated the activity, redefined roles, and led the discussion.

Literary luminary (third-grade student). Read book to entire group and assisted where needed.

Summarizer (kindergarten student and third-grade student). Kindergarten student dictated summary of story to third-grade student. Third-grade student facilitated discussion and summary.

Reactor (kindergarten student and third-grade student). Kindergarten student dictated reaction and related it to a personal experience. Third-grade student facilitated discussion or summary.

Illustrator (kindergarten student and third-grade student). The kindergarten and third-grade student prepared illustration together and presented illustration to the group.

Word wizard (kindergarten student and third-grade student). Kindergarten student chose three unfamiliar words. Third-grade student used previous knowledge, text, or dictionary to define word. Kindergarten student dictated definition in his/her own words, and the students illustrated the word together.

This activity proved very meaningful for both the kindergarten and third-grade children. Students were enthusiastic and energetic when meeting in their groups. They raised good, interesting questions, discussed their reading seriously, and stayed on task most of the time. Students were also able to identify problems they encountered. Some kids thought we had too many sessions, some felt the books were too long, and others admitted that they had been confused at first. The other teachers and I concurred with the students' remarks. We know the next session will be smoother because the students will be familiar with the process, we will use shorter books, we'll have each pair reread the book together before performing their role, and perhaps we will eliminate a couple of roles. If we do this, the groups will be smaller and more manageable. I plan to continue to refine and revise my use of literature circles in the kindergarten classroom.

▼ ▼ ▼ ▼ ▼ ▼ ▼ ▼ ▼ ▼ ▼ ▼

9

Intermediate-Grade Applications

IF THERE IS a "natural home" for literature circles, it would have to be in the intermediate grades. When kids make the jump from picture books to chapter books, when they build up some serious fluency and speed, then independent reading can really take off. The world of books is fresh and new and unlimited, and there is so much great literature to choose from, both fiction and nonfiction. From all around the country, we hear stories of fourth- or fifth-grade classes who have "invented" literature circles for themselves. Hey, all you need to do is lock a bunch of ten- or eleven-year-olds in a room with multiple copies of good books, and they'll start literature circles for themselves!

In this chapter, we hear from three intermediate teachers who have developed highly personalized models of literature circles, combining various elements to suit their kids, their school, and their curriculum. Sara Nordlund and Melissa Woodbury are teaching partners who work in warm, adjoining fourth-grade classrooms in a rural Michigan school. They recount the refinement of their kids' book clubs over several years. Teresa Bond Fluth originally described her Texas-style book clubs in an article in *The Reading Teacher,* from which this piece is adapted. If you are looking for other intermediate-grade models, you can read about the classrooms of Marianne Flanagan (page 40), Theresa Kubasak (page 42), Karen Smith (page 32), or Sandy King (page 71).

Literature Circles in Fourth Grade: The First Six Years

Sara Nordlund and Melissa Woodbury

HART UPPER ELEMENTARY, HART, MI

A lively discussion was taking place. The students were talking about how both mothers and teachers can "turn the power up with their eyes." The kids had just finished reading a passage from *Frindle,* by Andrew Clemente, where the mother uses that special, powerful gaze. I smiled as they gave examples and thought about how far our literature circles had come—all the way from our classrooms at Hart Upper Elementary School to this discussion on a warm, sunny July day in my own backyard.

At the end of the school year, we invited our students to join us for backyard literature circles. For three mornings in July, the students came loaded down with lawn chairs, highlighters, pens, and enough snacks to feed many classrooms. We enjoyed several mornings of reading, discussing, and laughing together about *Frindle.* At the end of our last meeting, we took pictures and signed one another's books. We had tried many variations of literature circles before; backyard literature circles was just the latest version.

Our History with Lit Circles

When we first heard about literature circles about six years ago, we were excited about trying them in our classrooms. We spent that first summer preparing, collecting books, running off role sheets, and discussing how literature circles would be managed. We were determined that by the end of the year our students would increase their reading levels, read more books, and choose to read for enjoyment. It would be great if we could say everything went just the way we envisioned it. However, as each new literature circle session ended, we had identified changes that needed to be made. And so changes were made—many of them—over the years.

Since we started literature circles, we have developed different forms of role sheets countless times. We have changed the format of the discussion sessions. We've tried having the students read aloud to each other in their groups, as well as having them read silently on their own. We've tried running lit circles every other day for six weeks at a time. All these variations were an attempt to find a lit circle format that worked the best for our students and for us.

In our fourth-grade rooms, literature circles are team-taught and combined into our language arts curriculum. Reader's workshop, writer's workshop, and guided reading (using our basal reading series) are also implemented. We had been looking for other methods to get our students to read more, not just because it is a school subject but because we wanted them to enjoy reading as much as we do as adults. When our literature circles first began, we used the role sheets from Harvey Daniels's book throughout the entire first year. These role sheets did help the students stay focused on their discussion, and at this point we wanted evidence in writing as to what the students were discussing. For our first experience in using literature circles, the discussion groups seemed to work pretty well.

As time went on, however, the students started viewing the role sheets as worksheets, and so did we. We thought we had an effective discipline system in place for those students who did not complete their role sheets and were not prepared for their next discussion group. Unfortunately, the ones being disciplined were *us,* because it was the same students who didn't finish them time after time. The joy of literature circles was starting to diminish. The other problem was that the students did not seem to be putting a lot of thought into their role sheet responses. For example, one student who was often the word wizard kept saying he picked words because they were "funny." Looking at some of the words he selected, we noticed some really hilarious ones like *the, some,* and *hill.*

Our next step was to get the students to use the role sheets more as discussion tools and not so much as a paper to read aloud in place of discussion. In order to do this, we used several different strategies. For one thing, we gave kids a demonstration of the kind of in-depth conversation we were looking for. We grabbed a couple of other adults in the building and modeled a real literature group discussion in front of the students. We also tinkered more with the role sheets. Our new version was simply a laminated page with many different questions on it, rather than a blank form that students were expected to fill out. Now when the students finish their reading selection, they can choose questions on the card to ask their group, or they may ask a question of their own. This has really helped the students' discussions become more open-ended.

How We Do It Now

We don't jump into lit circles right away. Our year starts off with reader's workshop, in which students do individual independent reading and write to us in dialogue journals. This means we are having regular written conversations with kids about books. So by the time literature circles are ready to start, the students have had the opportunity to think and talk about books already, in writing.

> Dear Mrs. N.,
> I am reading *You Can't Scare Me.* It's good so far. I don't really know the reason I abandoned the one book. Yes I learned about many kinds of robots like Hoborogbug and anabots. My favorite robots were hobo and robug.
> Sincerley,
> Brandon
> PS. Do I spell sincerley right.

> Hi Brandon!
> You were pretty close on sincerely. You just had the "e" in the wrong place. I noticed that you said your robots were Hobo and Robug. What do they do? (Is the robot really a bug?) If I could invent a new robot I

would invent a robot that did my housecleaning for me. I HATE
HOUSEWORK! I would name my robot

Rocleanbot or

Robotcleanbot or

Ronomorehousecleanbot.

(That is pronounced Ro-no-more-house-clean-bot. Get it? No more?)

What new book did you find to read?

Love, Mrs. N.

Dear Mrs. N.,

I really do think you could would get rich off of a house cleaning robot.
And when I mean rich, I mean rich. If you want to learn more about
robots you just have to go to the school library and look up Robots. I
finished *You Can't Scare Me,* now I am reading *Amazing Bugs.* It's really
cool!

Sincerely,

Brandon

In addition to talking informally about books with us, the students need
to develop a sense of community with each other. So, from the very start of
school, we practice and model active listening on a daily basis. We talk about
what good listening looks like: eyes on the speaker, hands free, mouths closed.
We stress that put-downs have no place in our classroom, or anywhere. The students know that put-downs can be given with eyes, words, and actions and that
none of these will be tolerated. Our students are encouraged to feel free to
express their opinions, thoughts, and questions about the book without put-
downs from their peers.

In midfall, when it's time to start literature circles, we have a wide array of
book sets to choose from. Over the six years we have been experimenting with
lit circles, we have been accumulating good books in multiple copies. Mainly
we have ordered these titles through the book catalogs that arrive monthly in
our mailboxes. When students order books for their own home libraries, any
bonus points earned are used in ordering sets of six books for our classrooms.
When selecting books, we choose appropriate quality literature that will hold
students' interest over a period of time. We try to pick an assortment of informational books, Newbery winners, and other chapter books by a variety of
authors.

The atmosphere for literature circle meetings is really important. We give
our kids choices about where they read. After all, who likes to read a book in
stiff, upright chairs? So we try to set up our rooms to have the feel of a living
room, with couches, recliners, rocking chairs, pillows, rugs, and several floor
and table lamps. Just turning off the fluorescent overhead lights and using our
special "mood lighting" really changes the climate in the room. When it is time

for meetings, quiet music plays in the background as groups discuss. (We have found that this actually helps keep the noise level down.) Our one seating rule is that when discussing, kids must sit so they face one another, either in a circle or around a table. This promotes active listening within the group.

Currently, our literature circles run on cycles anywhere from two to three weeks. When groups are formed, the length of the books is taken into consideration. At the beginning of the cycle, we select an array of books that are comparable in length. The choosing process begins when we hold a session of book-talks. A selection of about ten titles are gathered together, and in a Siskel-and-Ebert manner, we share with our students what the books are about. We also invite students who have already read one of the selected books to share their opinions.

Once all the books have been reviewed, each student is given an index card and asked to list his or her four top choices. We promise that we will try to see that they get one of their top choices but ask them to be flexible in case the numbers don't work out. Once the cards have been gathered, we spend time going over each student's choices and placing him or her in an appropriate group. We try to aim for groups of four, but sometimes they have to be as large as five or six to accommodate choices.

When we ask the students to give us several choices, they get a sense of ownership, but we, as their classroom teachers, still have lots of freedom to create groups with specific students in them. When forming our literature circles, we look at group dynamics and the reading ability of the students, making sure that there are leaders and role models. We are also careful to make sure the special-needs students are not all placed together. Once the literature circle groups are created, the first session involves passing out the books and introducing group members to one another.

As soon as the books are handed out, we take over the building! Since our two fourth-grade classes do their literature circles at the same time, we have fifty people in about ten different groups. We try to spread the groups out as much as possible. Several groups go the gym to meet, where they are monitored by our shared classroom paraprofessional. Kids know that it is a special privilege to work outside the classroom, and they tend to rise to the occasion. Each room, then, has three to four groups with an adult in each room observing and monitoring.

All students have a folder where they keep journal entries about the book they are reading and discussing, along with a copy of the laminated role sheets (which they refer to but do not write on). The roles we use are character captain, connector, passage picker, discussion director, and a new one tied to our character education program, which we call "life-skill luminator." This person is supposed to mark places in the book where a character used or didn't use certain life skills, such as cooperation, tolerance, or honesty. This folder comes with kids to every session; they need it to save their notes while reading and to find good topics for conversation when meeting in the groups. The whole lit circle cycle lasts approximately two weeks. Each session lasts between fifty and sixty minutes, and we meet four or five times per week. Some groups meet longer than two weeks, and some are finished in six or eight sessions. (Literature circle groups that finish their book before the others go directly back to reader's workshop, reading and journaling about an individual book on their own.)

Each literature circle meeting has two steps: meeting and reading. When the group gathers, the first thing they do is discuss their reading from the previous day. There are several resources they can draw on for their discussion. First, they can refer to their journal for ideas about what they've read from the previous day. The journal is meant to be a discussion tool, not a product for the teacher. It may include drawings, phrases, questions kids have about their reading, or connections they have made between their reading and their own life. In addition to jotting in the journal, students also mark passages that they would like to share with their group. These passages can be read aloud and then talked about. Students may also use the role sheet list to pose questions for the group. We have found that the groups spend most of the time discussing marked passages and journal entries. They know they don't have to use the role sheets—but they are there to help if kids need more to discuss.

After the discussion is held, usually for twenty or thirty minutes, it is time for reading. The members remind one another how many pages they will read for the next day's session. Then kids are free to find any place in the room to begin their assigned reading. We encourage kids to mark passages and make journal entries as they go along. When groups finish their literature circle book, they fill out a simple book summary sheet that asks them to describe the setting, give the key characters' names, retell some plot highlights, and give a quick opinion about the book.

And what about us? Once the students are settled into their groups, we take a backseat and watch them progress on their own. When they read, we read, too. When they are discussing, we walk around and listen to the groups. There are definitely times that we need to step in and assist with disruptive students or to settle a disagreement on differing viewpoints, but for the most part our role is mainly to observe and make notes on our evaluation charts, which list five key group skills we watch for:

Completed the reading
Prepared for discussion
Cooperated
Listened actively
Remained on task

Monitoring these skills daily allows us to track kids' progress from session to session and assists us in filling out the literature circle rubric (see next page) at the end of the cycle.

LITERATURE CIRCLES

Name
Date

	Possible Points	Point Total
Works cooperatively with the group	10	
Is prepared for discussion group	20	
Uses active listening	20	
Stays on task during discussion	20	
Demonstrates comprehension of text through discussion with peers	20	
Completes a literature circle book review	10	
Total score	**100**	

Looking Ahead

Our goal continues to be helping students discover the joy of reading. In addition to fine-tuning our literature circles, we are always looking for ways to encourage kids to read beyond the classroom. Besides our summer literature circles, we have also tried an e-mail discussion group. We invited some of the students who had e-mail capabilities at home (and parent permission) to take a couple of weeks off of regular homework and read and discuss *Little House on the Prairie* with us at night. We set a number of pages for each day, and at a designated time we e-mailed one another our thoughts on the book.

> Dear Mrs. Woodbury,
> Today I read about Mary and Laura going to the first party. When they get home they tell Ma all about the party. Then Ma said "we can have a praty next Saturday." so they do. I just got to were everyone has come and that is it. I just filled out a book summary for half of the book. No I do not know what L.H.O.T.P. means.
> Melissa

> Dear Melissa,
> L.H.O.T.P. stands for *Little House on the Prairie*. I wrote that instead because it is a lot faster. GR stands for Grand Rapids, right? Are you interested in other LHOTP books? I read all of them when I was your age. Are Matt and Abby still dating?
> Love, Mrs. Woodbury

This was a great variation, and one we hope to use more often as more of our students get computers at home.

We feel that we are meeting our main goal. By adding literature circles to our curriculum, we have invited our students to become lifelong learners, to join in the joy of reading. Parents tell us at conferences that their kids are picking up books at home more frequently. That's encouraging. We will continue to refine and revise our book clubs in our classrooms, in our backyards, and in cyberspace.

Teresa Bond Fluth

FIFTH GRADE, ROUND ROCK INDEPENDENT SCHOOLS, CEDAR PARK, TX

For several years, I had been experimenting with book groups or literature circles in my third-, fourth-, and fifth-grade classrooms. My book groups had always been very teacher-led (meaning I gave tasks to be accomplished during each group meeting), and I was not seeing my students excited or engaged in interesting or productive conversation. So I began doing some classroom research with the notion that things needed to change.

I studied several different models of book clubs. I liked the format of the book clubs described by McMahon and Raphael (1997), where the four components are reading, writing, discussion, and instruction. This kind of discussion usually begins with the students sharing from their reading logs, and I wanted my students to keep a similar journal. However, McMahon and Raphael's model required all four components each day, and time did not permit this in my classroom. Wiencek and O'Flahavan's Conversational Discussion Groups (1994) provided a more flexible framework for me. These groups met every other day, with the students reading a piece of literature and writing an individual response the day before they participated in discussion. I felt comfortable with this type of book group format, yet I was still unclear how much additional structure I should give to the groups and their journal assignments.

I took heed of Nystrand, Gamoran, and Heck's (1993) advice that I couldn't expect great results if I just put the students in groups and let them "go to it" (p. 22). So we began early in the year to use five different reading roles I adapted from those introduced by Harvey Daniels (1994), tools designed to provide some structure while allowing for open-endedness: discussion director, passage master, illustrator, word wizard, and connector.

Getting Started

I modeled these five reading roles using the picture book *Jumanji*, by Chris Van Allsburg. I read the book to the whole class and modeled a journal entry for each role. I wrote about the importance of following directions when my best friend and I baked a cake and left out the baking soda, which was a connection (connector role) to *Jumanji* and the importance of following the directions to the game. I reread the passage where a lion chases one of the characters through the house and wrote about what an incredible description the author gives, making me feel that the lion was after me (passage master).

After I modeled a particular role, my students practiced the role on a novel we were reading as a whole class at the beginning of the year. We could then discuss each role in small simulated book groups, as well as a whole class. We would also practice the role on our read-aloud book. After we had tried out all these roles over a period of a couple of months, I began to see some of what my class and I called "dynamic discussion," where they were talking with one another about the text. I was ready to let my students take control.

As a class we brainstormed ideas and suggestions for book group discussions and journal writing. I kept a poster on the wall of the five reading roles and encouraged students to use these roles if they so desired. Other journal writing ideas included putting yourself in the place of a character, making predictions, writing about what you liked and disliked, and writing about changes you would make to the story. Book group discussion suggestions were to take turns talking, look at the person who is talking, bring your journal, and ask questions. I wrote these journal writing and discussion ideas on posters that were always accessible to the students and groups.

Students were surprised when I told them I would not assign them reading roles or tell them what to write about in their journals. The only requirement was that they spend some time every other day writing *something* in their journals. I emphasized that our brainstormed lists and the reading roles poster were there to help them if they were stuck for ideas to write about. I encouraged them to write what they were thinking about and what they might want to discuss in their groups.

Students were exposed to five novel sets (five books in each set) through book-talks by me; a "book pass" allowed them to look at each book closely. The focus for this book group was conflict, and I chose novels on several levels that involved some sort of conflict. Book choices were *Noonday Friends, Hatchet, Island of the Blue Dolphins, Number the Stars,* and *The Lion, the Witch, and the Wardrobe.* The students listed their top two choices and I then placed them in groups.

Once groups were formed, they were given a calendar and a due date for when they should have completed their novel. As a group, they were to make reading assignments for each school day until the due date (approximately three weeks)—for example, Monday, March 5—pp. 34–46; Tuesday, March 6—pp. 47–59; etc. Each class day, they would be given at least twenty minutes to read their novels. The remaining twenty-five minutes would be spent either writing in their journal or participating in book group discussions (journals and book groups flip-flopped days).

This is where I gave up much of the control of book group time. The students knew the guidelines (calendar, schedule of journals and discussions, posters of journal ideas and discussion guidelines) and I was curious to see what types of journal entries would be written and what kinds of discussions would follow.

My Classroom Research

Thinking about Vygotsky's (1978) theories of the zone of proximal development and internalization, I was curious whether my students would internalize the reading roles they experienced under my direction. At the beginning of the year, my mini-lessons on main idea, summarization, cause and effect, etc., did not seem to elicit critical thinking or discussion in my students. They could apply these skills to the novels they were reading in book groups, yet did not seem to take their thinking any further than what was taught.

When I read Daniels's book and understood the importance of guiding my students' critical thinking (in their zone of proximal development) using reading roles, I also saw the importance of giving my students ownership in this thinking by making their reading tasks open-ended. My job was to teach the type of reading role and let the students' thinking take over. Vygotsky uses the example of teaching the four arithmetic operations and how they "provide the basis for the subsequent development of a variety of highly complex internal processes in children's thinking" (p. 90). I saw the teaching and modeling of the five reading roles as providing the basis for my students to develop a variety of complex internal processes regarding reading. Perhaps the reading roles coupled with more student control was the key to eliciting "dynamic discussion" in book groups.

Thus, my research questions became, Are my students internalizing the reading roles modeled, and which roles are used most frequently? What types of connections are students making and why? For my research project I paid special attention to one group consisting of Brandon, Andrea, Lana, and Carri. These four students chose the book *Noonday Friends,* by Mary Stoltz, to discuss together. The story revolves around two best friends, Frannie and Simone, and their families. These girls deal with the financial problems, worries, and disappointments their parents experience. They have a difficult time maintaining their close friendship because each girl has family responsibilities that leave little time for socializing, except during the lunch hour at school. When a quarrel finds them not speaking to each other, the girls realize the importance of compromise and small gestures in relationships.

For my analysis, I collected data for a four-week period in March, during the initial experiment allowing my students to have free rein with their journal assignments. My data sources included field notes on the book group discussions, as well as student journals and audiotaped discussions and transcripts. My analysis proceeded through three phases: examining journals, analyzing my field notes, and listening to and transcribing audiotapes.

I began by looking through the student journals for evidence of the use of specific reading roles. What I found in the students' journals indicated consistent thinking about the text using the reading roles, without my direction. Using a tally chart for each role, I concluded that the connector role was used most frequently by the entire group. I discovered that Brandon used the illuminator and connector roles the same amount of time and that Lana used the discussion director and connector roles equally. Carri overwhelmingly used the connector role, and though Andrea wrote little, she also used the connector role most frequently. In addition to reading roles, students also made predictions, criticized the author, put themselves in the character's situation, and relayed feelings about events in the story. These types of journal entries occurred less frequently than any of the reading roles.

My field notes from observations of the group confirmed that connecting was the most prevalent kind of response. Many times students would read from their journals using a word wizard, discussion director, passage master, or illuminator role, which would lead to connections from the other members. The most common reason for making a connection came when students were relating to a character or situation. Most often, one student's connection would prompt the other group members to connect to their own lives. For example, in the book, Simone and Frannie (best friends), get into a fight that fascinated my students.

Carri: Why does Simone think Frannie isn't pretty for picking her scabs?
Andrea and Lana (*together*): I pick my scabs all the time! (*Laughter*)
Andrea: I once fell on gravel when I was going to get some eggs for my mom, and I slid five feet on my shin, my knee, and my hand. And then a couple of days later I had total scabs. It was the grossest thing.
Carri: When I first got my stitches, they were all like that.

My initial reaction to this conversation about scabs was that the group was straying from their task of discussing *Noonday Friends*. However, after listening to the full conversation and revisiting the story myself, I realized that this scab incident is the breaking point of the strong friendship between the two girls in the story. That the students chose to discuss it makes perfect sense. In addition, the dialogue shows that the students were relating to having and picking scabs, which to them does not seem like such a terrible thing to do. They were relating to Frannie and her puzzlement about losing a friend over such a common occurrence. Further discussion by the group revealed their understanding that picking scabs wasn't the only reason Simone was upset with Frannie. They discussed how friendships usually end after things build up, and the scab picking incident was the last of several incidents in the characters' friendship.

Often kids would make connections while trying to clarify something in the text. In the novel, Frannie's younger brother needs to stop rushing down the street because he has a stitch.

Andrea: Wait, I have to say something. What does it mean by a stitch?
Brandon: A stitch is like a pain.
Carri: Or you run and are like, ack!
Lana: It's called a stitch in your side. It's kinda like when you get a cramp.
Andrea: Okay, I get it.

Other examples of connections made in this type of context included understanding the words *ambush* and *jubilant*.

The third reason for making a connection during discussion involved disagreeing with a group member. This happened very diplomatically, with students sharing their experiences or that of others (as shown in the example below) to prove a point to another student. Andrea has an interesting theory on the future of Lila, another girl in the book, who thinks about her future dating and how much fun it will be. Lila is a rather wealthy and conceited character who befriends one of the girls, bragging about what her future will be like. The main characters in the book get frustrated when they realize how much easier Lila's life is than theirs. Andrea had already stated her dislike for Lila in the discussion.

Andrea: I don't think Lila is going to get many boys or dates because, um, she has a good childhood, and *I think* that having a good childhood means not so good of an adulthood, you know?
Carri: Hey, I have a good childhood!
Lana: Hey, I have a good childhood!
Andrea: It doesn't . . .
Brandon: I do.
Andrea: It doesn't mean that you're going to have a bad adulthood. It means that you're going to have, like, as much as you have, that's what I think, as much as you have good as a child. You're not going to have that much as good when you are an adult.
Lana: Miss Fluth probably had a good childhood and now she has a good adulthood.
Andrea: Her class isn't that good. We talk a lot.
Lana: No . . .
Andrea: We talk a lot.
Lana: Some people do . . .
Andrea: She gets frustrated.
Lana: So, everybody gets frustrated.
Brandon: Yeah, we've been in the same class for three years.

The rest of the group disagrees with Andrea's idea that if you have a good childhood, you won't have as good an adulthood. Although the group agrees with Andrea's negative feelings toward Lila (as evidenced in other discussions), they can't agree with the point she makes. They argue by relating their good childhoods, their teacher's good childhood, and how all people get frustrated. All of these connections help to support their rebuttal to Andrea's statement. When disagreeing with a group member, students tended to use their own experiences or the experiences of those close to them to support their argument.

Conclusions

The students took charge of these book groups to facilitate their understanding of the text. Through writing about the reading roles they had learned (internalized) in their journals, dynamic discussion blossomed in each book group. Although students were not given specific journal assignments, they chose to write using the reading roles as models the majority of the time.

Of the reading roles used by the students, connector was used most frequently. Their connections helped them and their peers make sense of the text by linking their own lives and those of their peers to the characters and situations. The students made connections to past events in their lives, their families, and relationships with friends and peers. They used these connections to understand the text by relating to a character or situation, to clarify something in the text, or to disagree with a group member. Because I did not specify what to write in their journals, the students chose to write about things that had meaning to them. This in turn helped to make the discussions meaningful and dynamic.

I discovered that fifth graders successfully lead book groups, stay on task, and demonstrate critical thinking in discussions and journals. They accomplished this by choosing their own responses to the literature. However, I feel book group success also involves modeling different types of reading roles and brainstorming discussion and reading guidelines together.

10

Middle and High School Applications

IT CAN SEEM pretty daunting to work literature circles into the middle or secondary school program. The typically overstuffed curriculum, brief class periods, and clanging-bell schedule make teachers feel like there just isn't time to cram in anything extra or try something new. In English classes, we also have "the canon problem," that list of Great Books and authors who must be covered by everyone in the class, from *Beowulf* to *To Kill a Mockingbird*. Letting kids pick their own books may be getting really popular in elementary schools, but very few secondary curriculum guides encourage teachers to divide their class into small groups around books of choice (yet!). This means that middle and high school teachers have to do two things: (1) fight for class time for independent reading, so they can do true literature circles, and (2) adapt key literature circle procedures to those required books, so that kids can enjoy peer-led discussions even when the literature is preselected.

These three teachers are bringing literature circles to their adolescent students in a variety of ways. With some colleagues, Margaret Forst designed a new semester-long elective course specifically built around literature circles and explicitly aimed to develop habits of lifelong reading. Nancy Steineke shoehorns lit circles into her sophomore English class and uses careful discussion practice to create engaged groups around kid-chosen novels. Nancy's procedure for helping kids select books was outlined on pages 77–80, and her more complete thoughts on small-group work are highlighted in her forthcoming book, *Reading and Writing Together: Collaborative Literacy in Action* (2002). Working with some titles required by her curriculum, Sharon Weiner is adapting key elements of literature circles to make the experience more personal and engaging for her middle school readers. Yet another model of literature circles for teenagers, featuring Jenny Cornbleet and Tina Peano's classes at Best Practice High School, can be found in Chapter 5.

Margaret Forst

LAKE FOREST HIGH SCHOOL, LAKE FOREST, IL

Like so many language arts teachers, Margaret Forst says that her number-one goal is for students to become lifelong readers and writers. But Maggie backs up these ordinary espousals with extraordinary actions. On the writing side, she has guided one of the nation's most honored student literary magazines for more than a decade. But lifelong reading? She was worried about that goal. It seemed that too many kids were escaping from high school without firmly establishing the habits of regular, engaged, personal reading. Even though her progressive school district already mandated fourteen days of reading workshop per semester in all English classes, it still didn't seem to be enough. So Maggie designed a new semester-long elective course—Contemporary Literature—that put book clubs at the center, and pushed it through the school approval process. Because the class was not leveled as honors or remedial, the first kids who signed up were a very mixed group, including some strong readers, some struggling ones, and some kids eagerly seeking one more English credit in order to graduate.

Before the first section of the class ever met, Maggie did something really smart. She wrote a letter to every employee of the high school, inviting them to come and join the book clubs in Contemporary Lit. You can come for just one book, she explained, or stay with us through the whole semester. A dozen adults who could get free during that period, including paraprofessionals, substitutes, several teachers, and the school's technology director, signed on. Suddenly Maggie had added a whole new dimension to literature circles. The adults who volunteered to meet twice a week with kid readers were (guess what?) lifelong readers or aspiring lifelong readers themselves. These were living models of the exact thing this class was designed to nurture. In a very real sense, the success of the course was guaranteed the day Maggie signed up these grown-ups to serve as coreaders.

The course began with three weeks of training. The whole class read one book together: *A Lesson Before Dying,* by Ernest Gaines. (Looking back, Maggie says that this selection proved to be too downbeat, and she plans to try another one next year.) As they worked through the book, Maggie offered the students and adult partners a series of mini-lessons on different ways that readers can interact with text. Usually, the strategy involved a particular kind of thinking, embodied in a short piece of writing done either at home or in class. One day they'd try out dialogue journals with a partner, another day they would practice pulling a key quotation from the text, the next day they'd track a character through the chapters, and another time they'd bring in a bit of background research (in this case, about a topic like capital punishment). They'd take each of these tools into a small discussion group and try them out with that day's reading from *A Lesson Before Dying*. Then they'd come back into the whole group to share ideas about the book and talk about how the interaction tool had fed the discussion. Finally, each strategy was added to a list kept on a whiteboard in the front of the room, a reminder to everyone of different responses they could use in the future.

Also during this training period, the class took one day a week to grow another important list: books we might like to read. Both Maggie and class members gave book-talks about favorite titles. They looked at the *New York Times* best-seller lists, the Oprah list, and book reviews from various magazines and newspapers. The adults were especially helpful in generating titles since they tended to be a little more familiar with contemporary books than the kids. Gradually, a list of "possibles" developed, inscribed on another slab of whiteboard leaned against the wall, right beside the response strategies list.

Once they had completed the common book and built a repertoire of response strategies, it was time to swing into the regular schedule. During the last week of *A Lesson*, Maggie asked people to decide on their first-choice book and to create a group of two or more. This was done through purely informal, ad hoc negotiation, and Maggie says it works fine every time. Some of the titles chosen were *A Heartbreaking Work of Staggering Genius, Back Roads, Hannibal, White Oleander, Plainsong, High Fidelity,* and *Bridget Jones's Diary*. Most groups ended up with several kids and one or two adults. At their first gathering, they had to figure out how to get the books (library, borrow from a friend, buy) and decide on the first chunk of reading, say through Chapter 4 by next Tuesday.

Now the regular schedule of the course kicks in. Mondays the class meets as a whole to do its mutual maintenance work, like discussing the book reviews from the Sunday newspaper, making lists of possible books to read, dealing with timing and logistics issues, or setting up future groups. Tuesdays and Fridays are book club meeting days. Wednesday is a just-reading day. Thursdays are used for people to connect with other groups, using dialogue journals and other tools to talk about the different books they are reading. When extra time turns up on any of these days, it's used for more reading. Even on the Tuesday and Friday meeting days, some groups like to talk for just fifteen minutes and then get back to reading, while others meet for the whole period.

On book club meeting days, Maggie's role is not wandering and monitoring but being a group member herself. She usually starts by placing herself with whichever group looks shakiest, and then gradually works her way out to the stronger ones. (Of course, there are other adults in almost every group, so she would hear about it if things went badly awry.) When she is in a group, Maggie tries not to teach but just be her real reader self. She shares her feelings, opinions, insights, and noticings, but mainly she listens to the kids and draws them out.

Though she tells the story with some embarrassment, Maggie's role in *The Poisonwood Bible* group shows just how honest a reader she is willing to be.

Halfway through Barbara Kingsolver's anguishing novel, she told her group, "I can't stand this any more! I don't want to read one more word about this husband. He's a jerk and he's always going to be a jerk and I don't want to read another three hundred pages of him being a jerk. I've already met plenty of jerks like this. Life is too short! I'm going to read something else." And she left the group. Maggie says she felt really guilty about letting the group down, although she did notice that they carried on entirely unaffected by her dramatic departure. Meanwhile, she picked up a more congenial book, caught up on the reading, and joined another group—where she continued to be not Maggie the schoolteacher but Maggie the passionate, demanding, engaged, lifelong reader.

The adult mentoring in the book clubs is powerful but subtle and not at all teacherly. Maggie is careful to instruct the adults, "You are not in charge of the group. Just be another member, along with the kids." Since the adults are basically off-duty volunteers, they usually arrive in a nonpedantic frame of mind, and this isn't too much of a problem.

Sometimes the pairing of an adult with certain kids can be downright magic. When Andrew signed up for Contemporary Literature, he brought an unpromising record. Years earlier, he had failed freshman English and dropped out of school. Now he was back without a single English credit on his transcript, hoping to get back on track and eventually graduate. At the same time, the school's technology director, David Miller, turned up, cheerfully open to any matchup. Maggie asked if he'd pair with Andrew, who was having a hard time finding someone else who wanted to read the short suspense novel that interested him. David bought the book, read it, and joined Andrew in a spirited discussion. Following Andrew's lead, they read a couple more in this genre together, and then David started suggesting other titles and authors. They embarked on a study of Harry Potter books, reading the first two in the series before the year ended and the third one over the summer. When the long-awaited fourth volume was published that August, David mailed a copy to Andrew's house.

Though Maggie's book club course looks very loosely structured, there is some very careful management in the background. Each week, readers are asked to write two notes to the teacher explaining what is happening in their book, how they are responding to it, and what is going on in their group. Maggie logs these in with a check, check-plus, or check-minus, and sends back a short written comment. All readers keep a portfolio containing all the artifacts of their reading—lists of books read, written or drawn responses, notes to and from the teacher, completed projects, etc. Over the semester, the kids do three or four projects that ask them to reflect on and synthesize their reading in a different way. One project asks for a reading autobiography:

> Who are you as a reader? Write a letter about yourself as a reader so far
> this semester. Have your reading habits changed? Have you discovered

anything new about yourself as a reader? What do you like to read? What books have you enjoyed the most?

The ambitious final project asks kids to think about the bigger picture of literature and the wider family of readers they have been entering, to pull all their reading together:

> From what you have read, what would you suggest are some of the characteristics of literature of the late twentieth century and early twenty-first century? Of course, your conclusions will be highly personal ones that may or may not be true of contemporary literature as a whole. However, you should think about the books you have read and see what characteristics these books share. Formulate a central idea and use several (three to five) books that you have read this semester to support that idea. Remember the focus of your paper is to formulate an answer to the question through your limited reading and support that answer with the body of literature that you have read. Aim for a multiparagraph paper between three and five pages long. You might begin by reading over your journal entries and other writing on the books you have read. Spend some time thinking about this. If you are having trouble coming up with a central focus for your paper, please see me for a conference.

Like most other high school courses, this one must be graded. But Maggie doesn't give out any letter grades until the very end. She just lets kids know the ingredients of success along the way and encourages them to accumulate evidence. She says there's virtually no whining about grades, because everyone knows what it takes to get an A or a B, and most kids achieve it.

Contemporary Literature
Your final grade for this course will be based on the following:
—your class participation in and preparation for reading groups
—the consistent pace of your reading as determined by your reading lists
—your reading folders
  • submitted consistently and on time
  • contain all required items
  • exhibit high quality journal entries
  • demonstrate organization in a user-friendly manner
—your projects
—your final reading portfolio
If you wish to go over and above the minimum requirement, feel free to add a visual component, research an author, or add anything you wish.

Margaret Forst is certainly operating "second wave" literature circles here, by anyone's standard. She's created a flexible, open, and deeply student-centered structure. There's complete freedom of book choice, no restriction on the kinds of interaction around texts, and a rich assortment of group partners. Time is allocated to what really matters: reading and talking about books. As a result, kids are reading six to sixteen books per semester, sometimes two and three at once, as they finish up one group and get ready to jump into another. Indeed, Maggie's high school literature circles look very much like "real" adult book clubs, the ones where lifelong readers get together in living rooms and community centers. Hey, she even lets kids bring food to their—whoops, that would be against the rules.

But of all the special ingredients Maggie has combined here, the one most worthy of immediate replication by other schools is the adult volunteers, which could be expanded to include not just school employees but parents, community members, retired people, and others. Here's a letter Maggie sent to this year's adult readers, letting the kids explain in their own words what the mentoring had meant.

Dear Wonderful Reading Volunteers,

Thank you for making our Contemporary Literature class a success. I would like to share some of the students' comments with you so you can see from their words what a wonderful reading experience this has been for everyone.

Christine: "In my other classes, my ideas weren't as free as they should have been. I was also very quiet in discussions, because I guess it was more intimidating in a bigger group. But having the chance to read in small groups made me more comfortable. . . . I thought having teachers join in on the book clubs was a great idea. It not only brought more opinions, but also allowed us students to feel more on an equal level with them. When there were teachers in the group, it wasn't like teachers versus students. We were all just equal members in the group. It was a good way to meet other teachers in the school and to build a friendly relationship."

Tessie: "I got many good ideas from people in our class. I want to start a reading journal so I can ask questions and maybe be able to go back and answer them."

Tiffany: "It was a satisfying feeling to be able to go through a book and figure out for myself what I thought was important and what was not. When I found a quote or theme that was interesting to me or meaningful to the story, it was beneficial to have a reading group to report and discuss my ideas with. The reading groups functioned both as a teaching tool and as a medium where I was able to bounce ideas off people."

Caroline: "I think that I gained insight because of my classmates and teachers in my book groups. I saw how they looked deeper than just the surface of the book and really analyzed the character's thoughts and motivations."

Sarah: "The teachers that came did an excellent job of letting the students learn. When we enjoy something or have found the symbolism behind a certain situation, the information becomes much more meaningful to us. The teachers would put things in their point of view, but they never ran the discussion based solely upon their findings."

Brittany: "I have never felt so comfortable in a class and had this much inspiration to read."

Kelly: "I know that I will continue to read into the summer and into the years to come. . . . I have learned this year how fun it is to get lost in the words of literature and find myself taking part in the story as if I were one of the characters."

Heather: "The class's atmosphere was always comforting, and I was never nervous to give my opinion in a group discussion. I have not only grown into a stronger, faster reader, yet also a person who finds reading fun, something I never thought possible."

As you can see, you have been vital to a very important part of these students' learning. I can't thank you enough.

Sincerely,
Maggie
P.S. I had tons of fun, too.

Nancy Steineke

VICTOR J. ANDREW HIGH SCHOOL, TINLEY PARK, IL

Our book-choosing process takes one whole class period for the kids and a couple of days of fine-tuning by me (see pages 77–80). Then, the day the chosen books get passed out to new groups, I like to immediately follow with about fifteen or twenty minutes of SSR time so that students can get a bit of a feel for their books before they first meet. Then, when the groups do gather, the tasks are mostly organizational. There are several jobs to be completed.

Warm-up with membership grid. Often, we teachers want students to move directly into a task when what the group really needs at first is some "get to know you" time. The membership grid is a simple interviewing activity where students keep notes on new information they gather about their classmates' interests, opinions, or background (see page 49). The grid is the first item on the agenda of each lit circle meeting.

Ground rules. By now, students have a pretty good idea of what behavior creates success versus failure in group activities. Therefore, at the first meeting I have each group develop a list of three to five ground rules that everyone agrees to follow. I might have students think about how they'll deal with a member who hasn't done the reading/notes, how to share equally in discussion, or how not to get on one another's nerves. Students often bring some baggage with them from their previous experiences in dysfunctional groups, so this is a way to clear the air and lay the cards on the table so that all members are clear on one another's expectations. Here's an example of the ground rules one group negotiated.

> Takes turns talking and doing discussion things
> Come prepared
> Be nice to each other no matter how much pain you're in

I like that third rule. I'm glad students also recognize that personal baggage needs to be put aside in order for academic activity to take place. I have each student list the group rules on a sheet of loose-leaf paper labeled Lit Circle Processing, along with the first and last names of the group members. This sheet comes out at each meeting for review, reflection, and goal setting.

Reading calendar. One of the things I like best about literature circles is that it promotes student responsibility and decision making. At this first meeting I give each group some calendars with the lit circle meeting dates and any other important dates (holidays, prom, etc.) marked. I tell students that the book needs to be finished by the last meeting date but that they need to decide what reading is due for the other dates. It's interesting to listen in on the conversations and the strategies. Often, inexperienced groups will start by figuring out how many pages are in the book and then dividing by the number of meetings. Sooner or later, though, someone else will suggest that finishing a certain number of chapters for each meeting might be a more logical approach while someone else will recognize that it makes sense to assign more pages to the meetings that have more reading time between them. Each member of the group keeps a copy of the calendar, and they also turn in a copy to me. Of course, some groups completely mismanage the reading schedule at first and then need to change it. That's okay; it's part of the learning process.

Large-group processing. While the students are still sitting in their groups, I have one member from each group stand and share their ground rules as well as tell how the group decided on its reading schedule. Then I give the groups a few minutes to review their own rules and schedule, since the sharing might have jogged some refinements to their own.

Processing. Before the groups disband, I want them to immediately begin to recognize and reinforce their positive accomplishments, so on the same sheet that lists their ground rules, I have them discuss and list three specific things that helped the group get along, get the jobs done, and enjoy one another's company. If time permits, it's nice to share these quickly in large group as well because it publicly affirms behavior that contributes to group success. Also, often the kids aren't specific in their observations (i.e., "We cooperated"); this gives me the chance to prod them for an example that illustrates the skill. Last but not least, I tell the members to turn to their group and say, "Thanks for your help; I'm glad you were here today." Yeah, it sounds phony, but when I don't remind the kids to frequently thank one another, I notice a drop in positive interaction. Hmmm. Imagine how differently we might feel at school if we were frequently and genuinely thanked for our hard work.

Preparing for the First Discussion

Though role sheets are often suggested for literature circles, by the time the kids are in high school, I want them to focus on the typical elements that a real reader might bring to a group discussion: questions, passages, connections, illustrations. When each student prepares in this manner, there is usually plenty to discuss. Ideally, there is too much to discuss, which forces students to choose their most promising discussion items to throw on the table when it is their turn to contribute. I always find it helpful to show students what high-quality notes look like by showing them work from previous students. (Of course, the samples are from novels other than the ones they are reading.) Besides the usual name, date, and hour, the paper must be headed with the title of the book and the page range due for that discussion. I emphasize that high-quality notes cover *all* the pages, not just the first ten! The paper is folded in half lengthwise to create two columns. The left-hand column is for notes, the right-hand column is for passages, and the back side is for connections. A separate blank sheet of paper is used for the illustration.

The First Discussion

On discussion days, I plan some sort of ten-minute individual activity so that I have time to take a quick look at the notes. I can always give students more time to read, but I've found a good ongoing assignment is writing a character journal, summarizing the book so far from the point of view of the most interesting character. This gives kids one source of ideas to discuss when their groups gather. Before the first notes are due, I go to the office supply store and buy a date stamp. During the ten minutes the kids are writing in their journals, I can skim and stamp an entire class's notes. The stamped date prevents kids from trying to sneak in late work, but that won't work if you leave the stamp lying around on your desk. Hide it!

After the notes are checked, it's time for the groups to move together. Between the membership grid warm-up activity, the reading log, and discussion notes, there should be enough to keep them busy for at least twenty minutes. Keep in mind that English teachers can gab for hours about what they've read, but high school students aren't English teachers; it's always better to have them begging for more time rather than finishing early and then having extra time to start throwing wadded up candy wrappers at another group.

For the first meeting, I use an agenda similar to this:

1. Warm-up with membership grid (5–10 minutes).
2. Read character journals aloud and discuss (5–10 minutes).
3. Take turns guessing at, explaining, and asking questions about one another's illustrations (5–10 minutes).
4. Discuss questions, passages, connections (10–20 minutes).
5. Group processing (5 minutes).
6. Large-group processing (5 minutes).

Before the groups meet, I make very clear the kind of behavior I expect to see as I observe the groups. First, on a poster, an overhead, or the chalkboard, I make an "I'm Looking For . . ." list:

1. Desks touching
2. Plenty of space between groups
3. Members focused only on each other
4. Equal participation, taking turns
5. Smiling and friendliness
6. Books open, everyone on the same page

Besides the general requirements of the list, I also give each group an accountability sheet.

Each member signs his/her name in a blank. As I monitor the groups, I also try to do some specific observation, checking off skills being used, circling those absent, jotting down exactly what students say or do that is a specific example of one of these skills. Though the number rating (1 is low and 5 is high) is always present on this form, I don't necessarily assign it myself. Usually I let each student rate himself along with a note explaining why. Direct observation is an important guide for deciding on the following day's lesson. Also, my observations can be useful to the group during end-of-discussion processing. I always leave some time for skill discussion, refinement, and review for the day following a lit circle.

The Day After That First Discussion

Many times there is not enough class time at the end of a lit circle meeting to fully discuss the small-group processing. Rather than rushing through it,

I set some time aside the following day. After that first meeting, it's helpful for all the groups to see what strengths and frustrations they have in common. Here are the lists one of my classes developed after their first discussion:

Things Done Well
Stayed on task
Used twelve-inch voices
Asked a lot of questions
Encouraged each other
Listened to each other's ideas
Compromised on different answers
Asked for sections to be reread
Made good eye contact
Didn't interrupt the speaker
All our desks touched

Goals
1. Work faster
2. Pay better attention to the speaker
3. Ignore other groups
4. Ask more questions
5. Sit closer together
6. Use twelve-inch voices
7. Have more fun
8. Take turns reading
9. Share work evenly
10. Include others

After the lists are made, students return to their lit circle groups for a quick meeting so that they can review their specific improvement goal, possibly changing or modifying it so that they are working on the element most critical to improving their next discussion. Once the goal is set, they need to figure out three actions the group can take to achieve the goal. For example:

Goal: Include everyone equally
1. Let the person who talks the least go first
2. Address each other by name
3. Take turns in discussion rather than letting one person ask everything from his notes

The first course of action for a troubled group is to recognize the specific problem. Then they need to think of some ways to solve it. Goal review now becomes a part of the meeting agenda.

The Second Discussion

For all meetings there are some constants, namely the "I'm Looking For . . ." list, the lit circle accountability rating form, the membership grid, and the lit circle notes. As groups progress, though, the meeting agenda begins to evolve:

1. Membership grid (5–10 minutes).
2. Read character journals aloud and discuss (5–10 minutes). A variation of this might be for members to trade journals and respond in writing as if they were another character or possibly even the same character returning to the entry at a later date.
3. Review the goal and action plan from the last meeting (5 minutes). Discuss how each person is going to meet that goal in today's discussion.
4. Take turns guessing at, explaining, and asking questions about one another's illustrations (5–10 minutes).
5. Discuss questions, passages, connections (10–20 minutes).
6. Group processing (5 minutes). Use these three questions: What were three specific things we did well today that helped us meet our goal? What is one thing we can do differently so that our next discussion improves? What was an interesting idea that came up in our discussion that we could tell the rest of the class about? Remind group members to thank one another before disbanding.
7. Large-group processing (5 minutes). If you have an extra five minutes, use it for a quick roundup of one positive accomplishment and one goal from each group.

The Following Day

Students get back into their lit circles to discuss a couple of items. First, what solution worked best in helping the group meet its goal? Everyone should put a star on her processing sheet by that item. Next, under the new improvement goal, agreed on the day before, each person needs to come up with three specific things he can say or do to meet that goal. Last time the group came up with a group plan; this time each person is coming up with his own plan. In the example below, one group decided they needed to ask more follow-up questions, so each person came up with three all-purpose follow-up questions she could use in the next discussion.

Goal: Ask more follow-up questions
1. Where did you find that?
2. How does that make you feel?
3. What did that make you think about?

Ideally, each member will have different questions to use so that the discussion is truly extended.

Finally, each group reviews how they will explain the interesting idea from their book to the rest of the class, given that each group is reading a different book. This time there are no volunteers; everyone in each group needs to be prepared to present to the class after discussion, since representatives will be chosen at random.

Once again, I conclude with a short large-group discussion, usually no more than ten minutes unless students seem really interested and involved. It's important to remember that all groups do not have to share about every single processing question. I try to make the random element fun by using a transparency spinner. (The Kagan product catalog sells them for only a couple of bucks.) I have the kids number off, pick a group to start, and then spin; the person with the number the pointer lands on is the one who stands up and addresses the audience.

Since this discussion is taking place while the kids are still in their groups, it's important that whoever "wins the spin" stand so that it's easier for the rest of the class to focus on the speaker. Equally important is for the audience to swivel around in their chairs or desks so that they are always trying to make eye contact with the speaker. Letting half the class sit with their backs to whoever is speaking is a recipe for nonlistening. The message being sent is that this large-group discussion isn't very important anyway.

The Remaining Lit Circle Discussions

By the third meeting, the groups have developed a certain rhythm and familiarity that allows them to participate in more in-depth discussion. They are also refining the way they create their notes so that better discussion is created. Starting with the third discussion, I encourage each group to develop its own discussion agenda. I've noticed that groups can quickly fall into ruts, trudging through their questions on a death march toward their connections. Groups need to experiment with different ways to start. They might save the journals for last and start with each person's favorite passage, or each person might prioritize his discussion notes, picking only the best two items to bring up with the goal of using the text and follow-up questions to extend the discussion. At this point, after the day's agenda is set, I also encourage members to put their notes facedown because what they bring up from memory will probably be more spontaneous. Of course they can return to their notes for a page reference. Here's a sample agenda for a later meeting:

1. Membership grid (5–10 minutes).
2. Negotiate the discussion agenda (5–10 minutes). Now the group decides how they want to use their discussion materials. I encourage them to try a different agenda each discussion.

3. Review the goal and action plan from the last meeting (5 minutes). Discuss how each person is going to meet that goal in today's discussion.
4. Discussion (15–25 minutes).
5. Group processing (10 minutes). Compliment pass. Each member passes her processing sheet to the person to her right. That person compliments the owner of the paper on something specific that she said or did that helped the group that day. The writer signs his compliment. When everyone is finished writing, the papers are passed again. By the time the owner gets her paper back, she has a signed compliment from each person in the group. An important skill that must be practiced here is silent, patient waiting. Members will finish writing their compliments at different paces, but everyone must wait for all to finish writing before the papers are passed.

Sharon Weiner

MIDDLE SCHOOL, BAKER DEMONSTRATION SCHOOL, EVANSTON, IL

When I introduced literature circles to my seventh-grade class, I was exploring various ways of improving the quality of kids' literature discussions, in terms of both investment and insight. Admittedly, I was skeptical about the ability of kids to direct their own discussions with enough depth. Too many of my kids were unwilling to trust their own responses—they far too often wanted to know what the "official" interpretation of an event or character was or what I (the allegedly infallible teacher) thought the story "meant." I knew I needed to provide a structure to help kids develop and trust their own readings. So I briefed them with some background on *Beowulf,* and we jumped in.

On the first day, I gave kids a set of lit circle role sheets. They discussed and debated the roles, and worked in single-task teams (all the passage masters together, all discussion directors together, etc.), developing their responses to the first part of the tale, "The Story of Grendel." They discussed the similarities and differences in their responses to the same task. (The hard part here was persuading some kids to trust their own responses rather than look to the others.) I put same-task kids together so they would have confidence in the basic focus of their role, and so they could help one another fill out the preparation sheet. I think this gave them the confidence to begin.

The second day, the kids discussed "Grendel" in literature circles, with each member of a circle taking a different role. Even with just their previous day's preparation, I was amazed at the depth of their discussions. At the end of the day they decided to stay in their literature circles but to switch tasks for the second part of the tale, "Grendel's Mother."

On the third day, for the "Grendel's Mother" discussion, the kids came into class and immediately got into their circles and began their discussion. This was especially striking because I was late to class. I expected to walk into chaos. Instead I found (as I walked in fully six or seven minutes late) a smoothly operating class—four literature circles in earnest discussion. I have never seen a model for discussion that was so intuitive to kids and so well liked.

I have played with the model in several ways. Sometimes, we decide to have a researcher role. This individual finds and reports on interesting background information about an author or a topic, with support from the librarians and me. The research topic is up to the researchers, not me, and is therefore almost guaranteed to be of interest to the group. The one big rule is that the researcher must always clearly tie his or her information with details from the reading. The kids are often extremely insightful and original in their research topics. For example, one eighth-grade researcher brought in art books by concentration camp victims for a group reading of Elie Weisel's *Night*. I think this is a great way to individualize the teaching of research skills, and kids seem to love this role.

Literature circles are also a natural structure for novel or short story units that involve student choice. I put out more sets of novels or stories (sometimes kids bring in sets of stories) than there are possible groups in a class. Kids then arrange themselves by their interest in reading a particular story (but there must be complete groups). After reading the story at home and preparing for the discussion, they discuss the story in their literature circle. At the end of each discussion, kids choose their next story to be read in re-formed groups.

I have also organized circles around read-alouds. The kids are first organized into literature circles and choose tasks. Then I like to read (or have kids read) the selection twice—once for overall listening and pleasure, and once again for analysis. The second time, kids listen for their specific task—passage picking, illustrating, etc. This works well, because the kids focus on their jobs as they listen. They then discuss the reading in literature circles, with a copy of the selection for reference. This really helps kids see how listening for specific purposes alters the listening process, and they have become increasingly better listeners.

Another variation on the model is based on reading workshop activities. As students read books they have individually chosen, they respond at various times in their reading journal. Occasionally, I ask them to respond in the manner of the roles they now know so well—passage master, discussion director, summarizer, or vocabularian. Then I ask kids to share what they have written, in small groups or (on occasion) with the group as a whole. I think this has two benefits. It is, in a way, an approach to book-talks—to exposing the whole class to books that individuals are reading. This approach also offers kids who are reading the same or related books opportunities for discussion—something that often seems missing in reading workshops. As an additional benefit, kids are now much more aware of vocabulary than when they read purely independently.

To sum up, my students really love literature circles. They like the comfort of the structure, but also the flexibility of the multiple roles. They see that this one structure can be applied to multiple tasks—small-group reading, read-alouds, required books, or independent reading. They learn that understanding comes from more than one direction. Most important, they learn to trust themselves and respect one another as discussers and analysts. They bring up what is important to them, and in doing so seem to connect more deeply with the reading. I enjoy and value this approach to reading, but far more important, so do my students.

▼ ▼ ▼ ▼ ▼ ▼ ▼ ▼ ▼ ▼ ▼ ▼

11

Teachers and Parents as Readers

YOU MIGHT BE surprised to discover this chapter, which focuses on grown-ups as readers. Hey, isn't this supposed to be a book about getting kids into literature circles, with plenty of practical tips and management suggestions? Yes indeed, and I've found that there is nothing more practical for getting lit circles going in your classroom than being in one yourself. We always say that the goal of lit circles is to help children fall in love with books. Well, great, but if we adults aren't active readers ourselves, what are the realistic chances of transmitting a passion for literacy? How are we supposed to know how book clubs feel and sound, how they solve problems, how they mature over time? What's our own template? Our model?

In this chapter I want to share some thoughts about teachers (and parents) as readers, about the ways that we can recover reading in our own lives and connect with other readers. But don't worry. You don't have to start with *War and Peace* and you don't have to commit to a monthly book club right away (although once you join in some book discussions for yourself, you may do just that!). You can start really small with a few colleagues, reading and talking about short short stories, newspaper clippings, poems, or even topical cartoons from the paper. In Appendix A, I have included two step-by-step workshops that you can use informally with colleagues or in an inservice workshop to experience literature circles firsthand.

South Ocean Middle School

PATCHOGUE, NEW YORK

In a workshop for sixth-grade teachers, Diane, Greg, Joy, Susan, Manuel, and I are discussing the short-short story "Waiting," by Peggy McNally. The one-page, one-sentence, stream-of-consciousness piece recounts the circular and seemingly sad life of a substitute seventh-grade teacher in Cleveland. She dutifully drives to school every day but savors the donuts in the faculty lounge much more than the students. Her home life is also downbeat and repetitive. She lives with her widowed father and has just declined a young man's offer of a date, saying she needs to wash her father's car instead. A promise she has apparently made to her dying mother prevents her from breaking the dull cycle of her life. The story ends with the phrase "and you know the rest."

Most of the group members are initially troubled, even exasperated by this character. She seems to lack gumption and initiative. While waiting for life to happen to her, people suggest, she's fallen into a rut she seems unable or perhaps unwilling to escape. They talk about the story's artifice of being one 225-word run-on sentence and how the author's style underscores the monotonous, humdrum nature of the substitute's life. Diane, who's held back from the discussion until now, weighs in.

"You know, I really connected with this girl," she says. "I had a time when my life was on hold, too. When I lost my husband and I had to just survive, take care of my kids, go to school, and keep working just to save my house. I mean, I looked a lot like she did. I was keeping a commitment."

The other group members are quietly attending to Diane's heartfelt story. "I put my life on hold. I had to for nine years," she reiterates. "So maybe that's what this girl in the story had to do."

There's a pause while people digest. Craig, who is sitting next to Diane, turns to her and quietly offers, "But isn't this woman's situation different in the story? She's single, but you had kids. It's kind of expected for parents to put their life on hold, to make sacrifices if they have to, for their kids. But she's doing this to herself."

Joy comments, "I wonder when this story was written, because in this day and age, I can't believe any woman would let herself be so helpless, with feminism and everything."

Diane comes back: "No, I think it is the same. She made a commitment to her mother, to her father, and this is what she's got to do. It's just, sometimes you have to make a commitment and stick to it." Craig nods, listening patiently as she continues. "When this all happened to me, my father was helping me out a lot. And then he was in a terrible car accident, and then I had to take care of him for two years, like he had taken care of me. So, altogether, it was nine years my life was on hold."

I ask, "During all that time, did you ever think you were going to come out the other side, to get off hold, and have more of a life?"

"I didn't know. I was just going through that stage, you know? But I'll tell you, when I did wake up nine years later and take the next step, I really rocked the boat, big time—for everybody in my family!" She smiles.

Susan ventures back to the story. "So maybe it's just about stages. Life is hard, and we all go through stages." There's a spurt of talk around the group as people remember times they were stuck in a stage of life. Sometimes it is a commitment to others that makes us limit ourselves; sometimes we climb into our own ruts. But we've all been stuck, not moving ahead, maybe even looking pretty comfortable in our rut, at least to people who would apply the same judgmental standards they are applying to the character in the story.

Joy muses, partly to herself, "You know, it's so easy to advise the people in stories and so risky to assume you know best for real people."

There's been a deep shift in the way this group is thinking about the protagonist in "Waiting." As we have connected her story—or the 225 words of it that are available—to our own lives, we've found parallels that surprise us. As we dig deeper into these connections, our understanding of the story—and even of our own lives—changes. Arguably, our new understanding of the story is deeper, richer, and more nuanced.

And after the workshop, over weeks and months, there is a steady flow of e-mails from Patchogue teachers reporting their excitement at implementing lit circles in their own classrooms, sharing all variations and adaptations they have made, and gleefully reporting, "It works!"

Finding Time for Reading

Obviously, when we adults try literature circles for ourselves, we enhance our ability to translate the activity for our students. But we gain much more than pedagogical insight from the experience. Through the magic of talk, in the company of good literature, with the gift of honest sharing, we become better readers, better colleagues, better friends, and better people. And these, come to think of it, are just the benefits we seek for our students.

But advising one's colleagues to be more active readers can sound arrogant and holier-than-thou. I once heard a conference speaker exhort a crowd of teachers that if you weren't up every night reading novels or writing for publication, you could never really be a great teacher. What a crock! What if you're trying to raise a family? Grade some papers? Fix the back steps? Have a love life? I mean, how much time for reading do most people/teachers really have—and if we did find a little time, do we have to spend it all on professional pursuits? What's wrong with sewing? Jogging? Or napping or tubing out?

To prove that this isn't a guilt trip in disguise, I'll tell a bit about my own odd and spotty reading habits. I recognize in my own teaching life the same pressures that squeeze reading out of busy educators' days, weeks, and months. First of all, I usually don't read *any* novels for about ten months a year. I'll scan professional books if they seem really urgent and practical, but novels, nah. It's mostly heart-pounding stuff like grant proposals, academic journals, and student papers. During the school year, my pleasure reading is magazines, by the dozens, everything from *Rolling Stone* to *Oprah* (don't ask!). I think that when time is short, I need short text.

Then there are the other two months, July and August. As soon as the last summer institute is done, and the last grades turned in, I cram in my year's fiction reading, alternating between the porch and the dock, depending on the angle of the sun. Luckily, I am married to a person who reads voraciously all year long, so my summer reading consists of Elaine's supreme picks of the year, culled from perhaps a hundred mostly current candidates. I'll read eight or ten novels by Labor Day, just enough for me to sound literate for yet another year.

So none of us has to be a perfect paragon of reading to be a good-enough model for our students. We just need to be reading something, something we can drag out during reading workshop, something we can weave into our mini-lessons. If we are so professionally overscheduled that we can't justify the time for "personal" reading, we could start by reading books written for the grade level we teach (picture books, YA novels), so we know what is available for our students. But the question for so many teachers still is, When? We have days that are full; we don't have any fallow hours lying around that we can assign to reading.

Of course, this crushing teacher schedule isn't just made up of official obligations; it is also full of habits that prevent us from reading. In an attempt to challenge our own reading limits, we came up with this list at a Center for City Schools staff meeting.

Top Twelve Ways to Get Reading into Teachers' Ridiculously Busy Lives
1. Turn off the *Tonight Show* and pick up a you-know-what.
2. Come to school a half hour early and read in your quiet classroom. Let kids find you.
3. Institute independent reading time in your classroom and read then (call it modeling).
4. Skip the Sunday paper and try a book instead. Ditto the daily paper. It's just upsetting you anyway.
5. Join a book club. Or start one at school or in the neighborhood.
6. Read during a planning period.
7. Get up an hour early and read. Then go to bed an hour early tonight. Instant habit!
8. Leave the car at home, take the bus or train and read.
9. Start a "book pair" with one other colleague at school.
10. Start an e-mail correspondence with a distant friend or relative around books.
11. Read during the boring inservice presentation (whoops—already tried that one).
12. Turn off *Letterman,* too!

Starting Your Own Teacher Reading Group

More and more teachers across the country are getting their staff development through study groups and reading clubs instead of auditorium lectures and lockstep workshops with out-of-town experts. This is a wholesome trend, both because it gives teachers more ownership of their own professional growth and because it allows people to get some real reading into their busy lives. Many times, these groups are initially established with the purpose of reading professional books and later stray into fiction. But now that we are consciously starting teacher book clubs in Chicago schools, we have learned to do it the other way around. Groups get hooked, energized, and bonded the fastest when they begin with novels, with narratives, with stories. So we prime the pump with popular novels and branch out to nonfiction books and professional books later.

While attending a literature circles workshop, ten teachers from Olive Mary Stitt School, in Arlington Heights, Illinois, decided to start their own book club. Always an spirited and adventurous group, the Olive teachers were excited about forming their own book discussion group. "I think we'll do a much better job in the classroom," reasoned third-grade teacher Tanya Klayman, "if we try this first ourselves."

With characteristic enthusiasm, for its inaugural book the group selected *The Poisonwood Bible,* Barbara Kingsolver's dense, thick novel about a missionary family in Africa. The initial plan was for the Olive crew to read half the book (nearly 300 pages) and meet to discuss it in a month; then the group would read the second half, meeting again a month further on. The idea was to hold these two meetings in the faculty lounge on a couple of Tuesday mornings, an hour before the kids came to school.

On the appointed day, as everyone gathered for the first session, there were problems. Yes, the food was laid out, plenty of tasty snacks; and the coffeepot, which had been dutifully plugged in by the janitor at 5:00 A.M., was brimming with brew. The trouble was, half the people hadn't read the book. Each chagrined teacher had valid reasons for not finishing the assigned pages. Assorted, very real life crises had intervened for some. Classroom and family pressures gobbled up time, and the next thing you knew, book club day had suddenly arrived. But that wasn't all. Gradually, some members began confessing that they were put off by the book, lost in its intricate plot twists, or just plain not "hooked."

The Olive faculty was feeling just like any class of students—or adults—when confronted by a really hard book and lacking adequate supports to connect with it. But instead of becoming paralyzed, the teachers reorganized. They divided the book into eighths instead of half and committed to meeting weekly instead of monthly. The adjustment worked better than they could have hoped.

To begin with, everyone arrived the next week having read the first few chapters, a much more reasonable and focused assignment.

As their reading group developed under its new rules, the Olive teachers were aware of the analogy between the management issues in their own book club and the ones they faced in the classroom. The fact that they had to dramatically alter the "lesson plan" for their book club offered a priceless classroom lesson. They watched their own apparently reasonable plans go up in smoke when 300 pages simply proved to be too much for most of the "students" in the group.

But a parallel they hadn't expected was the personal one. A closeness developed over those eight meetings that took everyone by surprise. As Chris Murphy put it, "We bonded as people, not just as a staff, like we never have before." As the discussion ranged, individuals shared aspects of their lives that had never come up even during ten or twenty years of close colleagueship. The Kleenex box went around the table more than once; tears of laughter were almost as common. By the end of the eight weeks, teachers were using words like *transformed.*

Of course, *The Poisonwood Bible* itself gets much of the credit for the intensity of the teachers' experience at Olive School. After all, if you spend eight weeks marinating in issues like family, marriage, faith, loss, and the colonization of Africa, you are likely to have some powerful conversations. Indeed, the trajectory of the Olive group reminds us that just as for children, the success of literature circles depends above all on the quality of the books; you simply must have significant, valuable, rich, and meaty books to work with. But the quality of literature is a necessary though not sufficient condition for a good book club experience. For good peer-led discussions to occur, you also need a plan, a pattern of mutual responsibility, and a workable schedule.

Our consultants at the Center for City Schools have been seeding adult book clubs around Chicago for several years now. The goal is to have kid book clubs, teacher book clubs, and parent book clubs all going in the same school and for them to come together around the same book or topic occasionally. For example, Brown School, on Chicago's West Side, was planning a K–8 unit on Africa, so Marianne Flanagan suggested the teachers begin by forming their own book club around (you guessed it) *The Poisonwood Bible.* Taking a lesson from Olive School, Marianne and principal Connie Thomas scheduled two months for everyone to read the book, planning an optional "halfway-through" meeting and a full afternoon's discussion a month after that. Because they were trying to jump-start a book club where none existed, it was important to make everything easy for the teachers, so Marianne delivered a copy of the book to everyone's mailbox along with a copy of the schedule, linking the book to the upcoming interdisciplinary unit.

The attendance at the halfway meeting was encouraging; twenty staff members stayed after school to talk. And at the big meeting a month later, the whole staff of fifty teachers, administrators, and staff members divided into four smaller groups and headed off to different classrooms for an afternoon's conversation. They shared their puzzlement, horror, and worry about the women's plight, their strong responses to the minister husband, and their impressions of the Africa depicted in the story, so different from the visions that they, mostly African American women, had previously held. They also talked about their joys and struggles with doing the reading, how it helped them empathize with their students, how this thing called book clubs might actually work with their students. It was an exhausting and exhilarating day for many. That was two years ago; today, many Brown staff members continue to meet regularly as the Westhaven Teachers Book Club, comprising teachers from the five schools in the neighborhood and meeting in a nearby public library.

Parents as Readers

In this book, we have put a good deal of responsibility on parents, especially those with primary-age kids. We expect them to read books aloud at home, scribe kids' quotes on Post-it notes, and come help us out in classroom book clubs. But as much as we depend on these practical favors, we know that the deepest, most important help parents can offer to literature circle teachers is to be readers themselves. When kids see their parents reading for pleasure, for work, to get information, and to accomplish life's many chores, this family modeling is precious and durable.

But we know that the parents of our students have some of the same grown-up problems that we do—like busy lives with little time for reading. And parents may have some other problems we schoolteachers generally do not share—like discouraging and disenabling experiences with reading in grade school, undiagnosed learning disabilities, or language discrimination experiences related to family migration. Even some apparently high-achieving parents can be turned-off readers if they were browbeaten and belittled in high school or college literature classes.

So if we want parents to support our literature circles, we may need to help them recover reading for themselves. And if we want them to model reading for their children, we may need to create a comfortable reading experience for parents, right at school, where their children might just happen by to watch. At our Center for City Schools, we have a remarkable person called Pete Leki who engineers just this kind of cross-generational modeling full time. Pete has started dozens of parent study groups and reading clubs, most of which carry on after he has planted the seeds and moved on. Here's Pete's report on one such group.

A circle of chairs at the end of a hallway. A basket of *pan dulce*. A pot of coffee steaming, scenting the quiet air with its rich flavor. It is SSR time for this parent book club at Waters Elementary School, in Chicago. Thirty minutes of kicked-back, peaceful, release time for parents to catch up or race ahead in their book, *Like Water for Chocolate,* by Laura Esquivel. The readers pause every once in a while to highlight a phrase or jot some musings in their reading journals.

Blanca O. leans back in her chair, sips at her sweet coffee. A classroom door opens and out streams two lines of children. Their heads turn as they notice the parents immersed in their books. They start to cry out greetings, but are hushed by the librarian, and reconcile themselves to a smile and wave. They are proud and happy.

The parents finish up their reading and break into full-scale conversation about the sad circumstances of poor Tita, shackled by family tradition to serve her mother and deny herself all the pleasures of life— except . . . cooking. The bitter and sweet of her life is poured into her meals.

The magic of food is well understood by these parents. The medicinal and healing qualities of *mole de guajalote* and *pasteles, chorizo de norteno* and *champandongo*. Soon the stomachs are growling and stories of back home are flowing. Books snap open as points are made. "What's with this Pedro, anyway? What a worm!" The circle quiets as Clara reads her journal entry, a memory of the smells of her own mother's household.

Are all our lives as full of such pain and ecstasy as Tita's? Could we write of our own lives, our own yearnings and disappointments, the way Esquivel did?

"Maybe," says Griselda, "but we would have to put a lock on that book!"

This is the third book of this school year for these parents. They've read *The House on Mango Street,* by Sandra Cisneros, and then plunged into a thick volume about parenting, *Que pasa con los muchachos de hoy?* [*What's Up with These Boys?*], by William Pollack. The meat of each workshop is the free-flowing discussion that swirls through the group, interrupted occasionally by my need for translation when the words fly too fast. Here, the participants reach back to their own experiences, empathize with one another's tough times, and laugh at all the craziness of life.

That the parents are on display is not accidental. We are modeling for our kids our love of reading and our excitement at sharing our opinions and experiences. Parents hunger for a chance to talk about their lives and how they intersect with the themes in these books.

Almost every session takes time to introduce parents to additional strategies for plunging deep into a text—dramatizations, abstraction and symbolization through different art media, letter writing to characters, poetry. These are the methods being used in the classrooms with our children. Parents are invited into the inner sanctum of teaching strategies and philosophies. At the end of each project the parents select a piece of their writing to share with the whole school, and it is published as a little booklet.

For *Like Water for Chocolate* we are putting together a book of recipes, set in the context of our family histories. In the style of Esquivel, each recipe's instructions are interrupted by asides describing family members' personalities or incidents they recall. The parents will enter the texts and compose the booklet during their computer class, held Saturday mornings.

Strong, long-term relationships are being grown here. Reading has become a habit. It is a glue that helps to hold our community together. Our lives and stories warm one another. As the doctor explains to Tita, "And let me tell you something I've never told a soul. My grandmother had a very interesting theory; she said that each of us is born with a box of matches inside of us but we can't strike them all by ourselves; just as in the experiment, we need oxygen and a candle to help. In this case, the oxygen for example would come from the breath of the person you love; the candle could be any kind of food, music, caress, word, or sound that engenders the explosion that lights one of those matches."

In these parent groups, Pete has been finding potential leaders, moms and dads who are eager to start book clubs of their own, to carry on and spread the idea to other schools in other neighborhoods. On periodic Saturday mornings, these parent leaders get together and, naturally, talk about books. At a recent meeting, when they gathered to talk about *The Color of Water,* they connected in a number of ways:

Brenda: Could you imagine someone telling you your mother's dead by telling you, "We have three rooms of furniture you could have"? They didn't tell her that her mother was dead. Rachel was remembering how her mother cried, how she could hear those sounds up to the time she wrote this book how her mother cried.

Pete: It makes you feel like, yes, she got through this and what can you do? That's just how it was for her.

Claudia: So if you look at writing, if you want to be a writer—when I talk to people and they tell me, "You need to write a book on that." And the more I read this and other things, Pete, I begin to think, well now, I got a story too, and I could tell it.

Claudia certainly does have a story, and so do all these other parents. And when their book club experience makes them feel like writers as well as readers, we know that our work has been successful. We know that time in a grown-up book club may even change what happens back at home, in families. Later during that same Saturday session, Earl Hitchcock reflected on changes in his daughter Denise's behavior after he and his wife, Lorraine, joined a book club and started reading books around their house. "The television is not on—not because we're telling the kids, 'Turn the television off! You got to do your studying.' But seeing us read, and particularly me I am sure, seeing us read some makes you more involved with reading. And she's turning the television off on her own rather than counting on us to tell her to turn the television off, and she's engaging in reading—and that's been a plus for me."

12

Assessment: Record Keeping, Evaluation, and Grading

IF ADULT book clubs are the basic model for literature circles, then assessment presents quite a puzzle. Just imagine a grown-up reading group gathered in someone's living room, finishing up their monthly discussion. Maybe they've read Anita Shreve's heartbreaking novel of love, motherhood, adoption, and loss, *Fortune's Rocks*. After two hours of intense talk, group members close their books and help the host take the empty snack plates into the kitchen. Finally, as people are putting on their coats, one group member suddenly starts handing out grades.

"Mabel, you had lots of Post-it notes in your book. A+ for you."

"Arlene, you didn't say a thing tonight. All you did was sit and cry. F."

"Jim, your personal connections were too far from the book. B-."

"Barbara, you had some good thoughts, but you interrupt too much. C-."

Would anyone ever come back to this book club, after being "assessed" the way kids get assessed in school? Probably not.

At the start of this book, I said that the main job is to bring book clubs into the schools without messing them up. Well, it's assessment that does most of the messing, that distorts and twists literature circles until they sometimes become unrecognizable, completely severed from their friendly, voluntary, spontaneous, book-loving, free-flowing heritage. There is tons of assessment pressure out there. The so-called accountability movement constantly presses for more tests, more scores, more grades, more ranking of children. To prevent literature circles from getting messed up by this external measurement mania, we need to be extra vigilant.

But we teachers have our own assessment concerns in the classroom. When groups of our students are spending large chunks of the day meeting in literature circles, we often worry, How can I evaluate this activity? How do I know what kids are learning? What records do I need to keep? How can I give grades? And what about report cards? These same concerns, of course, arise in connection with almost *any* decentralized inquiry-based activity in which student groups work without direct supervision while the teacher facilitates. At one level, these questions reflect a genuine concern about how teachers can document kids' growth, as well as eventually award a justifiable grade.

At another level, assessment questions sometimes reflect concern about classroom management and discipline. After all, grades are often used as a mechanism of control in the classroom, with the reward of a high grade or the threat of a low one used to steer children's behavior. When teachers think about decentralizing their classrooms in the ways that literature circles require—with kids working largely on their own—they start wanting a list of contingencies to employ if individuals or groups aren't productive. That's why, in Chapter 6, we talked at length about problems of classroom management in literature circles. Teachers interested in keeping their assessment system separate from their discipline system might want to have a look at that section.

Principles of Constructive Assessment

Here's some good news. Literature circles leave a very rich trail of evidence of kids' reading, learning, and thinking—if we know how to recognize, capture, and talk about all this data meaningfully. To begin with, we must approach the assessment of literature circles as we would any other complex, integrated classroom activity. Anything we do in the name of assessment must be theoretically congruent with the collaborative, student-centered nature of the instructional model. So we have to start with the questions, What are we assessing for? When we observe, record, measure, or judge, what are we trying to accomplish? What theories and principles guide our assessment efforts? To frame these issues, we have listed below some guiding principles of sound, authentic assessment. Later, we offer some specific ways to assess students in literature circles according to these standards.

1. Assessment should reflect and encourage *good instruction*. At the very least, the evaluation of student work should never distort or harm solid classroom practice. Ideally, assessment activities should unequivocally reinforce progressive curriculum and learner-centered teaching methods.
2. The best assessment activities are actually *integral parts of instruction*. While many traditional measures occur separate from or after teaching, the most powerful new assessment activities—such as conferences, analytic scoring scales, and portfolios—are ingredients of good instruction. When assessment overlaps with instruction in this way, it helps teachers to be more effective in same amount of instructional time.

3. Powerful evaluation efforts focus on the major, whole *outcomes* valued in the curriculum: real, complex performances of writing, researching, reading, experimenting, problem solving, creating, speaking, etc. Traditional assessment has been largely devoted to checking whether students are receiving the proper "inputs," the alleged building blocks, basics, or subskills. The new assessment paradigm dares to focus on the big payoffs, the highest-order outcomes of education, in which kids orchestrate big chunks of learning in realistic applications.

4. Most school assessment activities should be *formative*. This means that we assess primarily to ensure that students learn better and teachers teach more effectively. *Summative evaluation,* which involves translating students' growth to some kind of grade that can be reported outside the classroom, is just one small, narrow, and occasional element of a comprehensive, contemporary assessment program.

5. Skillful and experienced evaluators take a *developmental perspective.* They are familiar with the major growth models, both general cognitive stage theories and the models from specific curriculum fields (stages of reading, mathematical thinking, invented spelling, etc). Rather than checking students against arbitrary age or grade-level targets, teachers track the story of each child's individual growth through developmental phases.

6. Traditional norm-referenced, competitive measures that rank students against one another (such as letter grades and numerically scored tests) provide little helpful formative assessment and tend to undermine progressive instruction. Instead, constructive programs increasingly rely on *self-referenced growth measures,* where each student is compared with herself or himself. This means teachers must have ways of valuing, tracking, and recording such individualized factors as improvement, effort, good faith, insight, risk taking, rate of change, and energy.

7. Teachers need a rich *repertoire of assessment strategies* to draw from in designing sensitive, appropriate evaluation activities for particular curriculum areas. Among these broad strategies are
   Kidwatching/anecdotal records: open-ended, narrative observational notes, logs, and records.
   Checklists: structured, curriculum-anchored observation guides, charts, and records.
   Interviews/conferences: face-to-face conversation to access, track, and monitor student growth.
   Portfolios/work samples: writing, art, projects, video/audiotapes, learning logs, student journals, etc.

Performance assessment: criteria and instruments used for analytic scoring of complex performances.

8. It is never enough to look at learning events from only one angle; rather, we now use *multiple measures,* examining students' learning growth from several different perspectives as outlined above. By *triangulating* assessments, we get a "thick" picture of kids' learning, ensuring that unexpected growth, problems, and side effects are not missed.

9. A key trait of effective thinkers, writers, problem solvers, readers, researchers, and other learners is that they constantly self-monitor and self-evaluate. Therefore, a solid assessment program must consistently help (and require) students to take increasing responsibility for their own record keeping, metacognitive reflection, and *self-assessment.*

10. It takes *many different people working cooperatively* to evaluate student growth and learning effectively. In every classroom, there should be a balance between external assessment (district standardized tests, state assessments, etc.), teacher-run evaluation, student self-evaluation, parent involvement in assessment, and collaborative assessments involving various of these parties.

11. Teachers need to *reallocate the considerable time they already spend on assessment*—evaluation, record keeping, testing, and grading activities. They need to spend less time scoring and more time saving and documenting student work. Instead of creating and justifying long strings of numbers in their grade books, teachers can collect and save samples of kids' original, unscored products. This reallocation of time means that once they are installed, new assessment procedures don't require any more time of teachers than the old ways—nor any less.

12. Sound evaluation programs provide, where necessary, a database for deriving *legitimate, defensible student grades.* However, major national curriculum groups have recommended that competitive, norm-referenced grading should be de-emphasized and replaced by the many richer kinds of assessments outlined above (see Zemelman, Daniels, and Hyde 1998).

13. The currently available state and national standardized tests yield an exceedingly narrow and unreliable picture of student achievement, are poor indicators of school performance, and encourage archaic instructional practices. Therefore, professional teachers *avoid teaching to standardized tests.* Instead, they show colleagues, parents, and administrators the more sophisticated, detailed, accurate, and meaningful assessments they have developed for their own classrooms.

Assessing Kids' Growth in Literature Circles

All of the above principles suggest that literature circles naturally *invite* the use of state-of-the-art assessment approaches. Indeed, most of the teachers whose classrooms we've visited in this book have developed assessment tools and strategies that embody these progressive ideals. These teachers take seriously the precept of triangulation, and so they use a *variety* of assessment tools to create a deep picture of the whole activity (which is talking about books). Further, since lit circles are mainly a student-led, independent activity, these teachers encourage lots of student self-assessment. Here are some of the most common and effective approaches to assessment in literature circles.

Daily Stamp

When teachers worry about accountability for kids (did they do the reading?) and themselves (how can I get a grade out of this?), some kind of daily check-in grade can provide comfort. At Best Practice High School, Jenny Cornbleet uses a dating stamp purchased from a local office supply store. When kids come in for a literature circle meeting, she has them put their reading logs out on the desk while they work on another short activity. She quickly circles the room, glancing at each log just long enough to make sure it is authentic, on-topic, and ample, and then she stamps away: "Received, January 5, 2001." The ten points for each stamp all go toward the students' grades. She doesn't get into disputes about half-baked logs. If it isn't done completely, no stamp. This is binary grading, on/off, yes/no, all or nothing. Sometimes Jenny gets mushy and lets kids come in later in the day for stamping. But not tomorrow or the next day. After all, this grade is for keeping up and being ready. And it works. Once students know what they have to do to get the ten points, they generally do it—or accept the consequences when they flub.

▼ VARIATION: **Encourage Accountability Through Video Surveillance**

Each time literature circles meet in her classroom, Kathy LaLuz trains a loaded video camera on one book club group. She very dramatically checks the viewfinder (and rearranges kids' bodies, if necessary) to make sure everyone is visible. Then she says, "Have a nice meeting," and takes off. She usually doesn't come back to this group that day, because she doesn't have to; the camera is recording everything. Once in a while Kathy has a group take a day off from their discussions and asks members to review the group's latest tape, critiquing their process and writing her notes suggesting how they can improve. Other times, she just moves the camera to the next group and tapes right over the last meeting.

Many teachers feel under pressure to "get a grade" out of every single lit circle meeting and have accordingly devised a variety of daily point systems like Jenny's. In fact, I think one of the reasons that so many teachers have clung to the role sheets far beyond their usefulness is because they look like official schoolwork and are eminently gradable. At least when teachers award their points for reading response logs, Post-it notes, or other more open-ended forms of preparation, it's a step ahead. But always, if we look back at our living-room book club template, all this grading is bound to undermine spontaneity, trust, and risk taking to some degree.

Observation

When the teacher pays occasional visits to each literature circle, it is a natural opportunity to assess the progress of both individuals and the group, as thinkers and as a team. Some teachers keep it simple, taking *open-ended observational notes,* jotting down important or memorable comments made by kids, as well as noting reactions to the process of the group. Others like to use a simple *checklist* for this purpose, with kids' names down one side and a set of thinking and social skills on the other. Such a checklist might include yes/no items such as "Brought book and role sheet to the group," "Played role effectively," "Contributed to the group's productivity," "Listened attentively," "Built upon the contributions of others," and the like.

One observation form that teachers in our network use a lot was adapted from Samway and Whang's *Literature Study Circles in a Multicultural Classroom* (1995). Our version goes like this:

LIT CIRCLE OBSERVATION SHEET

Group Name _____ Date _____

Name	Prepared?	Participated?	Thinking Skills	Social Skills
Brenda	✓	✓	"This place looks just like my grandma's farm." (Visualizing/connections)	Invited Joe's opinion
Joe	✓	✓	"I didn't think this part was very realistic." (Making judgments)	Side talk with Dan
Mary	✓	✓	"I know how you feel, 'cause my dog died, too." (Connecting)	Good eye contact
Dan		✓	"I didn't read it."	Asked questions
Melinda	✓		No comments	Sat quietly

This form helps the teacher assess each member's effectiveness in four different ways while she is observing a group (the first two items are mechanical and gradable; the second two are deeper and more authentic):

1. Noting whether the student has come *prepared* (book in hand, journal filled out, apparently having read the day's chapters). This can either be checked yes/no or, with an eye toward grading pressures, can be awarded ten points, fifty points, whatever. In the example above, the teacher has smartly chosen an all-or-nothing point system, just as Jenny Cornbleet used with her stamp-in process. If you are ready for your literature circle, you get all the points. If not, it's zero. This is quick, over-the-shoulder grading. There are no threes, no 7.5s, no debates, and no calls from your mother, thanks.

2. Noting whether the student has *participated*. Now, it may be true that in real adult book clubs members don't get kicked out if they just sit and listen, but here in school, we may need to require overtly sentient behavior. Here's one teacher's rule: If I come and visit your group for ten minutes, I expect to hear everyone open their mouth, at least once. No points for mutes. (Yeah, I know, tough love.)

3. Recording *thinking skills*. The teacher writes down one memorable comment from each student, either as a quote or a summary. Then she tries to figure out what kind of thinking this contribution represented—connecting, visualizing, asking questions, predicting, evaluating. She may do this categorization on the spot, or save that task for later.

4. Recording the student's *social skills*. As with the quotations above, the teacher tries to notice just one noteworthy social skill, something each kid is doing in an exemplary way, or a skill that needs more work.

You'll probably find it takes at least ten minutes to notice and record all these things in a typical group. Yes, it does seem like a lot to chart in one observation, but you'll get good at it fast. With the schedules most of us use, you'll probably get to two groups per meeting day. This means it may be two weeks before you get back for another observation. But just think: this means twenty observations a year if you do literature circles all year long, and ten if you alternate book clubs with reading workshop. That's a lot of "thick" and sophisticated assessment.

Developing this kind of observation guides a teacher in several ways. At the most basic level, it documents students' efforts and "justifies" your use of class time for such an activity. Much more important, it gives you a chance to see how kids are reading, thinking, and interacting. If your observations show that Bobby is personally connecting with books week after week but never noticing anything about the authors' craft, never visualizing the scene, never asking questions about the characters, then you can do some good coaching, challenging him to broaden his response next time around, to try some new thinking.

Such observations also provide great formative input for the teacher. As you notice patterns in individual kids, you can coach them in conferences or literature letters. And when you notice patterns that are more widespread, you can plan mini-lessons around them for the whole class. If your observations show that many kids are lagging on using follow-up questions, you'll know it is time for a practice session at the start of the next book club meeting.

And finally, there is the self-protective side. This tool can help generate a long string of grades in your grade book, just in case that dreaded (probably mythical) parent suddenly shows up at your classroom door, demanding to know why little Dixie got a B- in reading. Okay, just imagine having a stack of these observation forms on hand if such a parent actually materialized. The records would allow you to say what the kid is reading, whether she comes to class prepared, how much she participates, what kind of ideas she has been contributing, what kinds of thinking she is using, what team collaboration skills she has mastered and which ones need work. Any other questions, Mrs. Fidditch?

Some teachers find it obtrusive or even threatening to invade a group and then sit silently, rating students. Even if you tell kids in advance that you are "just writing down what you guys are saying," the kids aren't dumb. They know you are there to judge at some level. If you or your kids are bothered by this weirdness, just leave your clipboard behind and sit in for a while. Then scoot back to your desk and make your notes privately, before the impressions slip away. Teachers making this choice may get to fewer groups each day, but they will be able to more fully join in the groups they do visit, which is a plus.

While formally observing groups can be helpful and informative, this is not the only role teachers should take when visiting groups. It is a special gift when teachers simply come to visit a literature circle as a fellow reader, fully open to being captivated by the book under discussion, the kids in the group, and the ideas at hand. When we are visibly torn between the role of evaluator and the role of fellow reader, we may undermine our fellowship with students in ways we cannot readily see. And, unless grading is a constant and official demand in a particular school, there's no *reason* to visit groups mostly in the evaluator role. After all, being a coach, model, and partner is much more powerful.

Students as Self-Assessors

Kids can also make good observers, as Nancy Steineke has shown in her high school classes. In Nancy's version of literature circles, every group is supposed to not just discuss their book but also consciously work toward improving a couple of specific discussion skills they have chosen for themselves. So, periodically, Nancy will have one kid in each literature circle become an observer for the day, with the job of tracking how well the group is working toward its stated goals. These temporary student observers use a simple grid on which they list the kids on the left and the skills they are working toward on the right.

	Using Each Other's Names	Asking Follow-up Questions
Joe	✓✓✓✓	✓
Betty	✓✓✓	
Luann	✓✓✓✓✓✓	✓
Gloria	✓✓✓	✓✓
Ralph	✓✓✓✓	✓✓✓✓✓

All the observer has to do is make a tick mark each time she hears one of the two focus skills being used. There's no evaluation or judgment involved; the observer's job is simply to collect information and later put it on the table for the group. No, the data won't be flawless; the observer will get distracted, miss things, get drawn into the book discussion. It doesn't matter—what's important are the general patterns that emerge. In the chart above, it's clear that the group is really conscious of using names and that the skill is evenly distributed through the group. It may be time to pick a new goal, as this one seems to be mastered. On the other hand, Ralph seems to be leading the push toward follow up questions by himself, while the others are still lagging. The group may need to revisit this goal and find some specific strategies for improving. Some teachers might worry about shifting one kid's attention away from the book for a day. But as Nancy notes, that kid will learn a lot about group dynamics during that day that will plug right back into their own behavior in future meetings.

Modern technology invites another kind of student-driven assessment. Kathy LaLuz, who starts every literature circle session by training a video camera at one group. She arranges the kids carefully in a U-shape so that everyone's face is visible, double-checks in the viewfinder, then heads off to spend the hour with other literature circles, letting the camera record this group's efforts.

At one level, the camera is a kind of surrogate supervisor, a mechanical presence that reminds kids to stay on task and be accountable.

But the kids also know that periodically Ms. LaLuz will ask them to spend a whole lit circle session watching one of their own tapes. They will write about their responses, comparing what they see in the tape with the thinking skills and social skills they are supposed to be working on. Perhaps they'll write a group memo to Ms. LaLuz explaining how they see their own strengths and weaknesses as a book club. Or maybe she will come by and say, "All right, guys, what did you see on the tape? What did you like and what did you wish you could have erased?"

Book Projects

Having kids do some kind of project at the end of a lit circle cycle has become pretty routine for many of us, but it is something we might need to question. Let's be honest. One reason we assign book projects is *because we know how to grade them.* When we are trying to observe a kid-led discussion, we may feel out of our evaluative element. How can I evaluate a free-flowing, live discussion? It just seems too subjective, too loose, too ephemeral. But a project? Hey, I can grade a project. I know a B project from a B- project at fifty paces. And let's also be honest, we've seen plenty of book projects that turned out to be mechanical, empty, and dull, even though they provided handy fodder for our grade books.

But we have also seen some deeply meaningful book reports. I'll never forget the day at Best Practice High School when some of Tina Peano's kids came to class in ripped clothes and dirty faces and started a visceral reenactment of the last stages of *Lord of the Flies*; everyone was on the edge of their chair—and just a little bit afraid. Or the classroom of fourth graders in Cleveland, who overcame the limits of the deadly diorama to create thirty gorgeously idiosyncratic rodent habitats from *Mrs. Frisby and Rats of NIMH*. Or Maggie Forst's high school kids, writing serious essays about "the nature of contemporary literature," just like real literary critics—which they believe they are.

We keep coming back to the question, What do real readers do? What do real readers do when they come to the end of a really great book? Do they put on a puppet show? No, usually they find someone to talk with about the book, to share their enthusiasm and to walk that delicious tightrope between getting someone interested in a book and not ruining the story by telling too much. And, of course, advertising a book in this way lets the reader hear what she thinks, by synthesizing and shaping her response to a book for someone else's ears. This kind of genuine after-a-book conversation is something we want to make room for in our classrooms. If book projects can help kids enjoy this kind of urgent sharing, then they can be natural and positive, and they can feed the group with more and more "book leads." But the more elaborate, extended, and artificial projects get, the further they diverge from what real readers do, and we should be increasingly wary of their value. In Chapter 6 we offered a list of book project ideas that teachers have used successfully. Here we'll just add a few operational lessons we have learned:

Successful Book Projects
Kids freely chose the book in the first place.
There are plenty of options (dramatic, graphic, written, etc.).

Kids can work together or alone.

There are time and resources available for preparation.

There is a genuine audience or outlet for the work.

Reports are staggered, rather than presented all at once.

The standards for effective performance are clear in advance, and developed with students where possible.

Grading Literature Circles

Is it possible to grade students for their work in literature circles, over a whole book or a marking period? Yes, but do you *really* have to? It would be so much better not to grade literature circle work at all. Can't you base your grades on some other classroom activities, so that you don't undermine the genuineness of the book club conversation? So that you don't replace the collaborative culture you're trying to build with competition? I know, I know. You're working in a school district that requires grades for everything.

Okay, I give up. This is the sea we are all swimming in. But let's minimize the constant intrusion of scoring, points, and tests into the daily interaction of the circles. After all, if our kids' groups are really "hooked on books" and working well with one another, we don't need any grades for management purposes. We only need to sample their performance enough to feed the system whatever grades it requires. And since we also want to nurture a high level of self-evaluation and involve students in keeping their own records, whatever system we devise should have a strong component of student self-evaluation.

We've already warned about relying too much on book projects. So, if not a project, then what? How can we get a grade out of literature circles? A grade that is valid and meaningful, that doesn't distort the behavior of the groups, and that provides a credible report to the outside agencies watching over this classroom? "Performance assessment" may be the answer. And if you have ever read any restaurant reviews, you already know how it works. Most food critics have some kind of point system for rating the quality of a dining experience. One of our local restaurant mavens uses this scale: food = 10 points, service = 4 points, atmosphere – 3 points, value – 3 points.

When we move this kind of scoring into school, it is called "performance assessment." We call it this because this approach to grading asks, What are the ingredients of a successful performance in this activity? What are the ingredients of a successful informational speech, a successful science experiment, a successful research paper? As these examples suggest, performance assessment is especially suited to complex, higher-order thinking activities—like literature circles.

If we want to design performance assessment rubrics for literature circles, of course we can do it ourselves. But it is much more fun, and more educational, to create them with kids. Here's how we do it in some of our schools. After the students have been through one round of literature circles, we set aside a meeting to develop our own performance assessment rubric. Going back and forth between journal writing, talking with partners, and sharing as a whole class, we ask kids to develop a list of ingredients or components of "an effective member of a book club." As we share ideas, we help the kids winnow the list down to a reasonable number of entries, eliminating duplicates and gently discarding wacko suggestions. Here's the list one group of third graders at Waters School recently came up with:

Traits of Good Book Club Members
Do the reading
Listen to other people
Have good ideas
Ask people questions
Stick to the book
Dress nice

Actually, this third-grade list is pretty much what older kids usually come up with—except for the wardrobe entry.

Now we ask the kids, Are all of these things equally important? Is dressing well for your literature circle meeting as important as having good ideas? No, no, they clamor. Okay. So now we announce that the rubric must add up to one hundred points, and we put kids in groups to propose point values for each component. Later, we reassemble as a whole class and haggle toward a point distribution agreement. Finally, we affirm the rubric; this is our scoring guide and we're sticking to it—at least until we revise it a month or two from now. When we're finished, we'll have something like this:

LITERATURE CIRCLES SCORING GUIDE—Room 206

Ingredient	Value	My Score
Do the reading	25	
Listen to other people	15	
Have good ideas	30	
Ask people questions	15	
Stick to the book	10	
Dress nice	5	
Total	100	

Now, this is a good process. The whole time we are listing, debating, and valuing, we are actually teaching kids the ingredients of successful work, marinating them in the criteria of achievement. Indeed, this rubric-creation activity is just one of the very few instances I know of where assessment becomes part of instruction in a constructive way.

Once your own class rubric is created, there are several ways to use it. You can score individual kids yourself. Or both you and the student can each fill out a form and average the results. Better yet, you can have students score themselves and then meet with you to review their ratings. You can adjust scores up or down for off-the-mark ratings. Given the seriousness with which kids grade themselves, you'll probably be doing more raising than lowering.

Now let's return to that mythical parent conference where Dad is demanding to see proof that Junior deserved a C in literature circles. You have all the kid's reading log entries, stamped and dated, you have a stack of observation forms bearing on his thinking and interacting skills, and you have a performance assessment rubric based upon clear criteria for achievement. Next!

Conferences

Some teachers have periodic *individual reading conferences* with students, and one good topic for these conferences is the child's work in the literature circle. Teachers can talk with the students about their own role in the group, the circle's problems and pleasures, and about the group's handling of specific books and ideas. Such a conversation helps the teacher access children's thinking directly and personally, and the information gained can help with everything from future book choices to re-forming the groups. Most teachers keep simple notes on these conferences, so they can reflect on them later in reconstructing patterns of growth, talking to parents, or arriving at grades.

Teachers can also conduct *group conferences with the literature circles* themselves. The teacher visits each group as the group is finishing up a book, asking the group to set aside one meeting in which they will reflect back together over what they have accomplished. At these meetings, kids review both the content of the book, the interpretations they have given it, and the process of their work as a group. As with an individual conference, teachers might let this meeting unfold spontaneously or work from a set list of questions they want to hear addressed. Similarly, they may want to make some notes during or after the conference—or simply tape-record the group conference and put a copy of the tape in each child's portfolio. This last alternative relieves the teacher of record keeping during the meeting, and as long as the goal of the conference has been to document and not to grade the group's work, simply *saving* the resulting tape may be plenty of "assessment." Once kids have learned the purposes and procedures of such assessments, they can tape and critique group meetings *themselves*. Groups can review the tape, make notes, and then have a special session to evaluate their own process. Finally, each kid can put a copy of his or her own written report in a personal portfolio. All these variations are good examples of how good assessment can actually be part of rather than separate from valuable class activities.

Portfolios

Some lit circle teachers use a portfolio system, in which kids save everything related to their experience of a book, either as a group or individually. This makes sense when you think about it. Well-run lit circles leave a lot of interesting collectibles. You've got the reading response logs, Post-it notes, or role sheets that helped set students' purposes for reading and guide their group meetings. (Yes, even though it is a pain in the neck, our teachers routinely have kids remove whole sets of Post-it note jottings from the pages of books that must be returned to the library. The trick is to first write down the page number on each Post-it and then to lay them out in page-number order on regular 8½ x 11 paper.) Added to this collection there may be some student observation sheets, some scored performance rubrics, and maybe a videotape of each group in action. Finally, if the kids did some kind of book project or extension activity, there will be the residue of that, too—a poster, a readers theater script, a written report, a piece of artwork. Some teachers also instigate separate teacher-student dialogue journals, so that kids are talking about their reading both orally with their group and in writing with their teacher. Obviously, such dialogue journals provide another rich source of insight for the teacher and a meaningful entry for a portfolio.

All these artifacts allow teachers a broad look at kids' growth; they invite us to track the sophistication of students' thinking, the extent of their preparation, and the nature of their interactions over time. There is no need to devise a separate test or worksheet when all these items are naturally occurring by-products and records of literature circle work. Such a portfolio of evidence provides a deep description of what a child has read and said and thought. While the individual pieces in this portfolio may not be scored or graded, the portfolio is a powerful assembly of raw material—evidence and documentation of the student's reading, thinking, and participation.

A Note on Record Keeping

Many teachers who are just beginning to use innovations like literature circles sometimes worry excessively about evaluation and grades. Perhaps because they are stepping out of the instructional mainstream, they feel obligated to keep meticulous written records of everything that kids do, say, write, read, or think. They feel ashamed if their records are jumbled and fragmentary, they feel inferior to colleagues whose records are more orderly, and they may even experience paranoid delusions of angry parents demanding to see "justification" for a child's disputed grade in this weird new "experimental" activity.

So, as you implement literature circles and find yourself worrying about record keeping, remember: doing the activity is the main thing. Very adequate documentation of kids' growth in this activity—or any other classroom structure—can be achieved by occasionally sampling their performance, by collecting the raw material of their efforts in portfolios, by talking to kids regularly and keeping track of what they say. While long lines of marks in a grade book may seem more scientific, you can also trust your memory, your impressions of kids. Your thoughts and judgments are not unanchored—you have valid, important, and consistent criteria inside you.

And while we're on the subject, who says that *teachers* should be doing most or all of the record keeping? Piling all the paperwork on teachers is one of those unexamined elements of schooling that, ironically, breeds dependency and helplessness among students. If there are records worth keeping in literature circles, they are worth being kept by kids. Students can keep track of their own role sheets, keep their own folders updated, enter metacognitive reflections in their reading response logs, write self-assessments at the end of each book, bind and save their own projects, and so on.

If all else fails and you feel yourself coming down with the left-brain flu, here are a couple of prescriptions:

- If a record-keeping procedure interferes with your relationships with children, get rid of it.
- If a record-keeping procedure interferes with natural conversation in the literature circles, get rid of it.
- If a record-keeping procedure becomes an end in itself, get rid of it.
- If a record keeping procedure is eating up so much of your time that you come to literature circles (or to school in general) stressed and upset, get rid of it.

13

Nonfiction Literature Circles: Moving Across the Curriculum

SOMETIMES I THINK we made a mistake calling these peer-led reading groups "literature circles." The name implies that the structure works only for fiction and only in reading or language arts classes. How wrong! If we had dubbed them "reading circles" instead, as our colleague Marline Pearson suggested years ago, we might long since have recruited a passel of science, social studies, and other "content" colleagues into the fold. And our students might have spent much more time with real nonfiction texts—biographies, information books, essays, science articles, and all the rest.

Yes, reading circles can definitely work for nonfiction text. After all, the underlying structure is simply good collaborative learning hooked to reading, right? Still, there are a few important conditions that must be met. Here's the bad news first: no, LCs probably won't work with your math textbook. Or the history or science textbook. So many teachers have tried applying peer-led discussion to that dense and inevitable reading called textbooks, and what happens? Nothing much. You don't see a lot of spirited discussions or free-ranging conversation—and you certainly don't see kids laughing or crying, having a deep emotional experience—that is, unless they have digressed pretty far from the book. (Well, they might be crying because they don't understand it.)

The problem is that textbooks are not "normal" text—certainly not narrative, but not even informational, in the sense that an article in *Time* or *Scientific American* informs us. School textbooks are a whole different genre. They are compendiums, storage systems for vast amounts of information, constructed without serious regard to supporting, engaging, or interesting their readers. Textbooks don't need to engage their readers, because their authors know that teachers will force kids to read them. After all, no one goes to a bookstore, buys a biology textbook, and then stays up all night reading it straight through ("I just couldn't put it down!"). Think about it. When was the last time you saw *Algebra I* on the best-seller list?

The point is, textbooks are reference books. They are best used as a place to look up information when you need it. No, you wouldn't take a science textbook to read on your beach vacation. But if your doctor told you that your hormone levels were messed up, you might pull the old bio text off the shelf and read up on the endocrine system. The trouble is, this is not how textbooks are generally used in school. Instead, we pretend that kids should be able to plow right through big sections of them, remembering most of the densely packed facts they encounter, and regurgitating those facts on tests. Whether teaching this way is wrong is another debate. But without question, this is a very narrow and peculiar kind of reading, not very much like the kind of reading that people do every day in their jobs, homes, and communities.

Some teachers buck these realities anyhow, figuring that if textbooks must be assigned, at least the kids can work through them in supportive groups. Sometimes these teachers chop their textbooks into small sections, jigsawing pieces out to student groups that operate in literature-circle-like fashion. This rarely has the energy or zest of real lit circles, but at least kids get to work with their friends, set their own schedules, and have some responsibility and voice in the process. But "textbook circles" aren't a very effective use of the lit circle "magic." Collaboration has a lot of social power; people can do jobs together that they can't do nearly so well alone. But when the tasks are mundane and convergent—like memorizing facts—even the magic of the small-group process tends to fade. Not even the best-structured group activities can bring real energy to work that's rote, predetermined, and unimaginative.

But no matter. School textbooks are just a drop in the ocean of nonfiction. The world is full of fascinating, important, debatable, and sometimes inflammatory nonfiction, from the daily newspapers to revisionist histories—for readers of all ages. To create reading circles that work like literature circles, we need to gather nonfiction materials that are discussable, that have some kind of narrative structure, some conflict or danger, some opposition of values, some kind of ethical or political dimension, some debate or dispute, some ideas that reasonable people can disagree about. Well, this leaves a lot to choose from—basically, the majority of nontextbook nonfiction being published today.

Twenty years ago, we used to have a hard time finding rich nonfiction books for young people. Now, that gap has largely been closed. For the youngest kids, the supply of informational picture books is growing daily. Primary kids love information, information about animals (dinosaurs, sharks, apes, owls, insects, whales) and places (Africa, the moon, rain forests, a farm, the pyramids) and people (babies, Indians, slaves, grandparents, Inuits).

For intermediate kids, there are biographies of noble historical figures as well as contemporary sports and entertainment stars. There are how-to books, adventure tales, and great science series like the Eyewitness books. Although they are technically not nonfiction, historical novels are one of the most popular and ample genres for readers of this age. There's no more natural curriculum integration tool than a historical novel like *Morning Girl* (exploration), *What's the Big Idea, Ben Franklin?* (the colonial era), or *Bud, Not Buddy* (the Depression). The literature on the Holocaust, immigration, and the history of different American ethnic groups is especially strong.

For teenage readers, the whole world of adult nonfiction opens up. The students we work with have recently enjoyed *There Are No Children Here,* by Alex Kotlowitz, the all-too-real account of two brothers growing up in a Chicago housing project. *Into Thin Air* and *Into the Wild,* both by John Krakauer, *The Perfect Storm,* by Sebastian Junger, and *The Last River,* by Todd Balf are true adventure stories with tons of science information and strong narrative lines. *The Big Test,* by Nicholas Lehman, gives kids a chance to learn about the sordid origins of the SAT test they will all face. More challenging reads offered are Dava Sobel's books *Longitude* and *Galileo's Daughter,* both of which dramatically recount inventions and inventors that changed the world. Patrick Diamond's *Guns, Germs, and Steel* offers a chilling and persuasive theory of why Caucasians have been able to dominate and exploit the other peoples of the world for two millennia. And *Chicken Soup for the Teenage Soul* offers short bits of helpful lore and wisdom.

In addition to whole books, teachers can also build nonfiction reading groups around shorter pieces taken from magazines and newspapers. Actually, every school subject worth teaching gets "covered" in the popular press, if we know where to look. We can gather articles about air pollution in the community, the role of serotonin in brain function, the latest genetic engineering breakthrough, racial quotas in police department hiring, or a controversial art exhibit. Another reservoir of nonfiction text is primary source material. My colleague Steve Zemelman assembled a set of historic documents about the African American soldiers who served in the Civil War, kicking off the unit of study by reading aloud Patricia Polacco's *Pink and Say,* a picture book based upon a true story handed down through the author's family.

Whether we are using nonfiction books or shorter pieces, effective "reading circles" will require the same discussion skills as fiction circles. Kids need to know how to keep a response log, mark important sections of a text, participate effectively in a group, reflect on and improve discussions, and so forth. For kids who have already done literature circles extensively, these skills should transfer fluidly to nonfiction text. If kids are at an earlier stage, some of the same training strategies described in Chapter 5 may be needed.

Just as with novels, we want kids to capture their responses as they read and bring to the discussion their questions, connections, feelings, judgments, words, phrases, and doodles. To harvest potentially discussable topics, we have kids jot in open-ended response logs or stick Post-it notes in key spots through the book or write notes right on the text if that's appropriate.

▼ VARIATION : **Try the Homogeneous-Heterogeneous Swap**

One of our favorite activities with older kids is the homogeneous-heterogeneous swap, which is based on a topical text set of short articles. Readers begin in a group where everyone has read the same article. Here, there are two stages of discussion. First, people just talk, having that good old-fashioned lit circle natural conversation about the text. Then, in the last five minutes, they come up with a "consensus highlight" from their reading—one aspect or idea that everyone agrees ought to be shared with people who haven't read this article. They talk this out, and each member jots down notes or key words about the agreed-on highlight. Then everyone swaps, finding her or his way into a new group where everyone has read a different article in the text set. This meeting begins with a round, in which each circle member tells the title and author of his or her article and then shares the consensus highlight developed back in the homogeneous group. General conversation follows. This is a concrete demonstration of curriculum jigsawing; everyone learns a lot about one topic and also gets a taste of some closely related material, without everyone's having to "cover" everything.

Teachers have developed some other tools for capturing readers' responses to nonfiction. On the following pages are two forms in the style of the role sheets introduced in Chapter 7. These sheets do not assign different jobs to different students but rather invite all readers to respond in multiple ways to the text at hand. The first version (Nonfiction Discussion Sheet) is designed for nonfiction groups where everyone is reading the same text, and it works pretty much like any role sheet. It sets purposes for the reading and encourages readers to "enter thinking." It reminds students that as they read they can visualize, connect, question, savor, notice, and evaluate. When members bring their completed sheets to a small-group discussion, they have an inventory of different "takes" on the text, ideas to sustain an extended conversation.

The second sheet (Nonfiction Jigsaw Sheet) is for "jigsaw" groups, where different members are reading different texts on the same subject (e.g., five articles about different types of water pollution) or different sections of a larger text (e.g., different chapters of a book on spiders). The sheet helps students have the kind of two-stage meeting that heterogenous readings require. First, everyone takes a turn identifying his or her text, and offering a quick summary and personal reaction. Once around the group, everyone can join in general conversation, comparing and connecting the readings. People can contribute their responses, passages, illustrations, or other notes wherever they fit, as the conversation unfolds.

Both of these handouts are subject to the same cautions as the literature role sheets. They can get mechanical if overused, and students may depend on

NONFICTION DISCUSSION SHEET

Name

Title of Reading   **Author**

While you are reading or after you have finished reading, please prepare for the group meeting by doing the following:

Connections: What personal connections did you make with the text? Did it remind you of past experiences, people, or events in your life? Did it make you think of anything happening in the news, around school, or in other material you have read?

Discussion questions: Jot down a few questions you would like to discuss with your group. They could be questions that came to your mind while reading, questions you'd like to ask the author, questions you'd like to investigate, or any other questions you think the group might like to discuss.

Passages: Mark some lines or sections in the text that caught your attention—sections that somehow "jumped out" at you as you read. These might be passages that seem especially important, puzzling, beautiful, strange, well written, controversial, or striking in some other way. Be ready to read these aloud to the group or to ask someone else to read them.

Illustration: On the back of this sheet, quickly sketch a picture related to your reading. This can be a drawing, cartoon, diagram, flowchart—whatever. You can draw a picture of something that's specifically talked about in the text or something from your own experience or feelings, something the reading made you think about. Be ready to show your picture to your group and talk about it.

NONFICTION JIGSAW SHEET

Name

Title of Reading   **Author**

Everyone in your group is reading something different but related. In order to have a good discussion, everyone will need to both share and connect. To prepare for your group meeting, please respond to the following items, either while you are reading or after you have read.

Summary and reactions: Jot down a brief summary of your reading and some personal reactions you had.

Connections: What personal connections did you make with the text? Did it remind you of past experiences, people, or events in your life? Did it make you think of anything happening in the news, around school, or in other material you have read?

Passages: Mark some lines or sections that you could read aloud to help other group members understand this text.

Illustration: On the back of this sheet, quickly sketch a picture related to your reading. This can be a drawing, cartoon, diagram, flowchart—whatever. You can draw a picture of something that's specifically talked about in the text or something from your own experience or feelings, something the text made you think about. Be ready to show your picture to your group and talk about it.

When the group meets, the discussion will have two stages. First, everyone will take turns identifying his or her reading by author and title, giving a quick summary and a personal reaction. Then, everyone will join in general conversation, comparing and connecting whatever seems valuable and interesting about the readings. You can contribute your passages, illustrations, or other notes wherever they fit.

them too much in discussions, taking turns reading their entries aloud rather than engaging in a free-flowing conversation. To prevent this, have kids hold their meetings with the *sheets facedown,* using them only when (and if) they run out of ideas to talk about. It's also a good idea to move on from role sheets to response logs or Post-it notes, which are more open-ended and natural forms of note taking.

Three Versions of Nonfiction Lit Circles

Next we have stories from three enterprising teachers who have developed their own versions of nonfiction reading groups. The models come from an integrated history and English unit in seventh grade, a college criminology class, and a fifth-grade classroom, respectively. Each of these stories holds many seeds for adaptations to other grade levels and content areas.

Kathy LaLuz

WASHINGTON IRVING SCHOOL, CHICAGO

It's time for a new round of literature circles in Kathy LaLuz's seventh-grade classroom, at Washington Irving School, in Chicago. Earlier in the year, the kids have worked through two cycles of regular book clubs, selecting and enjoying novels from Kathy's two-thousand-volume classroom library. The kids have been able to select books from bins and baskets labeled Adventure, Survival, Family, Romance, Biography, and more. Among the hot titles this year have been *Out of the Dust, Missing May, Ordinary People,* and *Roll of Thunder, Hear My Cry.*

This time, Kathy has planned something special. In connection with a social studies unit on Civil War history, the kids' book clubs will be reading slave narratives from the book *Remembering Slavery,* by Ira Berlin, Marc Favreau, and Steven Miller (2000). These autobiographical accounts, based on interviews of former slaves by the Federal Writers Project in the 1930s, provide first-person testimony, sometimes harrowing, sometimes puzzling, from the era of American slavery.

The idea for literature circles on slavery came directly from the students. Back in September, when Kathy was previewing the year's history curriculum for the class, several of the African American students expressed doubts about the courage of slaves. "Wouldn't nobody make a slave out of me," Dominique said. "I would have just ran away." Dominique couldn't understand why the slaves didn't fight back, didn't turn the masters' weapons against them somehow. A consensus quickly formed among these contemporary thirteen-year-olds: the slaves weren't as brave or as smart as today's African Americans. Slavery could never happen now.

Kathy was troubled and galvanized. She realized that her students knew little about the reality of American slavery, of its brutal and effective mechanisms of control. For the whole class, it was a matter of facing history, but for her mostly African American students, the stakes were especially high. It was a question of understanding and honoring their own ancestors. When Kathy discovered the *Remembering Slavery* book, she knew she had the right text: scores of interviews of former slaves from all parts of the South.

As Kathy puts together this special cycle of literature circles, she adds a couple of extra twists. She decides to jigsaw the readings so that each student in a group reads a different slave narrative. Kids in each group of seven are invited to pick a selection from an array of chapters. Jigsawing, Kathy explains in a mini-lesson, means that book club meetings will have a slightly different flavor from the "regular" ones where everyone has read the same text. In jigsaw groups, members need to give some information about their selection first, sharing highlights or summarizing events. After this initial round of informing, the discussion can then shift to connecting, comparing, and finding common elements. Jigsaw groups are especially powerful for content-laden nonfiction material, and that's why Kathy has picked them for this topic. As students report on the interviews they have read, they will need to explain (and help their fellow group members to understand) complex concepts like slave auctions, the varying norms of servitude in different regions, the underlying escape themes in field songs, and more. On the days these groups gather, Kathy reasons, there will be lots of clarifying questions, many puzzles over words, and plenty of surprises.

Kathy reminds kids that they will still use a reading log to capture their reactions and feed their group meetings. She reminds them to "notice" three to five sections of the text that struck them in some way. They can

- share a feeling or response
- tell what they were thinking or noticed
- ask a question
- make a judgment or interpretation
- draw a picture or diagram

As always, kids are required to fill one to two sides of a notebook page with these thoughts, labeling each entry with the page and paragraph number where the thought arose. The students will turn in their logs every morning so Kathy can look them over while the kids are doing their math. She gives a check-plus, check, or check-minus, mainly on the basis of scanning the quantity and specificity of the entries. Kathy does this not so much to get a grade as to constantly put kids on notice that they are responsible for coming up with great ideas for their discussions. Then, just before literature circles start at 1:00 P.M., she gives the logs back to the kids.

The first set of slave narratives gives the kids plenty to write about. When they return the next day, having read their first selections, the journals are brimming with thoughts, feelings, and questions. Iesha has written:

> p. 63, paragraph 1, sentence 1
> I was happy, surprised, and shocked that master never whipped Urele Muse whenever he ran away. I felt this way because most slave owners would whip their slaves half to death if they find out they ran away. I wonder why they used to tell kids that a runaway nigger would get them?

Meanwhile, Veronica was wondering:

> p. 161, paragraph 2
> If the people bought a really sick slave and the slave died, can't they get their money back or sue the people who sold them?

And Dominique, the young lady whose tough questions about slavery had inspired the whole unit, was asking:

> p. 114
> I read on page 114 that this girl's grandpa was the king in Africa, but now he was a slave. This page caught my attention because I didn't know they could make a king be a slave.

As Kathy reads through these initial journals, she thinks that this afternoon's meetings will be lively.

When the groups come together at one o'clock, they don't just plunge in. There are some procedures to be observed. Each of the two literature circles meeting in this time slot has a single group binder used for keeping records and structuring the meeting. A chart in the binder displays the kids' names and a string of literature circle meeting dates, like this:

	5/1	5/2	5/3	5/4	5/5	5/8	5/9	5/10	5/11	5/12
Iesha										
Dominique										
Jason										
Robert										
Marion										
Gilbert										
Antonio										

On a rotating basis, one member is designated "binder person" of the day, with several important responsibilities: to kick off the discussion, to make sure that everyone shares at least one question or concern they have brought, to transpose Kathy's check marks into each kid's box under today's date, and, after the meeting, to insert the actual reading logs in the binder, right behind this page.

The group meeting officially begins when the binder person says, "Who wants to go first today?" Then one kid will share something from his or her log, summarizing a thought, posing a question, sharing a feeling, or reading a key passage from the text aloud. Kathy's kids have been practicing these kinds of conversation-openers all year (and many of them, in previous years at Irving). They know how to jump in and build on the ideas of others, to question, prod, and piggyback. Sometimes a topic blossoms, leading to dozens of back-and-forth exchanges; sometimes it flops, but even then, each group member typically makes an attempt to pick up the thread that's offered before the group moves on. Well, that's how it is supposed to work.

Right now, the group near the door, the group that Kathy is not in, is starting their literature circle with a little "setting and joking," as it is called in the field of group dynamics. There is a well-known finding in the research on collaborative learning that certain kinds of off-task behavior can actually provide the "social lubrication" needed to help groups accomplish tasks later on. Well, in this particular seventh-grade group, social lubrication seems to involve poking one another with pencils, arguing about the binder, accusing members of not doing the homework, and stealing other people's reading logs. A glance from Kathy, who is thirty feet away setting up a video camera, puts them back on track. "Okay," says binder person Iesha. "Who wants to go?" With Marion taking the lead, the kids start telling about the seven different slave narratives they have read, sharing reactions and making connections.

I didn't know that slave owners could kill their slaves and not even be charged for murder.
I thought the slaves were brainwashed.
It just blew me away—it was a passage where it was, like wow.
I hate anything about slaves.
I wonder why the slaves didn't kill their masters with their own weapons. Because if they had them, why didn't they use them after all they went through?
It was so sad when . . . this lady had a cousin with two kids and one of them had to nurse the master's kid, a baby. And she fell down the steps with that baby, and when the master came home and saw the baby hurt, he just hit that child on the head with a board and killed her right there. And then he told some other slaves to throw her body in the river. When I read that, I thought they only beat them. I was shocked how he killed a four-year-old. It made me real mad.

She was four? The slave girl—the one who was babysitting?

Uh-huh.

I don't know why he did that, the master. I mean, killing her would be wasting slaves.

I agree and kinda disagree. I mean, if a girl fell down with *your* baby, you saying you wouldn't go off on her?

I could see it if he beat her, but he actually killed her.

If my baby was alive, that's all that would matter.

It was a accident.

She could have tripped on her shoes . . . or tripped on a step.

Why'd they give a baby to a four-year-old girl anyway?

It was the owner's fault!

How you gonna give a baby to a baby. I mean, really. How you gonna give a baby to a baby?

While these kids work, what is Kathy doing? Washington Irving's unique scheduling cuts Kathy's class in half for literature circles, which obviously makes supervising the groups (usually just two or three) much easier. Kathy further closes the monitoring gap by videotaping one group she's not with, every day. That means she can sit down and spend a longer stretch of time with just one or two groups, instead of hopping around between five or six different discussions.

Kathy is careful not to dominate the groups she joins. First, and mostly, she listens. She'll ask questions of fact or chip in a comment, but she doesn't run the conversation. But when she sees a problem develop, she's not shy. She'll say, "I think this is getting a little silly here. How is this connected to the book?" Or she'll ask, "What do you notice about participation? Is everybody contributing here?" Often, when she raises a question about either process or content, she will immediately get up and go visit another group, emphasizing that the kids must work things out for themselves.

Kathy says that her most important aim is to help her students grow, both as readers and as people. In a complex collaborative activity like literature circles, she has the opportunity to nurture the development of both cognition and character. And Kathy does a lot of coaching in both domains. At the end of almost any literature circle meeting, as in the other seams or transitions of the day, you'll see her take a child aside and give some quiet encouragement.

Today, she notices that one especially sensitive boy, Andrew, has been repeatedly shut down by the cheerfully aggressive kids in his group. Kathy is worried because he is getting in the habit of simply withdrawing from the conversation rather than fighting for airtime. She can tell from his dark and downcast expression that he is frustrated with his own response. As the class period ends and the kids file out for P.E., she walks with Andrew out into the hall, draping her arm over his broad shoulder, a good foot higher than her own. "Don't let them do this to you," she whispers. "You have so much to say. You gotta speak up. Make them listen to you. Can you do that tomorrow?" He nods and brightens. "Okay, Ms. LaLuz," he says, and ambles down the hall.

Marline Pearson

MADISON AREA TECHNICAL COLLEGE, MADISON, WI

I teach at a two-year technical college and have been using literature circles—which I renamed reading circles—for three semesters with my criminology classes. I have two sections of forty-five to fifty students each. Frankly, I've never witnessed such engaged, enthusiastic, and serious discussion among so many students in a classroom in my fifteen years of teaching. This testimony comes not only from what I have observed by walking around and listening to my students as they talk in their reading circles but also from reading the process checker sheets that each student fills out about their experience with the circles.

Let me add that my skill with reading circles has evolved over time. Three semesters ago, I was pretty positive about reading circles, but my students' experience with this technique has improved each semester as I've begun to troubleshoot and work out the bugs. There are several things I've learned from my mistakes and oversights in using this strategy over the past three semesters, and I'd like to share them.

Tell Your Students Why You Value Reading Circles

At the outset, I spend some time explaining why we're doing reading circles and why I value them. In fact, this leads me into a short discourse on my philosophy of learning and teaching, which values student-generated as opposed to teacher-directed discussion. Reading circles start with what the students think about the reading. They give students the chance to answer the following sorts of questions: Which passages are meaningful, puzzling, controversial, or striking and why? What connections occur in your mind as you read—to your own life or what you've read or heard about? What feeling does it evoke in you and how do you express it visually? Finally, what big issues and questions does the reading raise? My experience is that students really like this format because they feel they truly are discussing what's on their mind.

I also try to acknowledge that students have rarely had the opportunity to do this in class and that some may have had lousy experiences with class discussion. Typically, teachers set the discussion questions and issues and often don't give much time for students to think about their responses. This encourages passivity and a just-look-up-the-answers approach. It fosters the opposite of authentic or critical thinking. I'm always amazed how so many students can go through school and never really get any encouragement for authentic thoughts.

I always tell my students, "To do my job as a teacher and facilitate learning, I need to know about your thoughts, your experiences, the connections you make, and the meaning that you give to class materials. Above all, I need to know the questions that are important to you. Learning is a process of connecting new information to current knowledge and experience you possess." Unfortunately, too much teaching is like "bulldozing"—that is, the teacher plows through the material without stopping to check out how students are experiencing it. In the end, far too many students are silenced rather than stimulated by their experience in the classroom. Reading circles are a good tool, I think, for fostering some genuine discussion and giving me a sense of how learners experience ideas.

I also tell my students that I personally value collaborative work and that we all need practice in this. We need practice listening to one another to develop our own thinking. I explain that I will be circulating around and that they should flag me immediately if they need any clarification on roles. I point out that because each role reflects a different learning style, some roles may feel natural and others awkward. The bottom line, I tell them, is that I want the circles to work and to feel useful to them. If they don't work, then we need to try something else.

Starting Right: Train Your Students Well

Probably the most important thing I've learned over the past couple of years is the necessity of thoroughly training students in the reading circle process and then demonstrating it. My first experience using reading circles was literally the day after I myself was introduced to it. I rushed out and tried it with my students, doing minimal training and virtually no role modeling. Of the eight groups, five worked very well, despite the lack of training. But still, having three groups of disgruntled and/or confused students is not a pleasant situation. I have now worked out a fairly efficient way to train students and model the process with the class. It takes one or two class periods, but it is well worth the effort. And the training can be done on the material you want them to read anyway. This semester, after paying close attention to training, I can report that every single group was highly functional and engaged from the start. As of this writing, the groups are on their third round of reading circles and their enthusiasm and success are still holding.

How I Train Students

I give students a two-page article to take home and read. The next day in class I announce I'm going to train them to do reading circles and explain what they are and why I value them. I pass out the master sheets describing the roles and go over them with the class. Then I divide the class in half. Half the class is told that they will have ten minutes to go over the article (which they've already read the night before), pick out two passages that they find meaningful, and then jot down their reasons for picking them.

Meanwhile, the other half of the class is told to go over the article and jot down one or two connections. I choose these two roles because they are often the most confusing. After ten minutes, I ask for volunteers to share their chosen passages and elaborate on them. I then invite others to respond to the passage masters. We might review four or five passages before going on to review creative connections in the same way. I find that one student's passage or connection tends to evoke a response or idea from another student. Before we know it, we're into a good discussion on the article and the whole class now knows what was meant by those two roles.

My role in all of this is that of discussion director and facilitator: I invite everyone's participation, bring the groups back to the topic if they wander off too long, and stay aware of the time limits we've set for the group. I also point out that the discussion director's job is to come to the group with one, two, or three big issues or questions that the article raises. Using the overhead projector, I write/show them four issues that I would raise as the discussion director for this particular article. I advise them that the discussion director should *not* immediately start the group with her or his prepared topics, since these issues may come out naturally in the course of the students' discussion of passages and connections. In the beginning, I discovered that discussion directors tended to take on too much of the responsibility for selecting issues. I suggest they simply stand ready to raise their questions if they don't naturally arise in the course of the discussion.

During this initial training, the other role I assume is that of illustrator. I display a transparency drawing that I have done for the article and then ask the students to interpret it. Because I'm not very artistic, they quickly get the point that we're talking about expression, not about great "art" when it comes to the illustrator role. This approach helps my students relax about being the illustrator—an important consideration, since almost all of them initially blanch at having to draw. After my funny introduction to this role and their practice with it, I discovered that the role had become very popular. By the second round of reading circles, my students were asking me to tape their illustrations to the wall. My classroom became decorated in a unique and delightful fashion, and all of the students had a good time looking at all the drawings.

This "fun" approach to reading circles also helps the students understand that the goal is to have a natural, free-flowing discussion of what *they* understand from the readings. I tell them not to be totally driven by the roles, which are just there to help. I also keep reminding them that they are to be active listeners and that they need to respond to the things others say. This is something we also track with the process checker sheets.

At the end of the training, I give the students a two-page article, put them in groups, and let them divide up the roles. They are asked to prepare roles for reading circles for the next class period. I tell them I'll be checking at the door for their role preparation.

One final note about training: expect that it will take a while to smooth out the rough edges of your own experience with reading circles. It is new for you, the teacher, as well as for the students. Stay with it and you will be rewarded.

Metacognitive Tracking with the Process Checker Sheet

I've found it very useful to allow the students some time to reflect, do some self-evaluation, and then write something short about the discussion in their reading circle. When I was first introduced to the original literature circles model, there was a "process checker" role sheet to be filled out by one group member, who judged the participation of each member of the group. I have now given up having students evaluate other members of their groups. I guess in the beginning I thought I had to do this—almost as if it were a way of saying, "Participate or else!" My thinking now is that if students don't really get into it, then why do it? It's useful to me as long as it's useful to students. Also, I feel that if there was a problem earlier, it was probably more my fault for not training the students, clarifying the process, or allowing the students enough time and practice to do well.

Now into my third semester, I am into my third version of process checker sheets—a version that requires my students to evaluate only their own participation. This sheet basically asks the student to respond yes or no to the question of whether or not the discussion worked—that is, was there some genuine "connection" with one another's thoughts and ideas? If the answer is no, then students are asked to try to write about why they think this connecting did not happen. I offer some possible reasons: lack of preparation, boring article, different personalities or learning styles, etc. I hope that these suggestions will give students more freedom to be honest. If the answer is yes, then they are asked to describe one or two of the high points of the discussion, the topics or questions the group really latched onto. At the bottom of the checker sheet, they are to evaluate their own participation with a plus, an equal sign (meaning so-so), or a minus.

After the students have completed their self-evaluations, I collect the sheets by group and clip them together. I review them immediately to see if the group is working well. What I read on the checker sheets tells me what the "hot" issues are and thus tells me what to focus on in the rest of my teaching. For example, I might use some of the students' comments in a reading circle to start off the next class. This clear attention to what the students think is important—as well as the notes I write on each checker sheet when I return it to the student—indicates to the student how seriously I value the effort expended in a reading circle. It is probably especially important that a teacher take the time to write comments back to the students. My own comments are nonjudgmental and nonevaluative. I just share a reaction or ask clarifying questions. I tell the students that these sheets are the clearest way for me to gauge the usefulness of this format and to tap into what they're talking about.

In short, I really like my latest checker sheets because they offer the student some time for reflection and clarification of ideas as well as for a bit of metacognitive work. They give students the chance to write about the content and the process of their own discussions.

Other Important Tips

It is important to start small by using short, one- or two-page articles. Moreover, although reading circles do not need to be done every class period or even every week, students do need to practice the techniques thoroughly if they are to gain the skill it takes to make reading circles worthwhile. Do reading circles shortly after training the students and then do them again within a week or two.

Don't underestimate—as I did in the beginning—how much time students need to flourish in a session of reading circles. When I first tried them, I tended to frustrate students by ending the group meetings too soon. Either give students more time—it shows you are really serious about authentic student discussion—or give them shorter pieces to discuss. Preparing roles at home also saves time.

It certainly helps to check role preparations at the door and then give the students real consequences for not being prepared, including not getting credit, sitting outside the groups, or not being permitted in the classroom until they have completed their role preparation. After I did this a few times in my classroom, everyone got the message and I didn't need to do it anymore. It's important to remember what we as teachers are up against when we institute reading circles. In trying to create a more active classroom, we are attempting nothing less than a change in educational culture. Thus we should hardly be surprised if a number of students are resistant to reading circles in the beginning. Aside from its being a new and frightening thing to do, many students have had bad experiences with classroom discussions and collaborative activities. Although well-planned and well-executed collaboration can be wonderful for everyone involved, we all know how frustrating a sloppily planned and carried-out collaborative activity can be. Good collaboration takes the careful planning and monitoring of a skillful teacher.

Finally, a tip about student absences: a source of hesitation on the part of many teachers in using collaboration is their concern for the effects of absences on group cohesion. One way to deal with absences is to give credit (points) for participation in reading circles. Students can still get credit if they phone a circle member and ask that person to carry their role to the group. The person they call must be willing to jot down the role preparation of the absentee and discuss it over the phone in order to be able to relay it to the group effectively. So far, this has worked very well for me. To be sure, I can imagine situations where someone might abuse the privilege, but I think the other students would put a stop to this on their own; if not, I would intervene.

Judith Alford

MAPLEWOOD SCHOOL, CARY, IL

I started developing exploration circles as a way of giving my kids more choices in the classroom and improving their self-esteem. From the beginning of the year, my students had been making some choices about bulletin board displays, seating arrangements, and classroom tasks. By the time we got to choosing topics to study and books to read, a lot of their earlier insecurities, like constantly checking with me to see whether their choices were okay, had disappeared. I believe part of that "checking in" was testing me to see if I was really going to let them choose. It was not always easy to keep my fingers out, especially when the bulletin boards all turned black and stayed that way the whole year. But the kids loved it. I wanted other colors but stayed true to my promise that they could choose.

To allow for the greatest amount of freedom and student choice, I had worked out a special half-hour block of time in which groups of students could work on whatever they chose without formal curriculum restraints. This also gave me an opportunity to work with the children for part of the day without having to grade them. I renamed this activity exploration circles instead of literature circles. The students brainstormed topics they wished to know more about and then formed groups around their common interests. Mostly, I stayed out of their group formation process.

In this format, specific task responsibilities evolved out of the groups themselves. Kids decided on what materials to use, who would write, who was to gather pictures for the final project or presentation. We brainstormed a list of ways to handle the reading involved, including the group's assigning the pages or different kids reading different books on behalf of the group. During the process they set dates for completing readings, projects, or other tasks. They learned to adjust the dates according to their group members' progress and the progress of the rest of the class. Whole-class progress meetings were held every couple of days.

Three Cycles of Exploration Circles

We did three kinds of exploration circles, and each time students used a different method to choose their partners. During the first cycle the entire class brainstormed topics of interest. The topics were written down and photo-copied. Each student then prioritized five interesting topics by numbering from one to five, one being the most interesting. The students were grouped by their number-one choice. If there was no one else interested in a given topic, the student could change topics or choose to work alone. Only three students chose to work alone.

Another opportunity to change topics was provided if the group had difficulty finding information in our school learning center or the public library or could not find an expert who could supply them with additional information. Two boys, Timbo and Air J., decided to combine their topics of steam engines and diesel engines into a report on railroads. Students could also change their topic after one week if it turned out to be not so desirable or, in their words, "boring." After one week, they had to have arrived at a topic that they would stick with and ultimately present to the class.

One group of boys decided to find out about cars. They began cutting out and collecting over a hundred pictures of cars from magazines, newspapers, and calendars. They glued them into a huge, butcher-paper collage. This was going to be their finished project. When they went before the class, the students pressed them for what they had learned and why they did the collage. The class realized that this group had not done enough on their topic, and told them so.

Then the boys dug out some books about car engines and made a second poster about automobile engines. The boys decided they had made the collage because they liked the way the cars looked. During their conversation they decided to survey the rest of the class concerning their favorite cars. The boys then numbered each picture in the original collage with a permanent marker and developed a graph on butcher paper so the class could record their choices.

During their second presentation, the boys demonstrated they had learned that most of the class liked sports cars. They had also learned that constructing a graph based on a field of one hundred choices was not as easy as it looked, but they had been able to measure the paper and divide it to record the information. When the boys later wrote in their journals about their group's process, they mentioned they were glad I didn't tell them what they had to learn about cars and that I didn't yell at them about not working enough the first time around. They enjoyed making choices about their project and liked being treated as if they had a brain to make decisions.

Our second cycle of exploration circles was more like traditional literature circles. I provided some good novels for them to choose from. I ordered five copies of various paperbacks and did a brief book review about each. The books were *A Gathering of Days,* by Jean Blos, *Indian Chiefs,* by Russell Freeman, *Six Months to Live,* by Lurlene McDaniel, *Let the Circle Be Unbroken,* by Mildred Taylor, *Faithful Friend,* by Beatrice Siegel, and *The Sign of the Beaver,* by Elizabeth Speare. After I presented the book reviews, the students were given a ballot listing the names of the books. They numbered the selections from one to six according to preference. Group size was limited to five because I had only five copies of each book. All the students received either their first or second choice.

Groups decided how they would handle the reading. The choices were to read silently during class and at home the number of pages decided by the group; to read the book together in a group during class; or to appoint someone who would read the book to the group. While the group reading *Indian Chiefs* began reading the book together, the different reading abilities soon became a frustration to both the more able and the slower readers. Then they decided to assign pages, determine when the reading should be done, and then discuss the pages as a group. The rest of the groups decided from the beginning to assign pages and discuss the readings in class on a given date. Reading the pages independently appeared to be a good face-saving device for the less swift readers. Parents were encouraged to help with the reading process. The faster readers were able to read ahead and enjoy the book at their own pace, too.

In the third cycle, kids had an even more open choice. I invited students to brainstorm any kind of project they wished to do. The students discussed what they wanted to do, categorized the ideas into three options—free choice, having me read a book to the whole class, or working together in book-buddy teams—and then rated these options as their first, second, or third choice. The kids decided that "free choice" was what they wanted to do. (The few students who still wanted me to read to them were allowed the option of doing that while the rest of the class worked on their projects.)

Ice Man and Short Stuff chose to study humor. Blue Eyes, Heavenly Joy, and Boomer decided to do a play. The two groups then joined to do a humorous play. This group built their own sets, collected props, and rehearsed on their own time. Combining the two groups allowed them to have enough participants to enact the characters and pursue humor, too.

Several students chose to read another paperback and discuss it with a friend. It was exciting to see four students who at the beginning of the year had expressed hatred for reading choose this option. They selected books at their comfort level and asked my assistance only in gathering materials to complete their final project.

Looking Back on Exploration Circles

Problems: To prevent students from always choosing the same friends to work with, the topic selections and book selections were done by secret ballot, with no opportunity to discuss ideas at recess. I feel this is justified, since at other times of the day, kids have plenty of opportunities to work with their friends. (And sometimes I do select groups keeping in mind abilities, personalities, etc.)

Benefits: The greatest benefits are that the majority of students eagerly participate in group and class discussions, they are empowered by their choices, they stretch their learning beyond teacher expectations, they are excited about what they are doing, and the whole process gives room for individuals to be individuals. Kids love not only jigsawing what they are reading in literature circles, but sharing what they are reading for book reports or other projects. They love suggesting what the class might do next and suggesting books for the teacher and others to read.

Feelings: At first I had worries of, Am I doing a good job? What should a teacher do here? But once I realized it was okay for a student to say no to a suggestion from me, and once I started getting used to the feeling I wasn't needed, the students kept me more than busy. They wanted me to copy pages, gather materials, schedule learning center times, check out filmstrips, and read and respond to journal entries. I was simply a facilitator, offering open-ended questions to help students solve their own problems or find their own answers to their questions. I didn't want them to do it any other way.

Much like the writing process, literature/exploration circles are a process of moving from dependence to independence. But each class and year is different. It depends on the personalities of the children and teacher, the expectations, and the exposure to choice. It appeared the more choices I gave most students, the more willing they were to give others choices as well.

▼ ▼ ▼ ▼ ▼ ▼ ▼ ▼ ▼ ▼ ▼ ▼

14

Troubleshooting and Problem Solving

MOST OF THE time literature circles do work—honestly. Because they are based on the genuine and enduring literacy phenomenon called book clubs, they have an inherent integrity that usually helps them make the jump to classrooms successfully.

But this is school, and in school things don't always work the way we are promised in workshops and professional books. So in this chapter, I'll talk about all the things that can go wrong, the questions that teachers ask and the problems they share in workshops. The solutions offered here are mostly stolen from observations of other teachers, people who faced the same difficulties and worked out their own creative solutions to these common problems. But first, a gentle warning.

The most prevalent problem that teachers face as they try to implement literature circles is *patience*. In conversations and surveys, many teachers have confessed their tendency to worry, to expect too much too soon, to intervene prematurely, to rush in and take over, to lose faith in the kids and the process. So here's the most important caveat of all: wait. Don't panic. It will take hold in time. No educational change is ever instantaneous. Complex changes take even longer. If you really want to transfer responsibility and authority to your students, you are talking about a significant break with kids' past experience with school—and yours. Changes this large require some transition time, and you'd better be ready to live through it.

Indeed, when their patience starts to fail, truly progressive teachers—the real innovators—don't immediately complain about the kids. Instead, they start to question *themselves*. Not blame, mind you, but openly question. They wonder, Why am I so impatient? Am I getting itchy because, at heart, I really want to take over again? Maybe I miss being the center of attention and the source of control—presenting, telling, demanding, "really teaching."

Indeed, this "teacher ego problem" may be the unseen iceberg that has sunk thousands of instructional innovations. Many of us originally chose teaching as a career partly because of our need for personal display, for performing, for being the star of the show. So when we experiment with activities, like lit circles, that *take the teacher off stage,* we may feel deep ambivalence. Sometimes, if our own ego is not being satisfied, we may start finding reasons why a given student-centered innovation is "unworkable" or "unsuccessful" and needs to be dropped in favor of our return to center stage. As teachers, all we can do is be vigilant and self-critical, and steer around the ego iceberg. As far as literature circles are concerned, it is key to their success that teachers not dominate the process or the groups. The teacher must find personal gratification in the creation, facilitation, and support of the student-run discussions.

A Typology of Common Problems

Before we look at a couple dozen specific problems and solutions, I want to offer a "big picture" view of the things that commonly go wrong in book clubs. After watching literature circles develop for more than a decade, I've identified five main types of struggling groups, along with their symptoms.

Off-task: The group strays far from the book, digresses a lot, is easily distracted.

Shallow: Conversation is superficial, fact-oriented, and stays at lower levels of thinking.

Mechanical: Members take turns rigidly, offering minimal contributions, then bow out. There's no give-and-take, no interaction. They often become an off-task group after a few minutes.

Flagging: Group starts with a burst but quickly runs out of topics, becomes quiet and sluggish, or veers off-task.

Asymmetrical: Group has unequal distribution of responsibility, ideas, and airtime. One or two kids may dominate, do all the work; others contribute little or nothing.

Obviously, these problems can be either mild or severe, and we don't expect perfection from students in school any more than we do from adults in their living room book clubs. Slight cases of group dysfunction don't stop people from having worthwhile and useful conversations.

However, severe cases of off-taskness or shallowness can stop lit circles in their tracks. While the above symptoms may seem quite varied, their origins and solutions may not be as different as you might expect. When I observe any of these dysfunctional groups, I tend to mentally review a list of possible causes that looks like this:

1. poor book choice
2. failure to do the reading/prepare notes

3. regular reading residue
4. incomplete training
5. role sheet overdose
6. skillification
7. assessment intrusion
8. personal or culture problems

The first problem to suspect when groups go wrong is crummy books. I have seen this a million times. If the books aren't worth reading or talking about, kids will fill the motivational void with one or all of the patterns above, and it won't be any fun for the teacher when they do. Now, "crummy books" can mean a number of different things. It can be a literally meritless book, devoid of interest, like some of the synthetic products issued by quick-buck, third-tier publishers. It's always a red flag when a book lists no author on the cover or title page; you know it was probably written by a low-paid staffer in a dank basal basement. A crummy book can also be one that is forced on you, that's way too hard, that's dull and boring, that you chose by mistake and feel stuck with.

The good news is that "crummy books" is a totally solvable problem; change the books and this alone may heal the groups. I remember visiting one third-grade classroom in Cleveland where I saw the most spectacularly unsuccessful assortment of lit circles ever; the classroom was a veritable museum of how-not-to-do-it book clubs. At the time, the kids were reading from a box of fake books from some old activity kit. A month later, I returned to see the very same kids in the same groups totally engaged in powerful peer-led discussions of *Charlotte's Web*. Well, duh!

Once we make sure that the books are worthy, we need to check whether the kids have actually read them. Have they read the chapters selected for each day's meeting, and have they made entries in their journals to support and feed the group meeting when it happens? If most or all of the kids aren't prepared, the chances of a sparkling literary discussion are remote. This is a teacher management challenge; if the work isn't getting done, teachers need to delve into their repertoire of management tools to ensure that kids get ready.

All of the reading instruction that your students received during the years before they landed in your class will also affect how they operate in literature circles. If most of their past reading lessons (and all the high-stakes tests they took) stressed factual recall, you shouldn't be surprised when kids come to literature circles with questions like, What color was Molly's sweater in Chapter 2? If your students' prior reading lessons ignored personal connections, paying attention to craft and style, or questioning an author, why would they know how to think about text in these ways?

So, what we do about residue? This is not quite as simple as switching from crummy books to better books. Helping kids move beyond narrow reading habits is a project of many steps, over weeks and months. It is a bit like deprogramming a cult member. You have to be explicit about the problems with the old ways and the opportunities of the new ones. Every time you read a story aloud or talk about a book, you will demonstrate other ways to operate, new tacks to try, new angles into books and conversation. You will have to send a thousand consistent messages, showing kids how to visualize, question, connect, analyze, judge, and compare. Then, as they tentatively stretch out, you'll welcome and extend their initial attempts. None of this means that lit circles must wait until kids are "rehabbed." Indeed, joining in a literature circle can be part of the solution for readers with narrow backgrounds. What a great structure within which to practice thinking like a real reader.

Crummy books, lack of preparation, and reading residue can all undermine group functioning. But still, the most common cause of dysfunctional group behavior is simply incomplete training. Somehow the kids still don't yet command the repertoire of social skills and thinking skills that are needed to make peer-led discussion groups work. Maybe they plunged into literature circles too fast, maybe something was skipped in the initial training, maybe a given class needed more or different preparation than the teacher realized. All I'm saying is that if kids don't yet know how to do lit circles right, it is because we haven't yet shown them everything they need.

But as I have said throughout the book, lit circle training is never really over. After the initial intensive training, we continue to use the mini-lessons that start each meeting and the sharing sessions that follow them as occasions for ongoing or maintenance training. With any of the problem patterns, we can develop lessons that address them as kids continue along in their groups. If group problems are severe, we may have to jump back to intensive training, take out some short stories, and spend a few days on some make-up training.

The next few causes of group struggles are rare. Mechanical or flagging groups sometimes result from excessive use of role sheets or other structured tools, anything that looks like a worksheet. These devices seem to inherently encourage members to take one turn, do the minimum, and sit back. When this happens, we need to switch to more open-ended response harvesting tools, like Post-it notes or response logs.

Other off-track group behavior can result when well-meaning teachers try to "infuse" some required curriculum content into lit circle meetings. If we ask kids to "make a list of metaphors" from their lit circle book, we may think we are killing two birds with one stone, covering some mandated concepts and supporting book clubs all at once. But what we may be killing is the discussion. Since the whole idea of lit circles is for kids to develop their own discussions, no matter how imperfectly, we throw in skill lessons at our peril. There are plenty of other times of the day when we can teach metaphors, semicolons, and prefixes. If we undermine the unique autonomy and respon-

create in their lit circles. They may need more training, using one of the models in Chapter 5. Take a look at the way Barbara Dress teaches kids about "fat" versus "skinny" questions on page 72. Or put your strongest group into a fishbowl, to demonstrate good conversation for the rest. Or read a story together as a whole group, asking everyone to think up three fat, juicy, open-ended questions for discussion. Then use the kids' own strongest questions to demonstrate what kind of prompts spark natural conversation about literature.

On the other hand, mechanical conversations could mean that the kids have been using role sheets for too long and it is time to move to open-ended reading logs or Post-it notes, along the lines described on pages 56 and 58. When groups are listless, we also have to ask, Are kids reading books they have freely chosen? Are they meeting in groups they have freely entered? If kids are passive, dependent, and uncreative, it is sometimes because they are feeling *controlled* and are therefore being submissive. Maybe we teachers are hovering a little too close and need to back off.

4. What do I do about kids who are uninterested or unmotivated, or who misbehave in literature circles?

Well, what would you do if you told your class, Please take out your science books, and one child absolutely refused to do it? Which is to say, your repertoire of strategies for dealing with misbehavior or inattention in literature circles is *exactly the same* as it is for any other instructional technique you might choose to employ. You have conferences with them, write them notes, talk to the parents—whatever it takes to get the kid working effectively.

After all, in order to have a productive classroom, all teachers must find ways of enforcing their own standards of engagement. And while they operate with empathy and sensitivity, committed teachers do enforce those standards. Just as it is *not okay* by most of our standards for a kid continually to refuse to do any science, it is similarly *not okay* for him to misbehave in or undermine his literature circle.

On a brighter note, I find that lit circles are often the *answer,* not the problem, for kids who are disaffected, marginalized, or unsuccessful in school. This structure offers a chance to be active, to do something, to make some choices, to interact with peers, to get some positive attention. While the transition to literature circles may be especially bumpy for kids on the margins, the final payoff is often greatest for them.

5. How do you handle kids with special needs in literature circles?

Literature circles are one of the most powerful structures for making heterogeneous grouping work and also one of the very best opportunities for kids who are different to really shine. Including students who are at developmentally lower levels or who have designated special needs should not present any problem in real literature circles—in fact, it's a plus. The varied experiences and perspectives brought to book discussions by kids of different backgrounds are *assets*.

When lit circles are working well, kids pick books—and work in discussion groups—that are roughly at their own level. However, the possibility to move up or down the scale of difficulty, work with different kids, see other skills and interests modeled, is always there. And because the teacher isn't making whole-class presentations, she is available to help.

Most kids who are labeled as learning disabled or special ed are actually able to do just fine with higher-order thinking—for many, it is the lower-order operations (like decoding text on a page) that gives them trouble in school. If these kids can just get the book or the story into their heads, then they have tons to say, as much as anybody, about feelings, events, values, ideas, conflict, people. So when special education students select books for their literature circles that are simply too hard for them to plow through fluently, teachers provide help. They make sure that someone—an aide, parent, peer, or consulting special education teacher—is available to read the book aloud or that the book is available on audiotape in the classroom.

Many of the most popular kids books are now available on audiocassettes. For those titles that aren't sold commercially, homemade solutions are required. Smart teachers use student teachers, parent volunteers, and other captive labor to record tapes of missing titles. Just as building a classroom library is the work of a career, the same goes for books on tape. If you are going to have a literature-rich program that invites higher-order thinking, you must make accommodations for kids with special needs. When teachers provide these kinds of assistance, they ensure that *all* kids get to experience the essence of literature circles, which is not decoding but discussing the ideas in and around books.

6. Won't the top children be shortchanged in literature circles?

"Gifted and talented" kids are an important part of a rich literature circle mix. On a day-to-day basis, since free choice of books is a hallmark of LCs, these kids will probably be reading thick, challenging books and discussing them in the company of some other "gifted children." But if the circles are really working right, the groups won't be segregated; they'll often shift, and the partners won't always be other certified "giftees." Instead, some group members will be other sorts of kids—either because those kids have "picked up" to a harder book or because the gifted child has "picked down" to an easier book.

When this happens, literature circles are serving gifted kids very well. Often, children in this category have one or two highly developed areas of excellence—art, music, language, or math. But they may be greatly lacking in the street smarts, physical awareness, cultural knowledge, people sense, or emotional maturity that some other, so-called low-level kids enjoy. Truly, when the subject is literature and the task is discussion, diversity is a benefit to everyone.

By the way, if "gifted parents" are your real concern, here's a rejoinder that seems to elicit their support for literature circles: Well, would you rather have us go back to the old way, where the whole class reads the same book, pitched at the average readers in the group?

7. What about shy kids who don't like group activities?

Literature circles should be one of the solutions—not another problem—for quiet children. This structure offers shy kids a chance to speak up and be heard, not in the scary arena of the whole class, but in a three- to five-member group whose friendship, we hope, feels more solid and safe as days go by. The informality, the predictable structure, the low-stress atmosphere, the absence of right-answer pressure, and the welcoming of differences—all these features of lit circles help to encourage risk taking by kids who are tentative.

Always, of course, teachers must balance the potential of an activity like literature circles to "bring out" a shy kid with that child's right to be shy. They may reflect on their own experience in adult reading groups, where a very wide range of involvement is accepted, and people who rarely say anything may be considered members in good standing. If viewed as a learning-style issue, perhaps shyness shouldn't be "treated" or "overcome," but simply respected and accommodated. Thus, some caring teachers may decide, after giving literature circles every opportunity to invite a shy child in, that it's okay for one or two such kids to pursue their independent reading alone or in pairs, while most others work in groups. This is one of the toughest, sometimes heart-wrenching choices that professional teachers make.

8. What do I do about students who come to their circles unprepared?

This question comes up a lot. It seems that whenever we teachers consider implementing literature circles (or any other classroom innovation) our minds always seem to jump right to the kids who might *not* do well, instead of the ones who'll pitch right in. We overlook the twenty-three kids who will do the work cheerfully—and immediately start visualizing the troubles of the three who won't get it or who might cause problems. This kind of half-empty thinking seems to be imprinted on our teacherly DNA, and sometimes it blocks us from thinking realistically about change. If we find a classroom activity that quickly engages 80 or 90 percent of the kids, this is a triumph! We should have a parade, not moan about the handful that aren't on the bandwagon yet.

So, yeah, there will always be kids who don't do the reading or finish their lit logs. There will also be kids who skip their math homework, blow off the quiz, and talk during your lectures. What we need in all these instances is a firm and direct policy. In the case of literature circles, we can say this: Your book club offers a lot of freedom, choice, and creativity, but it is also a serious school assignment. It is a real loss for you to neglect your reading or your notes for literature circle meetings. It is also a disservice to your group, which depends for its success on the participation of every member.

If the reluctant or unmotivated students are highly grade-oriented, some teachers will set up a point system in the early days of literature circles. Typically, they'll give kids ten points for arriving prepared for each lit circle meeting, meaning they've read the assignment and have their reading log filled out. This approach works best when the points are over and above regular class work—free or bonus points—and awarded strictly on a checkoff, all-or-nothing basis. You don't want to be arguing with a kid about what's a seven and what's a six while you are trying to get literature circles to work. Whatever point system is devised, it's best to phase it out just as soon as students will read for the pleasure of the literature and the conversations.

In practice, the peer pressure within groups often takes care of the sloth problem. Many teachers have testified that once the circles are established and valued, kids vigorously police each other. As teacher Kristen Overcash reports, "They're kind and thoughtful unless someone comes to the circle unprepared—in which case they're harder on one another than I ever am on them."

9. What about the kid who reads ahead in the book, and then spoils the ending for everyone in his group?

This sure is annoying. That's why you need clear and explicit rules about reading ahead. Of course, we would never want to discourage a kid from getting hooked on a book, maybe staying up half the night to get to the end. That's a priceless literary experience that no young reader should miss. But it is the talking, not the reading, that is the problem. So teachers make it clear: *you can read ahead but you can't talk ahead.* This lit circle problem is a perfect topic for a collaborative mini-lesson. You ask the class, "What can you do if you have read ahead in the book and you want to be sure not to blab the ending to the other members? Let's make a list of strategies."

One kid suggests, "Put a rubber band around the part of the book that you have read extra. That will remind you not to talk past that point in the story."

"Good idea, really tangible and concrete. What else?"

"Before the meeting starts, flip through the book and be sure you remember how far the group has read for today, and what happens up to there."

"Another good one. Let's put these strategies on the wall, and we will refer to them as the issue arises. Okay? Off to your groups."

10. Can a group abandon a book if they are not enjoying it?

Different teachers have different answers to this one. Some feel that sticking with a disappointing book is a realistic, character-building experience. They argue that real reading groups sometimes pick turkeys and everyone still reads the thing—then they all come to the meeting and dump on it a month later.

These teachers also argue that you can have just as full and lively a conversation about a bad book as a good one. When did it lose you? What was wrong with this character? Why did this language ring false? People can support their opinions with sections of text just as well when panning a book as they can in praising it.

Other teachers differ. They point out that discriminating grown-up readers dump books all the time—life is too short to read worthless books. They don't want kids to suffer through bad choices, so they allow them to swap a loser for another title. The stipulation, of course, is that the group has to catch up with everyone else and meet the classwide ending date. No one is cutting any corners here; you can dump a book, but you can't quit reading altogether. In fact, the kids who re-choose are actually reading more than the other groups, when you add the false start to the whole replacement.

11. What about kids who dominate their group?

This is a perfect topic for an opening mini-lesson or a conversation during a sharing session. You know the drill by now, right? You start by saying, "I have been noticing that in some groups one person does a lot of the talking. What steps could we tale to make sure that everyone participates more equally?" List and enforce the results. Rinse and repeat.

Nancy Steineke has a nice idea that shuts up dominators without singling them out as culprits and that is a wholesome exercise for the whole class. At the start of a lit circle meeting, she'll give a mini-lesson on distributing the conversation among everyone in the group, not relying on a few people too much or drowning out the quieter voices. Then she gives every kid five poker chips, each good for one conversational entry in the group. Once your chips are gone, you're done for the day. Now the groups have to survive on balanced participation. Most of the dominators, given their personalities, use up their chips right away and have to sit and listen to others for the first time in a while.

12. What do you do when students are absent from a group? when they return?

Sandy King has a nice way of handling missing members of literature circles in her third-grade classroom. She has a menagerie of jumbo stuffed animals, and she puts one in the seat of any absent child. On many a day, Paddington Bear has served as passage master or word wizard for a group! Sandy's message to the children, of course, is, You can do just fine with the members who are left.

One of the reasons we usually put five kids in a lit circle is that we know one of those five will be absent on any given day, and we believe that four (or even three) is still plenty of people for a good book-talk. As long as the remaining members have done the reading and brought some notes, some questions, some topics for discussion, the group can proceed just fine. After all, in many fully enrolled groups of five or more it still only takes one "hot topic" to launch a stimulating conversation and keep it going.

For the student who misses a session, literature circles are a relatively easy assignment to make up. Obviously, the child has to catch up on the reading, and should do the missing journals or notes, turning them in to the group or teacher, as appropriate. When the absent kid returns, it is a valuable exercise— for everyone—for the group to offer the returning member a summary of the missed discussions; students may refer to the previous day's logs to cue their memory about this.

13. What happens when kids pick books that are too hard for them? too easy? Does the teacher continue to let kids make bad choices?

Literature circles are designed to be essentially self-leveling, with kids picking books that seem both interesting and readable to them. Sometimes students do pick books that are too hard, often in an attempt to place themselves into a certain circle of kids regardless of their own real reading tastes or abilities. This becomes the subject of one-to-one conversation and guidance. The teacher may need to have the student try reading a bit of the chosen book in a conference, which will probably make any comprehension problems very plain. After this kind of conference, the two can talk about selecting another, more accessible book—perhaps in the same genre.

But there's a fine line between helping kids avoid a too-hard book and encouraging well-calculated risk taking. After all, kids in literature circles should feel free to try a challenging book, too. So when a kid does pick a book that's above his fluency level, but doable, the teacher may endorse the choice and provide help. This may mean having an aide, peer helper, or parent read all or parts of the book aloud—or getting the book on tape so the student can listen to it as he reads. With this assistance, the kid can get enough of the story to be a valuable member of later literature circle conversations.

Students in lit circle classrooms do sometimes get into below-level reading "ruts," selecting, say, one Babysitters' Club title after another. This phenomenon tends to co-occur with the problem in Question 14 below—groups that don't reshuffle often. When this syndrome occurs, teachers start by asking themselves, Well, haven't *I* ever gotten stuck on one genre of "beach books" or one author—reading a whole string of mysteries or gothic romances in a row? Readers do enjoy plateauing with a beloved genre—indeed, that's often what we mean by "pleasure reading."

If a teacher is still concerned, she can use a variety of strategies to give the kid a nudge. She can write a dialogue journal note to the stuck student, suggesting other titles. She can conduct a book selection conference, giving the student a quick, tantalizing summary of four or five non–Babysitters' Club titles.

If the teacher has set up a classroom evaluation system that gives points for range, breadth, or risk taking in reading, a reminder of this fact might be a nice bit of iron-fist-in-a-velvet-glove guidance.

14. Every time we select new books, my kids always end up in the same group with the same friends—how can I ensure some mixing?

The reason for this might simply be that your groups are finishing at different times and there are no others available to re-form with. That's one reason why many successful lit circle teachers establish *ending dates* for each cycle, meaning that all groups commit to finishing their books on the same day, which in turn guarantees that everyone will be available when new groups get formed. If your kids still act clannish when they have the whole classroom to choose from, the first recourse is to talk about this problem with them openly, reminding them that one of the best features of lit circles is variety, in both books and discussion partners.

If reasoning doesn't work, blind voting probably will. Next time kids finish a cycle and it's time to pick new books, have them turn in a prioritized ballot of three or four choices for their next book. In order to ensure this will work, you should do this unannounced, so kids don't have a chance to conspire on the playground to pick the same book/group again. Then you can take the lists and compose the groups privately, with reshuffling a high priority. Who knows? You might give a kid their third or fourth choice for the sole reason of forming a new, promising group. That's some real *facilitation*.

But before we get too smug about this forced socialization, we should use the living-room test again. What happens in real adult book clubs? Do we change members after every book? Are you kidding? Hey, we have been the same eight people meeting every month for ten years. If someone proposed adding a new member it would probably spark a huge debate over "changing the dynamics of the group." Obviously grown-up reading groups are rooted in the idea that much is gained when book clubs stay together for a while. Indeed, many of our Chicago teachers are experimenting with stay-togther groups, especially during the second semester. The idea is to mingle everyone through a series of different groups early in the year, so kids get to know a host of other readers, their styles or preoccupations. Then we invite kids to find a few reading soul mates, and then let those groups work together through several books in the winter and spring.

15. What if kids pick a book I haven't read?

Great! There's much to be learned when a child is reading a book *we* don't know. Then we can honestly and congruently ask, What's it about? Why did she do that? What do you think will happen next? In fact, many teachers find that when they haven't read a book, they can be more probing with kids.

It works the other way around, too. If the teacher decides to read the book and join a group as a fellow reader, she can do some wonderful teaching. After all, as Robert Probst (1988) reminds us, one of the best experiences kids can have is seeing a teacher read a book for the very first time, enjoying a close-up demonstration of how a mature reader makes predictions, constructs meaning, and connects with a book. It's important that book recommendations flow *both ways* in the classroom—that teachers get turned on to books by students, just as much as they recommend their favorites to the kids. If you are worried about the appropriateness of kids' book choices, see the next item.

16. What about books with questionable content—ones with sex, violence, racism, or rough language?

Some of the very best books for young people violate the taste of grown-ups and make us worry. Steven Chbosky's *The Perks of Being a Wallflower* is chock-full of sex, drugs, violence, and bad words—and it is also one of the sweetest, most insightful young adult books in recent years. Kids *need* to read this book and ones like it. But what about the real concerns of parents about such subject matter?

Some of our literature circle network teachers have solved this problem skillfully. When kids pick books for a new round of LCs, they send home a simple permission letter with a copy of the book saying, "Your child has selected this book to read in a literature circle beginning next week. You may want to read it also. Please let me know if you have any comments." There's a place for the parent to sign off that they have reviewed the book. Once parents have said okay, teachers and kids are free to proceed. If the parent objects, the kid picks another book.

Sometimes teachers themselves are disturbed by the book choices kids make, even with the informed approval of their parents. Some object to the graphic horror of Stephen King, the formulaic repetition of the Hardy Boys, the degrading female stereotypes in the Babysitters' Club books. When it is the teacher's turn to assign books to the whole class—which most of us still do during other parts of the school day—then we are free to demonstrate our literary standards and, ideally, to explain them. But the purpose of literature circles is to build fluency and a love of reading by choosing one's own books—and that right should not be gratuitously abridged by the tastes of others, even the teacher. That means we bite our tongue and let kids choose.

17. What about all the noise literature circles seem to create?

One anonymous sixth-grade teacher had a great answer to this question: "Noise! The voices of excited kids carry very far. They do get excited. I *want* them to be excited!" And she's right. Noise is almost a barometer of kids' engagement in literature circles: if it's loud, it's probably working.

Noise is really only a problem if one of three conditions exists: (1) The kids can't hear one another well enough to work. (2) The teacher is going crazy. (3) People outside the classroom, like other teachers in the corridor or the principal, are annoyed. All three problems need to be solved, and all have the same solution: "the twelve-inch voice." Here's how our colleague Barbara Dress solves this problem. She tells kids that they have been using their "ten-foot (or three-mile!) voices" and need to grow a "twelve-inch voice." She has them practice adjusting their volume so they are inaudible from the next literature circle. She even has intermediate-grade kids kneel on their desk chairs so their faces are brought together and they do literally talk at a one-foot distance and keep their voices down. In Sandy King's room, where Barbara trained the students, the official command that now starts literature circles is "Butts Up!"—for obvious reasons. In Nancy Steineke's high school classroom, the first order of the day is for literature circle groups to assemble with their desks touching, a physical reminder of the closeness of the group and the need for short-range voices.

18. How can I get more skills instruction into my literature circles?

Literature circles *do* teach reading skills. They teach about the nature of different genres, about authors' ways with words, about how characters reveal themselves, and a thousand other valuable "skills." Every time a literature circle meets, multiple skills are being practiced, reinforced, or strengthened. However, these skills are being learned *inductively*, through practice and use, not *explicitly*, through teacher presentation. And the particular skills addressed will be different for every child every day, and the *sequence will be completely unpredictable.*

To do literature circles is to affirm a belief in incidental learning, in learning by doing, in scaffolded interaction. That's why teachers set aside this one special time of day for kids to just read and just talk, running their own learning. Teachers still control the rest of the day's schedule, and they can conduct skill lessons then. What most teachers find, though, is that the learning from real reading and talking feels more powerful than from teacher-directed instruction, and they reallocate more and more time away from teacher presentations and into literature circles, workshops, and other student-directed structures.

19. Can I use literature circles to teach a single required book? or sets of required books or readings? How about required nonfiction materials in content areas? Can I use circles to teach my integrated, thematic units?

Of course. Since we've already repeatedly had our say about the importance of student choice, we won't reiterate it here. As long as kids' school experience is well balanced and they are having plenty of student-directed time elsewhere in their day, in other structures like workshops or journals or negotiated-inquiry projects, then it's fine to harness literature circles to a bit of prescribed curriculum. That's exactly what Sharon Weiner is doing in Chapter 10.

If the choice is between studying a book in literature circles or in a whole-class lecture-discussion, then literature circles may offer more engaging format. They allow for active participation by everyone at once, rather than the laborious turn taking and passive turn waiting of the large-group approach. The small-group format also invites kids' real questions into the mix and safeguards against teacher domination of all conversations. Indeed, once teachers have tried using the "basic" literature circles model—where kids pick their own books—they often prefer to use this structure, rather than the older, teacher-centered approaches, for *all* literature study. This is how the influence of literature circles begins to reach out across the entire school program, transforming everything—giving students more voice and more choice all day long.

Literature circles can also be used to teach required authors, genres, or other sets of texts. Curriculum guides don't always prescribe the exact books to be read; sometimes they just want certain types of materials to be covered. So if your kids are mandated to read, for example, a Shakespeare play, a book on insects, a Roald Dahl novel, a Hemingway story, a research report on nuclear energy, or a canto of *Paradise Lost,* you can offer them several of each to choose from. Then, you can use the lit circle roles and structures to facilitate a more student-centered discussion.

This procedure, which brings a degree of student choice and voice even to very official school activities, is closely akin to the structure called "text sets" and is especially attractive to teachers of science, social studies, and other "content-area" fields. Rather than requiring, for example, that each student in a history class read superficially through the accounts of all Civil War battles, kids can join literature circles that pick just one battle from a "text set" of battle accounts to read and discuss. Later, the groups can connect in a wider discussion, jigsawing their articles and looking for similarities and differences in the individual battles.

20. Can you have literature circles where each member reads something different, instead of everyone reading the same text?

This is exactly how a lot of primary grade teachers operate their literature circles as a matter of routine (see Chapter 8). It's also a variant of the strategy of "text sets" we just looked at above. When each member of a small discussion group has read something different, the discussion procedures obviously need to be adjusted. Each member has to identify and summarize his or her reading first, and perhaps answer any questions, before wider sharing and comparing can go on. When such heterogeneous groups meet to discuss the reading of individually selected literature, it typically becomes a sharing and "advertising" session, in which kids savor or pan books they have read and answer questions from their peers. Such meetings don't do much to support reading in process (nor to question or push anyone's thinking), and so they usually happen only after books are completed.

Heterogeneous literature circles seem to work better when they are based on some kind of theme—related by topic, genre, author, or some other point of similarity. Then each group member has more to do than wait her or his turn. If we are all reading mysteries, then there are genuinely common features and overlaps to be listened for, noted, and explored, and the conversation can become cumulative. The nonfiction and jigsaw role sheets on pages 204 and 205 are designed to help orchestrate just these kinds of heterogeneous literature circle meetings.

21. I feel uncomfortable evaluating my kids' literature circles—it seems so subjective. What should I do?

This reminds me of Marianne Flanagan, the fifth-grade teacher we visited earlier in the book. When she first started lit circles, Marianne was worried about assessment, too. Periodically, she would resolve to do some evaluation, to get around to each group, to take some notes, and to write up kids' participation. But then what usually happened was that she would sit down in the first group, immediately get drawn into the conversation, and become so involved with the kids and the ideas at hand that the whole period flew by. Marianne didn't even get to another group, much less evaluate anyone.

Of course, what happened was far more valuable. Marianne has given an authentic, heartful, extended demonstration of adult reading and thinking to the kids in one group. In other words, she has been *teaching*. But also, if you ask her later about the individual kids in that group, she can talk in elaborate detail about how everyone is doing, what chapter they're on, what they think of the book, what they've read before, what kids they work with best, what kinds of questions interest them, and all the rest. So she *is* assessing children all the time, *using teacher observation and judgment*—but she evaluates not as an outside judge but as a side-by-side participant-observer. Most of Marianne's evaluation activities are not definably separate from her teaching—and her teaching is always, in part, evaluative.

If Marianne or any other teacher wants or needs to take the final step, making the outcomes of this kind of teacher observation visible and official, she can implement a few of the evaluation strategies outlined in Chapter 13.

22. My principal doesn't believe in progressive activities like literature circles, reading workshop, or writing workshop. I need ammunition to prove that these are worth the time and will raise test scores.

Literature circles and other collaborative, workshop-style approaches to literacy instruction do work, and their effectiveness has been documented in sixty years of quantitative and qualitative research. My colleagues at the Center for City Schools and I prepared two summaries of this research, which appeared in the October 1999 *Educational Leadership* and the March 1999 *Phi Delta Kappan*. On pages 7–9 of this book, I cited a host of studies pointing to the effectiveness of literature circles in particular. Appendix B offers more detail from the Chicago study highlighted there.

More broadly, you should draw your administrators' attention to the urgently important body of research being done by Fred Newmann (2001) and his colleagues at the University of Michigan. Their work shows that classroom activities that are highly authentic—meaning that they require deep engagement, involve extended conversations, and make explicit connections to kids' real lives—*raise standardized test scores,* including those in troubled urban schools.

I certainly hope that this book has helped you start and shape student-led book clubs in your classroom. If you have more questions about literature circles (and who doesn't?) please join our ongoing conversation on the web at **www.literaturecircles.com**. On this website, teachers from around the world exchange ideas, variations, materials, and tools with one another; we tell classroom stories about our kids' book clubs; and we hold each other's hands electronically as we experiment and grow as professionals. See you there!

Literature Circle Workshops for Teachers and Parents

Teacher/Parent Workshop 1—A Half Day with a Short Story

The following plan will look familiar, because it is similar to the one used for training high school kids in Chapter 5. If you want to begin by reading a whole book instead of a short story, skip ahead to the second workshop.

1. Read a good short-short story, something one or two pages long. Sandra Cisneros has many such stories in her collections *The House on Mango Street* and *Woman Hollering Creek*. In Chapter 5, I recommended *Microfiction,* by Jerome Stern. This volume is an especially good source of nasty, zippy little stories that make a nice respite from the usual bland workshop fare. First read the story silently and then, in groups of four or five, join in open-ended discussion for about ten minutes. Simply invite people to talk freely about wherever the story took them.

2. Stop the group meetings, and ask each circle to share one thread or sample of their conversation: something that got discussion going, generated some feeling, sparked a disagreement, or otherwise got people engaged. (In this step, we are honoring the literature first, before we start analyzing the discussion process—a vital element in all literature circles training, for kids or grown-ups).

3. Now, stop and ask everyone to reflect back on the short group meeting, looking for two things. What *social skills* were used to make this discussion work? And what *thinking skills* were used to comprehend the story and talk about it? Have each group reflect back on their brief meeting, making a list of ingredients they noticed, perhaps by dividing a sheet of paper in half and listing "social skills" on one side and "thinking skills" on the other.

4. Now create a whole-group list by inviting people to contribute items from their small-group lists. Do social skills first; digging out the

thinking skills is usually a bit harder, since these are generally deeper and more implicit. Here are lists of social skills and thinking skills developed by a group of teachers in a recent workshop:

Social Skills	Thinking Skills
take turns	make connections with personal experience, current events, other books, authors, other stories, artworks
listen actively	
make eye contact	
lean forward	
nod, confirm, respond	make pictures in your head
share airtime	visualize the scene, people, events
include everybody	
don't dominate	put yourself into the story
pull other people in	reread to clarify
don't interrupt	check and confirm facts
speak directly to each other	savor the story, language, events
receive others' ideas	question the author, characters, text
be tolerant	
honor people's "burning issues"	analyze, interpret
piggyback on ideas of others	make inferences
speak up when you disagree	draw conclusions
respect differences	make judgments
disagree constructively	evaluate the book, author, characters
don't attack	
stay focused, on task	attend to author craft and style
support your views with the book	notice words and language
	read passages aloud
trust each other	look for patterns
be responsible to the group	draw/illustrate/map sections of text

5. As you look at the lists you have created, the big point should be clear. A lot of deep and relatively sophisticated social and thinking skills go into the making of a successful peer-led book club! This means that in the classroom, we must either teach these skills to students or provide structures that supply them—or perhaps do a mixture of both. In one sense that's what literature circles training really consists of: creating an environment that optimizes kids' socializing and thinking and helps them gradually acquire more skills in both domains.

6. Discuss how these discussing and reading skills could be developed among your own students. What do they already know how to do? What skills need to be added?

7. Have everyone read Chapters 1–3 of this book, to provide a basic description and definition of the strategy, illustrated with classroom stories at several grade levels.

8. Have participants discuss their own experiences with literature circles or reading discussion groups in their classrooms. If they have already tried some form of literature circles, what is going well? What needs work? What do they still have questions about when it comes to fostering good talk about books in their classroom? If they haven't yet tried book clubs, what problems can they foresee cropping up among their own students?

9. If you own a copy of the companion videotape *Looking into Literature Circles,* watch and discuss it. The tape is only fifteen minutes long and is suitable for multiple viewings in a short period of time. You may want to begin by viewing the tape once with the group straight through for enjoyment, asking for general impressions of the literature circles at the end.

10. After a brief discussion of the first viewing of the tape, focus on specific skill development with a second viewing. Ask participants, while viewing the tape, to keep a double-entry journal with two columns, one for social skills, the other for thinking skills. As they watch the three different age levels of literature circles in action, have them keep a list of the social skills and thinking skills being developed by participants. One group of teachers came up with the following list after studying the video:

Social skills shown in the video
- taking turns
- building on the ideas of others
- drawing others into the discussion
- being prepared with questions and topics
- being comfortable with pauses and silence
- taking personal risks
- being respectful of differences in the group

Thinking skills used in the video
- clarifying facts
- asking questions
- connecting to personal experience
- speculating
- analyzing
- visualizing (drawing)
- questioning

Teacher/Parent Workshop 2—A Novel in Two Meetings

This workshop/demonstration uses the Newbery Medal novel *Maniac Magee,* by Jerry Spinelli. You can do the same workshop with another book; just be sure to find one with a really good first chapter for reading aloud. As befits a group of adults, this workshop is designed to plunge people pretty quickly into literature circles using simple reading response logs, just as we might do with a classroom of children. The workshop is presented in the form of directions for the group facilitator:

Session One

1. *Read aloud.* Read the prologue, "Before the Story," from *Maniac Magee.* (With a different book, this could be the first chapter, the introduction, or some involving sample of the text.)
2. *Respond.* Invite pairs of participants to talk for two minutes about any reactions or responses they had to this read-aloud. Stress open, personal response.
3. *Share.* Ask a few people to share a highlight or thread of their conversation.
4. *Explain.* Briefly talk about the concept of LCs: mention that they meld a reader response approach with collaborative learning.
5. *Form groups.* Divide the participants into groups of four or five each and make sure everyone knows what group they're in.
6. *Introduce response logs.* Define response logs, reminding people of the many ways that skillful readers think: connecting, predicting, questioning, analyzing, visualizing, etc.
7. *Give assignment.* "Read the book before our next meeting and jot some responses in your log, either while you are reading along or after you finish the book. If you prefer, you can put your responses on Post-it notes, put right on the pages where the ideas occurred. We'll see you next time."

Session Two (at least a few days later)

8. *Explain.* Immediately after greeting groups, send them off to meet. Invite them to simply have a *natural conversation* about the book, wherever the story took them. They may use their response log entries however they help—or not at all. Announce the time available.
9. *Groups meet* (about 15–20 minutes). Visit the groups, gently and unobtrusively, to note how people are working and to provide help if needed. Try to remember some memorable comments from each group to help prompt the debriefing process, coming up.
10. *Reassemble the whole group and talk literature.* This is the most important step in getting teachers excited about literature circles. Invite each group to share one thread of their conversation, a point of agreement or disagreement, something that got a strong response,

something they spent some time on. Elicit one such topic from every group before moving to the next stage. This will probably stimulate good cross-talk and varying interpretations—encourage these as much as time allows. The more the passion and controversy builds, the better the demonstration.

11. *Debrief the strategy* of literature circles, including the response logs and the group meetings. Ask people to notice what worked and what didn't work in their book club meetings. Finally, ask teachers to talk about how they could adapt this structure to the age students they teach. Discuss different formats and possibilities for using literature circles in content areas. That's it.

Research on Best Practice Cluster Schools: Chicago Annenberg Challenge, 1995–1998

Percent of students who *meet or exceed* state goals on Illinois Goals Assessment Program (IGAP)

Third-Grade Reading

	1995	1998	Change
Jenner	21	27	+6
Waters	26	48	+22
Field	41	44	+3
Irving	36	62	+26
Citywide Average	45	45	0
BP Cluster Average Gain	31	45	+14

Third-Grade Writing

	1995	1998	Change
Jenner	65	69	+4
Waters	50	81	+31
Field	68	82	+14
Irving	73	83	+10
Citywide Average	86	76	-10
BP Cluster Average Gain	64	79	+15

Sixth-Grade Reading

	1995	1998	Change
Jenner	25	34	+9
Waters	44	44	-
Field	23	43	+20
Irving	57	58	+1
Citywide Average	47	46	-1
BP Cluster Average Gain	37	45	+8

Sixth-Grade Writing

	1995	1998	Change
Jenner	71	95	+24
Waters	87	81	-6
Field	78	92	+14
Irving	98	93	-5
Citywide Average	**88**	**86**	**-2**
BP Cluster Average Gain	**84**	**90**	**+6**

Eighth-Grade Reading

	1995	1998	Change
Jenner	26	47	+21
Waters	50	59	+9
Field	34	45	+11
Irving	58	61	+3
Citywide Average	**49**	**50**	**+1**
BP Cluster Average Gain	42	53	+11

Eighth-Grade Writing

	1995	1998	Change
Jenner	59	100	+41
Waters	52	94	+42
Field	59	81	+22
Irving	96	100	+4
Citywide Average	**75**	**75**	**0**
BP Cluster Average Gain	**67**	**94**	**+27**

Book Lists:
Literature Circle Favorites

The following list is far from definitive. It contains the favorite titles of students whose teachers have contributed to this book, some books used in workshops by teacher-consultants from the Center for City Schools, and a few of the author's own picks. This list is not censored for content or language; there are some strong, raw books here, including *Nightjohn, Remembering Slavery,* and many of the adult titles.

K–2 (Picture Books to Easy Chapter Books)

American Girl Series. Middleton, WI: Pleasant Company.

Andrews, Jan. 1985. *Very Last First Time.* New York: Atheneum.

Brown, Marc. Arthur Series. New York: Random House.

Brown, Marcia. 1947. *Stone Soup.* New York: Scribner.

Browne, Anthony. 1986. *Piggybook.* New York: Knopf.

———. 1990. *Changes.* New York: Knopf.

Bunting, Eve. 1989. *The Wednesday Surprise.* New York: Clarion.

———. 1991. *Fly Away Home.* New York: Clarion.

———. 1994. *Smoky Night.* San Diego: Harcourt Brace.

Cameron, Ann. 1981. *The Stories Julian Tells.* New York: Pantheon.

Cleary, Beverly. 1965. *The Mouse and the Motorcycle.* New York: Morrow.

Cohen, Miriam. 1980. *First Grade Takes a Test.* New York: Greenwillow.

Flournoy, Valerie. 1985. *The Patchwork Quilt.* New York: Dial Books for Young Readers.

Fox, Mem. 1984. *Wilfred Gordon McDonald Partridge.* Brooklyn, NY: Kane/Miller.

Garza, Carmen. 1990. *Family Pictures/Cuadros de familia.* Berkeley, CA: Children's Book Press.

Gilman, Phoebe. 1992. *Something from Nothing.* New York: Scholastic.

Henkes, Kevin. 1987. *Sheila Rae the Brave.* New York: Greenwillow.

————. 1990. *Julius, the Baby of the World.* New York: Greenwillow.

————. 1991. *Chrysanthemum.* New York: Greenwillow.

————. 1996. *Lily's Purple Plastic Purse.* New York: Greenwillow.

Howe, James, and Deborah Howe. Bunnicula Series. New York: Simon & Schuster.

Lobel, Arnold. Frog and Toad Series. New York: Harper & Row.

Martin, Bill Jr., and John Archambault. 1989. *Chicka Chicka Boom Boom.* New York: Simon & Schuster Books for Young Readers.

Munsch, Robert N. 1980. *The Paper Bag Princess.* Toronto: Annick Press.

Numeroff, Laura Joffe. 1985. *If You Give a Mouse a Cookie.* New York: Harper & Row.

Parish, Peggy. 1963. *Amelia Bedelia.* New York: Harper & Row.

Polacco, Patricia. 1994. *Pink and Say.* New York: Philomel.

Scieszka, John. 1999. *The True Story of the Three Little Pigs.* New York: Viking.

Shannon, David. 1999. *David Goes to School.* New York: Blue Sky Press.

Warner, Gertrude Chandler. The Boxcar Series. Morton Grove, IL: Albert Whitman.

White, E. B. 1952. *Charlotte's Web.* New York: Harper.

Williams, Vera B. 1982. *A Chair for My Mother.* New York: Greenwillow.

3–6

Avi. 1991. *Nothing but the Truth: A Documentary Novel.* New York: Orchard.

————. 1995. *Poppy.* New York: Orchard.

Curtis, Christopher Paul. 1995. *The Watsons Go to Birmingham—1963.* New York: Delacorte Press.

————. 1999. *Bud, Not Buddy.* New York: Delacorte Press.

Dahl, Roald. 1984. *Boy: Tales of Childhood.* New York: Farrar, Straus, and Giroux.

————. 2001. *James and the Giant Peach.* New York: Puffin.

Danziger, Paula. 1994. *Amber Brown Is Not a Crayon.* New York: Putnam.

Fletcher, Ralph. 1997. *Spider Boy.* New York: Clarion.

Gardiner, John Reynolds. 1980. *Stone Fox.* New York: Crowell.

Hesse, Karen. 1997. *Out of the Dust.* New York: Scholastic.

Jiang, Ji-Li. 1997. *Red Scarf Girl: A Memoir of the Cultural Revolution.* New York: HarperCollins.

Juster, Norton. 1961. *The Phantom Tollbooth.* New York: Epstein & Carroll.

MacLachlan, Patricia. 1985. *Sarah, Plain and Tall.* New York: Harper & Row.

Naylor, Phyllis Reynolds. 1991. *Shiloh.* New York: Atheneum.

O'Dell, Scott. 1970. *Sing Down the Moon.* Boston: Houghton Mifflin.

Paterson, Katherine. 1977. *Bridge to Terabithia.* New York: Crowell.

Sachar, Louis. 1987. *There's a Boy in the Girl's Bathroom.* New York: Knopf.

Spinelli, Jerry. 1990. *Maniac McGee: A Novel.* Boston: Little Brown.

Taylor, Mildred D. 2001. *Roll of Thunder, Hear My Cry.* New York: Phyllis Fogelman.

Thesman, Jean. 1989. *Appointment with a Stranger.* Boston: Houghton Mifflin.

Middle/Teen (from Sixth Grade Up)

Angelou, Maya. 2002. *I Know Why the Caged Bird Sings.* New York: Random House.

Berlin, Ira, Marc Favreau, and Steven F. Miller, eds. 2000. *Remembering Slavery: African Americans Talk About Their Personal Experiences of Slavery and Emancipation.* New York: The New Press.

Burns, Olive Ann. 1984. *Cold Sassy Tree.* New York: Ticknor & Fields.

Buss, Fran Leeper, with Daisy Cubias. 1991. *Journey of the Sparrows.* New York: Lodestar.

Chbosky, Stephen. 1999. *The Perks of Being a Wallflower.* New York: Pocket.

Cisneros, Sandra. 1991. *The House on Mango Street.* New York: Vintage.

———. 1992. *Woman Hollering Creek and Other Stories.* New York: Vintage.

Cormier, Robert. 1974. *The Chocolate War.* New York: Pantheon.

Hesse, Karen. 1997. *Out of the Dust.* New York: Scholastic.

Hinton, S. E. 1967. *The Outsiders.* New York: Viking.

Lowry, Lois. 1989. *Number the Stars.* Boston: Houghton Mifflin.

———. 1993. *The Giver.* Boston: Houghton Mifflin.

Myers, Walter Dean. 1988. *Scorpions.* New York: Harper & Row.

———. 1999. *Monster.* New York: HarperCollins.

Paulsen, Gary. 1993. *Nightjohn.* New York: Delacorte.

———. 1999. *Hatchet.* New York: Aladdin Paperbacks.

Peck, Richard. 2000. *A Year Down Yonder.* New York: Dial Books for Young Readers.

Rowling, J. K. Harry Potter Series. New York: Arthur A. Levine.

Sachar, Louis. 1998. *Holes.* New York: Farrar, Straus, and Giroux.

Sagan, Carl. 1985. *Contact.* New York: Simon & Schuster.

Sanders, Dori. 1990. *Clover.* Chapel Hill, NC: Algonquin.

Sender, Ruth Minsky. 1986. *The Cage.* New York: Macmillan.

High School/Adult

Angelou, Maya. 2002. *I Know Why the Caged Bird Sings.* New York: Random House.

Bragg, Rick. 1997. *All Over but the Shoutin'.* New York: Pantheon.

Clarke, Breena. 1999. *River, Cross My Heart.* Boston: Little Brown.

Cushman, Karen. 1995. *The Midwife's Apprentice.* New York: Clarion.

Eggers, Dave. 2000. *A Heartbreaking Work of Staggering Genius.* New York: Simon & Schuster.

Esquivel, Laura. 1992. *Like Water for Chocolate: A Novel in Monthly Installments, with Recipes, Romances, and Home Remedies.* Translated by Carol Christianson and Thomas Christianson. New York: Doubleday.

Eugenides, Jeffrey. 1993. *The Virgin Suicides.* New York: Farrar, Straus, and Giroux.

Gaines, Ernest. 1993. *A Lesson Before Dying.* New York: Knopf.

Hamilton, Jane. 2000. *Disobedience.* New York: Doubleday.

Haruf, Kent. 1999. *Plainsong.* New York: Knopf.

Karr, Mary. 1995. *The Liar's Club: A Memoir.* New York: Viking.

Kingsolver, Barbara. 1988. *The Bean Trees: A Novel.* New York: Harper & Row.

———. 1998. *The Poisonwood Bible: A Novel.* New York: HarperFlamingo.

McBride, James. 1996. *The Color of Water: A Black Man's Tribute to His White Mother.* New York: Riverhead.

Morrison, Toni. 1970. *The Bluest Eye.* New York: Holt, Rinehart and Winston.

———. 2000. *Beloved.* New York: Penguin.

Patchett, Ann. 1997. *The Magician's Assistant.* New York: Harcourt Brace.

Proulx, Annie. 1999. *The Shipping News.* New York: Scribner Classics.

Sagan, Carl. 1985. *Contact.* New York: Simon and Schuster.

Sanchez, Carlos Cuauhtemoc. 1997. *The Last Opportunity/la ultima oportunidad.* Astrolog Publishing.

Schwarz, Christina. 2000. *Drowning Ruth.* New York: Doubleday.

Sender, Ruth Minsky. 1986. *The Cage.* New York: Macmillan.

Shreve, Anita. 1998. *The Pilot's Wife.* Rockland, MA: Compass Press.

Tan, Amy. 1989. *The Joy Luck Club.* New York: Putnam.

Wolff, Virginia E. 1993. *Make Lemonade.* New York: H. Holt.

References

Allington, Richard. 1983. "The Reading Instruction Provided for Readers of Differing Reading Abilities." *Elementary School Journal* (May).

———. 2000. *What Really Matters for Struggling Readers: Designing Research-Based Programs.* New York: Longman.

Alvermann, D. E. 1997. *Adolescents' Negotiations of Out-of-School Reading Discussions.* Reading Research Report No. 77. Athens, GA: National Reading Research Center.

Anderson, Richard, Elfrieda Hiebert, Judith Scott, and Ian Wilkerson. 1985. *Becoming a Nation of Readers.* Washington, DC: National Institute of Education.

Anderson, Richard, P. T. Wilson, and L. G. Fielding. 1988. "Growth in Reading and How Children Spend Their Time Outside of School." *Reading Research Quarterly* (Summer).

Applebee, Arthur. 1981. *Writing in the Secondary School: English and the Content Areas.* NCTE Research Report No. 21. Urbana, IL: National Council of Teachers of English.

Atwell, Nancie. 1998. *In the Middle: Writing, Reading, and Learning with Adolescents.* 2d ed. Portsmouth, NH: Boynton/Cook.

Beane, James. 1991. "Middle School: The Natural Home of Integrated Curriculum." *Educational Leadership* (October).

Bruner, Jerome. 1961. *The Process of Education.* Cambridge, MA: Harvard University Press.

Calkins, Lucy. 2000. *The Art of Teaching Reading.* New York: Longman.

Close, Elizabeth Egan. 1992. "Literature Discussion: A Classroom Environment for Thinking and Sharing." *English Journal* (September).

Cunningham, Patricia, and Richard Allington. 1998. *Classrooms That Work: They Can All Read and Write.* New York: Longman.

Daniels, Harvey. 1994. *Literature Circles: Voice and Choice in the Student-Centered Classroom.* Portland, ME: Stenhouse.

Daniels, Harvey, and Marilyn Bizar. 1998. *Methods that Matter: Six Structures for Best Practice Classrooms.* Portland, ME: Stenhouse.

Daniels, Harvey, and Steven Zemelman. 1985. *A Writing Project: Training Teachers of Composition from Kindergarten Through College.* Portsmouth, NH: Heinemann.

Daniels, Harvey, Marilyn Bizar, and Steven Zemelman. 2000. *Rethinking High School: Best Practice in Teaching, Learning, and Leadership.* Portsmouth, NH: Heinemann.

Dewey, John. 1916. *Democracy and Education.* New York: Macmillan.

Dupuy, B. C. 1997. "Literature Circles: An Alternative Framework for Increasing Intermediate FL Students' Comprehension and Enjoyment of Texts in the Target Language." *Mosaic* 5 (1): 13–16.

Evans, K. S., D. Alverman, and P. L. Anders. 1998. "Literature Discussion Groups: An Examination of Gender Roles." *Reading Research and Instruction* 37 (2): 107–122.

Fader, Daniel. 1976. *The New Hooked on Books.* New York: Berkley.

Fielding, Leslie, and David Pearson. 1994. "Reading Comprehension: What Works." *Educational Leadership* (February).

Fountas, Irene, and Gay Su Pinnell. 1997. *Guided Reading: Good First Teaching for All Children.* Portsmouth, NH: Heinemann.

———. 1999. *Matching Books to Readers.* Portsmouth, NH: Heinemann.

———. 2000. *Guiding Readers and Writers.* Portsmouth, NH: Heinemann.

Fox, M., and L. Wilkinson. 1997. "No Longer Travelers in a Strange Country." *Journal of Children's Literature* 23 (1): 6–15.

Glasser, William. 1990. *The Quality School.* New York: Harper.

Grisham, Dana. 1999. "Literacy Partners: Supporting Literacy Innovation in a Teacher Study Group." *Journal of Reading Education* 2: 1–8.

Hanning, E. 1998. "What We've Learned: The Reading Connections Book Club After Two Years." *Journal of Children and Poverty* 4 (1): 25–37.

Hansen-Krening, N., and D. T. Mizokawa. 1997. "Exploring Ethnic-Specific Literature: A Unity of Parents, Families, and Educators." *Journal of Adolescent and Adult Literacy* 41 (3): 180–189.

Harvey, Stephanie, and Anne Goudvis. 2000. *Strategies That Work: Teaching Comprehension to Enhance Understanding.* Portland, ME: Stenhouse.

Harwayne, Shelley. 1992. *Lasting Impressions: Weaving Literature into the Writing Workshop.* Portsmouth, NH: Heinemann.

Hauschildt, P. M., and S. I. McMahon. 1996. "Reconceptualizing 'Resistant' Learners and Rethinking Instruction: Risking a Trip to the Swamp." *Language Arts* 73 (8): 576–586.

Heath, Shirley Brice. 1985. *Ways with Words: Language, Life, and Work in Communities and Classrooms.* New York: Cambridge University Press.

Heath, Shirley Brice, and Leslie Mangiola. 1991. *Children of Promise: Literate Activity in Linguistically and Culturally Diverse Classrooms.* Washington, DC: National Education Association.

Hill, Bonnie Campbell, and L. Van Horn. 1995. "Book Club Goes to Jail: Can Book Clubs Replace Gangs?" *Journal of Adolescent and Adult Literacy* 39 (3): 180–188.

Hill, Bonnie Campbell, Nancy J. Johnson, and Katherine Schlick-Noe. 1995. *Literature Circles and Response.* Norwood, MA: Christopher-Gordon.

———. 2000. *Literature Circles Resource Guide.* Norwood, MA: Christopher-Gordon.

IRA and NCTE. 1996. *Standards for the English Language Arts.* Urbana, IL and Newark, DE: National Council of Teachers of English and the International Reading Association.

Johnson, David, Roger Johnson, and Edythe Holubec. 1994. *Cooperative Learning in the Classroom.* Edina, MN: Interaction.

Johnson, David, and Frank Johnson. 1998. *Learning Together and Alone.* Boston: Allyn & Bacon.

Johnson, Nancy, and Katherine Schlick-Noe. 1999. *Getting Started with Literature Circles.* Norwood, MA: Christopher-Gordon.

Kaufmann, G., et al. 1997. "Examining the Roles of Teachers and Students in Literature Circles Across the Classroom Contexts" in *Literacies for the Twenty-First Century,* edited by C. K. Linzer, K. A. Hinchman, and D. J. Leu, pp. 373–384. Chicago: National Reading Conference.

Keegan, Suzi, and Karen Shrake. 1991. "Literature Study Groups: An Alternative to Ability Grouping." *Reading Teacher* (April).

Keene, Ellin, and Susan Zimmerman. 1997. *The Mosaic of Thought.* Portsmouth, NH: Heinemann.

Kohn, Alfie. 1993. "Choices for Children: Why and How to Let Students Decide." *Phi Delta Kappan* (October).

Klinger, Janette, Sharon Vaughn, and Jean Schumm. 1998. "Collaborative Strategic Reading During Social Studies in Heterogeneous Fourth-Grade Classrooms." *Elementary School Journal* 99 (1): 3–22.

Laskin, David, and Holly Hughes. 1995. *The Reading Group Book.* New York: Penguin.

MacGillivray, L. 1995. "Second Language and Literacy Teachers Considering Literature Circles. A Play." *Journal of Adolescent and Adult Literacy* 39 (1): 36–44.

Martinez-Roldan, Carmen, and Julia López-Robertson. 2000. "Initiating Literature Circles in a First-Grade Bilingual Classroom." *Reading Teacher* 53 (4): 270–281.

McMahon, Susan, and Taffy Raphael. 1997. *The Book Club Connection.* New York: Teachers College Press.

Moffett, James, and Betty Jane Wagner. 1993. *Student-Centered Language Arts K–12.* 4th ed. Portsmouth, NH: Heinemann.

Newmann, Fred, Anthony Bryck, and Jenny Nagaoka. 2001. *Authentic Intellectual Work and Standardized Tests: Conflict Co-existence?* Chicago: Consortium on Chicago School Research.

Noll, E. 1994. "Social Issues and Literature Circles with Adolescents." *Journal of Reading* 38 (2): 88–93.

Nystrand, Martin, Adam Gamoran, and Mary Jo Heck. 1993. "Using Small Groups for Response to and Thinking about Literature." *English Journal* (January).

Oakes, Jeannie. 1985. *Keeping Track: How Schools Structure Inequality.* New Haven, CT: Yale University Press.

Pardo, L. S. 1992. "Accommodating Diversity in the Elementary Classroom: A Look at Literature-Based Instruction in an Inner-City School." Paper given at the National Reading Conference, San Antonio, TX, December 1992.

Peterson, Ralph, and Maryann Eeds. 1990. *Grand Conversations: Literature Groups in Action.* Ontario: Scholastic.

Probst, Robert. 1988. *Response and Analysis: Teaching Literature in the Junior and Senior High School.* Portsmouth, NH: Boynton-Cook.

Rief, Linda. 1991. *Seeking Diversity: Language Arts with Adolescents.* Portsmouth, NH: Heinemann.

Rogers, Carl. 1969. *Freedom to Learn.* Columbus, OH: Merrill.

Rosenblatt, Louise. 1938. *Literature as Exploration.* New York: D. Appleton-Century.

———. 1978. *The Reader, the Text, and the Poem: The Transactional Theory of the Literary Work.* Carbondale IL: Southern Illinois University Press.

Report of the National Reading Panel: Teaching Children to Read. 2000. Washington, DC: National Institute of Child Health and Human Development.

Routman, Regie. 1991. *Invitations: Changing as Teachers and Learners K–12.* Portsmouth, NH: Heinemann.

Samway, Katharine Davies, and Gail Whang. 1995. *Literature Study Circles in a Multicultural Classroom.* Portland, ME: Stenhouse.

Schmuck, Richard, and Patricia Schmuck. 2000. *Group Processes in the Classroom.* 8th ed. Dubuque, IA: William C. Brown.

Short, Kathy. 1986. "Literacy as a Collaborative Experience." Ph.D. dissertation, Indiana University.

Short, Kathy, Jerome Harste, and Carolyn Burke. 1995. *Creating Classrooms for Authors.* 2d ed. Portsmouth, NH: Heinemann.

Short, Kathy, and Kathryn Mitchell Pierce, eds. 1990. *Talking About Books: Creating Literate Communities.* Portsmouth, NH: Heinemann.

Sierra-Perry, Martha. 1996. *Standards in Practice, Grades 3–5.* Urbana, IL: National Council of Teachers of English.

Slavin, Robert. 1985. *Learning to Cooperate, Cooperating to Learn.* New York: Plenum Press.

Slezak, Ellen, ed. 2000. *The Book Group Book.* 3d ed. Chicago: Chicago Review Press.

Smith, Julia, Valerie Lee, and Fred Newmann. 2001. *Instructional Achievement in Chicago Elementary Schools.* Chicago: Consortium on Chicago School Research.

Smith, Karen. 1990. "Entertaining a Text: A Reciprocal Process." In *Talking About Books: Creating Literate Communities,* edited by Kathy Short and Kathryn Mitchell Pierce. Portsmouth, NH: Heinemann.

Steineke, Nancy. 2002. *Reading and Writing Together: Collaborative Literacy in Action.* Portsmouth, NH: Heinemann.

Taylor, Denny. 1998. *Family Literacy: Learning to Read and Write.* Portsmouth, NH: Heinemann.

Thayer, Louis. 1981. *Fifty Strategies for Experiential Learning.* San Diego, CA: University Associates.

Thelen, Herbert. 1954. *The Dynamics of Groups at Work.* Chicago: University of Chicago Press.

Vygotsky, Lev. 1978. *Mind in Society: The Development of Higher Psychological Processes.* Cambridge, MA: Harvard University Press.

Wheelock, Anne. 1992. *Crossing the Tracks.* New York: The New Press.

Wiencek, J., and John O'Flahavan. 1994. "From Teacher-Led to Peer Discussions About Literature: Suggestions for Making the Shift." *Language Arts* 71: 488–498.

Wood, George. 1992. *Schools that Work.* New York: Dutton.

Zemelman, Steven, and Harvey Daniels. 1988. *A Community of Writers: Teaching Writing in the Junior and Senior High School.* Portsmouth, NH: Heinemann.

Zemelman, Steven, Harvey Daniels, and Arthur Hyde. 1998. *Best Practice: New Standards for Teaching and Learning in America's Schools.* 2d ed. Portsmouth, NH: Heinemann.

Index